Surviving
HOLLYWOOD

YOUR TICKET TO SUCCESS

Surviving HOLLYWOOD

YOUR TICKET TO SUCCESS

Jerry Rannow

ALLWORTH PRESS
NEW YORK

07 06 05 04 03 02   5 4 3 2 1

Published by Allworth Press
An imprint of Allworth Communications, Inc
10 East 23rd Street, New York, NY 10010

Cover design by Joan O'Connor, New York, NY

Page composition/typography by Integra Software Services Pvt Ltd, Pondicherry, India

ISBN: 1-58115-255-8

Library of Congress Cataloging-in-Publication Data:

Rannow, Jerry.

Surviving Hollywood : your ticket to success / by Jerry Rannow.

    p. cm.

Includes bibliographical references and index.

ISBN 1-58115-255-8

1. Motion pictures--Vocational guidance.   I. Title.

PN1995.9.P75R36 2002

791.43'02'93--dc21

 2002009121

Printed in Canada

To Carly Cady, who read my spec TV script and
recommended it to her boss.

Contents

CONTENTS

Acknowledgments

My sincere thanks to my assistant, Karen Hamilton, advisor George Spelvin, the publishing whizzes at Allworth Press (Tad Crawford, Nicole Potter, Liz Van Hoose, Kate Lothman), and all the Hollywood professionals who have so generously contributed to this book.

Introduction

A WHIRLWIND TRIP

Okay, admit it. Who out there hasn't, at one time or another, had the fantasy of a glamorous career in Hollywood—of being an actor, writer, director, producer, star! We all dream about the possibilities that life offers, and the greater the dream, the more exciting the possibilities.

I'm sure that many of you are dreaming your Hollywood dreams at this very moment, which is why you're sneaking a free peek at this page to decide if it's worth it for you to invest in this book. Well, kiddo, this is the wisest career investment you will ever make. In your hand, you are holding a primer for survival in a business where the only certainty is uncertainty. Hollywood show business is the toughest, the riskiest, the most competitive and compellingly convoluted venture man or woman has ever devised.

This book guides you through an industry that can best be described as schizophrenic—functioning in abnormal ways—cloaked in a reality that can only be characterized as warped, resulting in variable behavior patterns brought on by frequent emotional and intellectual disturbances. It's a world of uncontrolled egos, where sometimes you feel like a nut and sometimes you are. But it's never dull, and as long as you keep your head screwed on tight, you can overcome and succeed.

Success in Hollywood show business is most often elusive and rarely happens overnight. And when good fortune comes a 'knockin', it may quite likely be fleeting and disappear as quickly as it knocked. It's a business where only the tough survive, and this requires a strength of character that is essential to keeping your mind from slipping out of its socket into a piping hot pot of bitterness and defeat.

Survival is the theme of a great many films and literary works. It has been a trendy topic on TV for a number of years because it is so important to what we achieve in life. My huge, unabridged *Random House Dictionary of the English*

Language (which I was easily able to remove from my library shelf with the aid of a forklift), defines "survival" in various ways:

1. A capacity for endurance under adverse conditions. 2. To remain alive. 3. To be unaffected in spite of some occurrence. 4. To bear up to affliction or misery. 5. To remain in existence in an atmosphere of competition. 6. To continue to live against the odds.

Synonyms for survival are: to persist, to succeed, to outlive.

In terms of survival in Hollywood, all of this would boil down to having a longer shelf life than the next person—with the kind of staying power that withstands the ups and downs of doing time in Tinseltown.

Hollywood show business demands a constant, vigilant quest for survival. Even when you've "made it," you never really have it made. A star one minute, a nobody the next. Look at a copy of *People* magazine from a few years back, and wonder whatever happened to all of those flavor-of-the-moment actors, directors, writers, singers—where do they go? Have they quit? Are they just laying low? Mounting a comeback? Or have they simply slid into the postfamous ooze, never to be heard from again?

Most everyone craves applause, likes to be publicly acknowledged. The fella who catches a foul ball at a baseball game holds it up proudly to receive the mandatory huzzahs, and show business is an attempt to catch that ball whenever it is hit in your direction. It's not so much a search for fifteen minutes of fame, but a life filled with spectacular catches that may depend on outside stimulus and basic self-esteem.

Survival in Hollywood is a combination of talent, training, and good, old-fashioned stubbornness. A successful career in show business requires a melange of mental flexibilities buttressed by a willingness to learn from mistakes. It's about being in the right place at the right time. It's a lot about luck—even more about manufacturing your own luck. Talent can finagle you through the door, but staying there is the tricky part.

Surviving Hollywood deals in straight talk about the real guts of Hollywood show business. This book will give tomorrow's "A-Listers" the ins and outs of what it takes to survive as a player in an industry where everyone is regularly misunderstood. Having sustained a thirty-year career in Hollywood as an actor, writer, and producer, I am familiar with the lay of Hollywoodland, and, through my own experience, can furnish you with a true reflection of the way things really are.

This book is a continuing story told through many recurring voices. Each chapter will be peppered with comments from actors, writers, directors, producers, agents, managers, network and studio executives—all of them skilled Hollywood professionals, passing on practical knowledge and sharp opinions gained from their years of experience. Some of these names may be familiar, some may not, but their knowledgeable contributions will impress and educate. These voices reflect the "heart" of Hollywood.

The names of all interviewees will appear in boldface, and their individual comments (called "Accounts") will often be set off in boxes apart from the general text, to give their thoughts and ideas a more specific focus. The participation of these interviewees was obtained through such means as mailed questionnaires, e-mail correspondence, and interviews in person or by telephone. At the back of this book, you'll find biographies of all the Hollywood professionals participating in this project. I know you will find their input interesting and informative.

Surviving Hollywood could aptly be titled "The Tinseltown Survival Kit"—jam-packed with valuable instruction, information, and revelation about careers in show business. It is not intended to teach you how to act, write, direct, produce, or ride in a limo. Rather, it addresses the basics of living the Hollywood life and developing your very own knack for surviving the day-to-day existence of a business gone wild.

Chapter 1

COMMITTING TO
A HOLLYWOOD CAREER

If you can dream it, you can do it.
—Walt Disney

I recently attended a party for a young friend, **Rachel Lawrence**, who was cele-
brating her high school graduation. Here's a kid who was the "star" in her high
school production of *Sweeney Todd* as well as a byline columnist for her school
paper. She was cheerleader captain, she was homecoming queen, and she has every
reason to believe that she is destined for a big-time show business career.

Rachel's parents have expressed quiet support for their daughter's plans to
become a Hollywood actress, but they confided to me their fear that she may not
have the commitment or the strength to survive in what they hear is a rather quirky
profession, and they can hardly be faulted for their concerns. They never want to
see their daughter hurt in any way. Mr. and Mrs. Lawrence understand full well that
even though Rachel has gone through twelve years of scholastic development, she
still doesn't know beans about who she is and is totally incapable of knowing what
she really wants. They dropped hints about show business being nothing but a risky,
uncertain search for that ever-elusive needle in a haystack. They presented their
daughter with solid facts that they had found on the Internet. Facts like: 70 percent
of the Screen Actors' Guild members make less than $7,500 a year as actors, and
less than 2 percent of SAG members make anywhere near $100,000 a year.

Of course, Rachel dismissed these facts with "Please don't worry. I can do it.
I'm gonna be in that two percent. Sure, I know the odds are big, but I honestly
believe in myself, and I'll never know I can do it unless I try." . . . And with that
logic in place, Rachel promised me she'd keep in touch.

Kyle Kramer was a student in my comedy writing class at the university
where I teach. He showed a fine talent for writing sitcom, as evidenced by his
spec script for *That '70s Show*. At the end of the final class, Kyle informed me
that he was heading for Hollywood to pursue his double-barreled dreams of acting
and writing. When I asked how his parents felt about it, Kyle said, "My parents

are probably the two most supportive people on the face of the earth. They even understood when I quit pre-med. Not only are they supporting me financially during these start-up months, they believe in me 100 percent. Without their support, I would never be able to do what I'm doing. . . . They urge me to fight for every inch and, in return, I strive to make them proud."

I advised Kyle that Hollywood can be a tough place to break into in one profession, but two. . . ? When he reminded me that I did it, I had to shut my big mouth. Kyle went on to say, "I do realize I've chosen two of the most difficult professions in the world to break into, but I wouldn't be going out there if I didn't think I could succeed." Kyle said he would e-mail up-to-date reports on his progress.

ROOTS OF PURSUITS: MENTORS AND MODELS

People who travel west with the intent of making it big in Hollywood do so for any number of reasons: maybe he or she has dreams of following in the footsteps of favorite actors on TV and in the movies; had teachers who saw their class-clown antics as potential for show business fame; or parents, cousins, brothers, or sisters who encouraged them early on to follow their wildest dreams.

"I grew up surrounded by humor," recalls writer **Bob Schiller**. "Both of my parents were natural wits. My cousin was funny and fed me Robert Benchley books as well as humor magazines. For as long as I can remember, I got pleasure making others laugh." (Schiller and his late partner, Bob Weiskopf, honed their comedy talents as staff writers on *I Love Lucy*, and they've been two of my comedy heroes ever since.)

My interest in performing began in grade school, when I discovered that the girls paid attention when I acted funny—or what passed for funny in my mind—and now it's become my life's work (although I no longer rely half as much on plastic buck teeth to get a laugh).

In high school, I was pushed even further into a possible show business career when I took a speech course presided over by a tall, sturdy, whitely crew-cutted man, Thoburn D. "Toby" Rowe. Mr. Rowe had an engaging sense of humor, and it was a real buzz to go into his class after an hour of geometry with the prematurely embalmed Miss Flexner. Up until this time, my ideas for possible careers had shuttled between becoming an architect, being silly on TV like Sid Caesar, or playing center field for the Chicago Cubs. Then, one day, Mr. Rowe (who was also the drama teacher) announced the tryouts for the school play. After much self-flagellation in the form of knowing there was nothing whatsoever that I had to offer the world, I read for a part that I didn't get because I knew I wouldn't. . . . But, when I was asked if I would be the stage manager and provide an offstage voice, I jumped at the chance. It goes without saying that I was the best offstage voice ever heard from offstage anywhere, and when I tried out for the next play I landed the crucial, yet smallest, role in the play. Thus I began a wondrous journey of teenage discovery—my first actual step into the practice of survival. I treasure those days, and honor the memory of my mentor, Mr. Rowe.

Mentor. Basically, this term means someone who is an influence—a role model who provides inspiration and, if you're lucky, some guidance. Most Hollywood professionals have had someone in their lives who influenced their career choices, and they know the value of continuing these relationships by keeping current on addresses; through occasional phone calls, e-mails, or correspondence, the mentoring process is kept alive and can continue to provide nourishment. In the preceding pages, I mentioned **Rachel Lawrence** and **Kyle Kramer**. These two young people are my "mentees"—ready, eager, new to Hollywood, and in their enthusiasm they have promised to keep me informed of their career progress.

ACCOUNTS:

Guiding Lights

The mentoring process can be found in a wide variety of places—at home, at school, on the screen, even within the offices of *BusinessWeek*, as was the case for **Charlie Hauck**. . . .

Writer/producer *Charlie Hauck*: "I was working in Pittsburgh as the bureau chief for *BusinessWeek* magazine when I learned that the third child my wife and I were expecting was, in fact, going to be twins. A *Business Week* editor in New York said to me, 'Hauck, do you realize you're breeding yourself out of a decent standard of living?' . . . Comedy writing came to mind because I was widely acknowledged as the funniest person covering the coal, steel, and aluminum industries. . . . I wrote some comedy material for Phyllis Diller, who was playing at a nightclub in Pittsburgh. She liked my material and encouraged me to go to Hollywood. I did."

Actor/writer *Robert Hegyes*: "My mother had a lot to do with it. She used to buy all these Broadway show albums and she'd play them for me. I memorized all the songs. . . . Also, my high school drama teacher, Bart Sheppard. He was great. I liked doing the school plays, and, most importantly, it was an opportunity to meet girls."

Actor *Jed Allan*: "At American University, I met Anne Bancroft, who was visiting her sister and saw the play I was in. . . .Well, she said some encouraging words that changed my life, and I went right to The Pasadena Playhouse to become an actor."

Actress/writer *Candace Howerton*: "My mentor was Ruth Burch, a casting director and producer of the La Jolla Playhouse. She and actor Mel Ferrer saw me in a children's theater production of *Tom Sawyer*. I played the ingénue, Becky Thatcher. Ferrer came up to me after the production and he told me he had never seen anyone as exciting as me, except his wife, Audrey Hepburn. I reacted in a very professional way and started to cry. Ferrer said if I ever came to Hollywood I should look him up and Ruth added, 'Come to Hollywood and I'll put you to work.' Of course I didn't know I would be working for her as a secretary! Neither she nor I ever called good old Mel, but she was my mentor. She paid for my first professional pictures, obtained agents for me and got me my first acting job. I was on my way!"

Writer/TV executive *Laurie Scheer*: "My role models were 'Daisy Clover' and 'Betty Schaeffer.' Daisy Clover is the child star played by Natalie Wood in *Inside Daisy Clover*. As a child, I wanted to be so much like her and to be part of her world. Betty Schaeffer is the script typist in *Sunset Boulevard*. She was a young woman writing scripts with William Holden. I loved that she worked in a bungalow on a studio lot—I knew that someday I had to do the very same and I did."

Actor *Hank Jones*: "After years of Hollywood pavement-pounding, I was lucky enough to land a job as a singer/comic on *The Tennessee Ernie Ford Show*. One day on the program, Ernie asked the cast, 'Of all the great people in history, who would you like to spend an hour with?' There were answers like Abraham Lincoln, Leonardo da Vinci, and Beethoven, and I said 'Stan Laurel.'. . . Then, one day, I received a phone call. 'Hello, lad,' said a soft, unmistakable English voice. 'Come on over, let's have a visit!' Stan lived in a smallish Santa Monica apartment, filled with a lifetime's worth of memorabilia. He generously gave me performance tips and commiserated about the feast-or-famine aspects of show business. He was much more outgoing and gregarious than his timid character on screen. His eyes twinkled with good humor, and he had the most marvelous belly laugh, so contagious you couldn't help but join in. I was in heaven! Finally, when it was time to leave, he said cryptically to me, 'Well, Hank, the next time you see me I'll have me hat on.' I really didn't know what he meant, but I smiled and said goodbye.

Weeks later, Stan Laurel was dead. Months after his passing, I was watching an old *Laurel and Hardy* short subject at home on television. In one scene, as he and Oliver were preparing to be hanged for some offense related to their glorious ineptitude, Stan said something that sent chills up my spine. He consoled his friend by telling him, 'Don't worry, Ollie, you'll know me up there . . . when you see me I'll have me hat on!'"

THE IMPORTANCE OF BEING IN EARNEST

When Hollywood beckons, you must wholeheartedly pledge yourself to the vocation you plan to pursue. Actor, writer, director, network executive, mini-mogul, media giant—whatever your goal, you must confine your thoughts to a single, unwavering frame of mind. Certain words should flicker brightly in the scope of your vision. Words like *purpose*—you have a specific aim, a resolve, a set goal for yourself. Another word is *determination*—you have a steadfast, unflagging adherence to a well-envisioned ambition.

In your deepest imagination you must picture yourself as successful and capable of overcoming anything that may get in the way of that success. The word *passion* should be foremost on your mind—as well as zealous *enthusiasm*, backed by an unflappable commitment to making it in show business. "You have to be absolutely committed," says actor **Lawrence-Hilton Jacobs**:

> Commitment is as important as the water that comes from the faucet or the air that one breathes. As corny as that may sound, I really mean it. You have to be that committed and that exacting for yourself, because you are going to have a lot of dim points of view on how to go forward. You have to depend a lot on your own raw nerve, your own roar, your own energy based on "I believe."

Commitment is an absolute necessity at this point. You have to be totally self-assured about how you are going to fit into the world of Hollywood. It's not always going to be easy to project that self-assurance, and a heaping helping of raw nerve may be your only ally when the going gets rough—and, believe me, things can get awfully prickly at times.

Once commitment is firmly in place, the muse takes hold—not a silent muse, but one that motivates desire and translates it into action. This kind of commitment, however, does not work on automatic pilot; it takes a certain amount of maintenance with a healthy squirt of mental WD-40 on a daily basis. Each morning when you wake, head directly for that trusty old bathroom mirror. After the initial shock has subsided and your face begins to lift and tighten to its natural state, flash yourself a series of smiles. Smile practice is a necessity in show business because a bright sunny smile with a full set of teeth is a hard thing for anyone to resist. A smile opens you up to people. It makes you appear happy, secure and confident even if you're not.

A constant nurturing of your muse is also a necessity, so during smile practice remind your mirrored image what your goals are and what you need to do to achieve those goals. Soon, this becomes a kind of mantra, which effectively serves to increase your determination to succeed, resulting in the rock-hard, resolute reflection you see smiling and murmuring greatness at you from the mirror. I would recommend that you recite this smiling mantra for about five minutes every morning. You may occasionally do it while driving alone in your car, but I do not advocate this practice in mixed company because it would only characterize you as just another one of those Hollywood nuts.

ACCOUNTS:

The Big Life Decision

Decisions to storm the gates of Hollywood appear in various guises. In my case, I had acted in loads of plays in high school, community theater, and then college, where I studied to be a high school English and drama teacher. This preparation enabled me to become one of the chosen few when I went to Chicago to audition for the National Company of *Bye, Bye, Birdie*. When, to my complete amazement, I got the part—and my Actors' Equity card—my professional career had officially begun. Next stop, Tinseltown!

For other professionals, the decision to storm Hollywood was strengthened in a variety of ways.

Writer/producer *Ralph Gaby Wilson*: "As an investigative reporter in Kansas City, late one night, while running across a plowed field, headed for a small forest with two thugs shooting at me, I said: 'If I'm lucky enough to make it to those trees, I'm lucky enough for Hollywood.' Besides, if they don't like your writing in Hollywood, they don't shoot at you."

Actress/writer *Candace Howerton*: "I was the Miss San Diego runner-up and appeared in college plays for the year-and-a-half I attended San Diego State College. Then, I packed my bags and 'ran away' to Hollywood. That's what I actually did, but I had done my homework. I had been in plays at the Old Globe Theatre, won an Atlas Award at the Globe for playing the sexpot in *Night of the Iguana*. What did I know about sex? I was a virgin. . . . Maybe that's why I won it."

Writer *Coslough Johnson*: "I came to Hollywood with a steady job writing training, sales, and promotional films (what we called 'industrial films'), and I had no real thought about writing television. Several years later, when I was directing a film for the government about some clay-like explosive and they insisted I blow up a goat, I realized that maybe I should try this television sitcom stuff."

PREPARING FOR THE BIG WHAMOO

As you can see, the circumstances that lead hopefuls to enter the golden gates of Hollywood vary considerably, but the desired goal is amazingly the same: to be an enormous success in show business. This takes huge gobs of planning and preparation. A great deal of concentrated thought is required for your journey to produce results. And, once you've thought it through, you have to act on those thoughts in order for them to take on some semblance of reality. Now, I'm sure you're aware of the fact that success in Hollywood doesn't find you; you find it, no matter what rock it may be hiding under. You don't wait for yourself to be used; you have to be the one who uses you. You must be resourceful, seek out paths, and invent methods that can give your career a good kick upwards. Look deeply within yourself for those qualities you possess that can project you into other people's minds. Oh, and any kind of contacts you have most certainly should be hauled out and brought into play.

When you hit town, visit the union offices. The Screen Actors Guild (SAG), the American Federation of Radio & Television Artists (AFTRA), the Writers Guild of America west (WGAw), the Directors Guild of America (DGA) and Actors' Equity Association (AEA) are all listed in the Hollywood area phone book. When you get to these offices, ask questions about membership. Explain that you know you'll be a member one day soon, and you want to make sure you're taking steps in the right direction. Unions can be very helpful to you. Most everyone likes to dispense wisdom, and knowing that you're a future dues-paying member will give them motivation to help.

It's also important that you keep in professional shape. Actors should act— take classes, do plays. Writers should write scripts, stories, plays—anything that will build up a portfolio. (More about these things coming up. Amazing stuff.)

ACCOUNTS:

The Professional Groundwork _____

Show business is a hit-and-miss industry, and you'll try a lot of things to break in—some will work, others will not, but that's not something you should dwell upon. Just put your head down and plow through that line. There's a goal line out there somewhere, and the only way you're going to cross that goal is by forging ahead with super-sized portions of staunch optimism. If at all feasible, having wealthy, supportive parents is a definite advantage.

Writer/TV executive *Laurie Scheer*: "I was lucky. . . . Some friends had already been working at ABC and I was able to get an interview within three days of my arrival in Los Angeles. By the end of that same week,

I had a job in the ABC Dramatic Development Department. . . . Such a thrill—I was working at a major broadcasting network with a degree in broadcasting. It was invaluable to me to learn the business from that standpoint."

Writer/producer/personal manager *Greg Strangis*: "My approach during my first Hollywood year was to learn as much as I could, meet as many people as I could, read lots of scripts, and try to determine where I could fit in. . . . I wrote stuff that really stunk, but I had to develop the writing muscle, and there's only one way to do that. Within a year, I was selling jokes to Garry Marshall for *Love, American Style*—blackouts at ten bucks a joke. I had arrived!"

Writer/producer *Lloyd Garver*: "I went to graduate school at Northwestern, and then came out to Hollywood. . . . I was very lucky in getting a job almost immediately writing questions and 'ad-lib' jokes for *Hollywood Squares*. However, I considered this my 'day job,' was open to any other kind of writing work, and was constantly writing spec scripts."

Director/producer *Tom Cherones*: "Starting in college, I worked at every job in six different public TV stations, but I wanted to earn more money and do shows that more than a handful of people would see. When I came to Hollywood, I could do anyone's job on a soundstage. My wife and I arrived with $7,000. . . . After five months, I finally got my first job (as a unit manager at ABC); we were down to one thousand dollars."

FAMILY HANDLING

Anyone aspiring to a Hollywood career is dependent on applause—on the acceptance of others. But approval is not something that is necessary to life; it is merely a longing and a desire. When a dependency on approval becomes the motivating factor in your decisions, you are courting discouragement, and it's time to change your thinking. The way you conduct your life is nobody else's business, y'know. *You* are solely responsible for your world.

In his book *Risking*, Dr. David Viscott warns: "When you ask other people for their opinion about your plans, remember that change and new, untried ideas frighten people. Don't expect encouragement. Expect others to discourage you in the same way they dissuaded themselves."

Your life belongs to you. Letting others direct your actions can be the biggest mistake of your life. Face it, most every parent, sibling, or other relative of a Hollywood wannabe is *not* going to be fully or even partly supportive of your decision to gamble your life on a fantasy profession. These people think they know the score, that they know all about how Hollywood ruins lives, and you will be reminded more than once that it's not a business for anyone in their right mind. They will worry that you're going to be corrupted, drug-ridden, and bitter for all those years you're going to waste failing to succeed. Family members know these things because the media has told them so.

In her book, *If Success Is a Game These Are the Rules*, Dr. Cherie Carter-Scott addresses this situation:

> Negaholics exist. They are the naysayers who have mantras of 'can't,' 'shouldn't,' 'it won't work,' 'it's not possible.' They are the people in your life who encourage you to stay small and play it safe. . . . They believe they are realists only saving you from disappointment, but in reality they are risk-averse. . . . You need to become strong enough to be able to deal with them when they attack your dream.

My own family never really understood what I was doing in Hollywood. I did receive faint enthusiasm when I landed a role or sold a script, but the question that followed was always the same: "So, what's next?" It was like they were saying, "Sure, you got lucky, but are you ready to go back to failing?" In many ways, I think this question reflected their own insecurities more than mine.

Actor/production executive **Jim Begg** echoes a similar experience with: "The difficulty was just making my family understand what I was doing. Nobody in my family had ever been in show business, and they did not know how to be supportive. . . . So, my advice is not to believe everything that mom and pop say. They're blinded by their love for you and not by reality."

One director friend of mine comes from a wealthy East Coast family, and when he announced to them that he was going to direct motion pictures in Hollywood, the East Coast cut him off, emotionally and financially, and nobody was happy about it. My friend has managed to live through this, but he can't wait to make it big so he can show the East Coasters they were wrong. He's still waiting to show them.

Your family has their opinions, and you have your goals. Never let anyone's discouraging words affect you. Let the negativity roll off your back. You are in charge of your own life. It's your full-time job. . . . Oh, and one other thing. Please don't react in anger to your family's behavior. That would be the worst blunder of all. Understand that they do support you—they just don't know how to show it.

Actor **Hank Jones** recounts his family difficulties: "[I had] some conflict with my parents at first when I told them I was going into show business. (I was at Stanford at the time.) Then when my first big role in a movie came out, my dad was going up to everyone at the premiere saying, 'That's my son! He's in the movie!' Glenn Ford almost hit him in the mouth."

CHARACTER IS MORE THAN JUST BEING ONE

Show business is a lot like the game of golf. You are constantly playing against yourself. It's never really you versus Hollywood, it's *you* versus *you*. Initially, the prospect of carving out your show-business niche may seem daunting, so it's important to equip yourself from within in order to survive.

Survival in Hollywood takes many shapes, but requires only one important attribute: *strength of character*. You hear that term a lot these days, and if you don't hear that term a lot, you heard it here, so trust me on this. Strength of character is the "foundation" by which you will succeed. It's a fortification—the thread that holds your career journey together.

Who you are—your strengths and weaknesses, your entire psychological makeup—comes to the forefront here. Your disposition, your temperament, your whole personality will either be an asset or a hazard that must be confronted and dealt with. You behave like a drip, and you'll lose points on the old success-o-meter—so rid yourself of that childish pout reflex and urges to get even. Work on yourself and develop a professional demeanor. You are a project in constant need of adjustment, and accepting this is very much a part of any professional's survival plan.

Character is a combination of . . . well, the characteristics that make up who you are. In Hollywood, there are some characteristics that will serve you more effectively than others. The first one that comes to mind is probably *persistence*. It's a basic stubbornness that fortifies you, a refusal to give up. Right alongside persistence is its first cousin, *perseverance*—a trait that keeps you solidly on the straight and narrow despite all those annoying orange barrels blocking your road to success. Then there's *fortitude*—a quality that taps into your courage and gives you the strength to bear up to pain, adversity, and the emotional pie in the face. These elements of character only touch the surface of our human makeup, but each time you discover them in your heart and develop them in your mind, you will possess the most important characteristic of all: *endurance*.

ACCOUNTS:

Character Reflections _____

I asked these professionals to reflect on what characteristics they valued most in their day-to-day work in Hollywood. Their answers ran the gamut.

Writer/actress *Jewel Jaffe Ross*: "It's persistence of the everlasting, never-give-in variety . . . of the 'If they don't love me I will die' variety. . . . It's dedication to the pursuit of career, to the detriment of every other life choice.

If you want to make it in Hollywood, drop all other baggage. Your career must come before friends, family, ideals, sleep, everything. Assuming a modicum of talent, a dash of intelligence, and the ability to put show business above all, you've got a chance . . . maybe."

Writer *Coslough Johnson*: "To me, the most important character element for survival in Hollywood is to keep your sense of humor. This will carry you through those jobs where you have to work with people who are ignorant, arrogant, opinionated and, above all, don't agree with you."

Writer/producer *Rich Eustis*: "The ability (difficult for any artist) to believe that anyone who doesn't think you're brilliant is crazy."

Writer/producer *Peter Lefcourt*: "Don't take yourself too seriously. Suffer fools well."

Actress/acting teacher *Helaine Lembeck*: "I don't know if it applies to Hollywood or life in general, but I think that you need to be honest with yourself. You need to listen to your own heart, listen to your own head and don't rely on other people's opinions because those people may not be there to help and support you."

Writers' agent *Gary Cosay*: "You have to have talent, discipline, and good judgment. . . . Also persistence—if you just keep pushing and pushing, eventually you will get an opportunity."

Actor *Jed Allan*: "Tenacity, ambition, charm, a big mouth. Forget loyalty—in Hollywood loyalty does not exist."

Writer/producer *Del Reisman*: "Ingrid Bergman was asked what element of character was most important for anyone in show business, and her response was, 'A short memory.' You have to forget the agony and get on with it."

Actress *Sondra Bennett*: "Confidence, persistence, and passion. Without those, you can undermine opportunity."

One element of character that has never failed to serve me well is *adaptability*. My ambidextrous mind has always enabled me to adjust quickly to change. I really owe it all to playing baseball when I was a kid. The grand old sport taught me how to skip, slide, swerve—to react instantly to whatever was coming my way. What can I say? Hollywood's gain was the Chicago Cubs' loss.

Chapter 2

HOLLYWOOD TRUTHS: DISPELLING THE MYTHS

*Strip away the tinsel of Hollywood
and you'll find the real tinsel underneath.*
—Actor/musician Oscar Levant

The mere mention of the word "Hollywood" conjures up all sorts of fantastic images in the public's mind. To the uneducated, it is a mythical city filled with show business folk all living glamorous, money-sopped lives. Sounds like fun, doesn't it? Perhaps we should scrutinize this a bit more closely.

Hollywood attracts dreamers—including you, right? I thought so. You dream of experiencing the lavish lifestyle of the rich and famous. You see yourself in a huge, glass-walled home, high on a Bel Air hill with an incredible view of the ocean, a pool the size of Brooklyn, a staff of loyal servants, all topped off by a security system that could befuddle James Bond. In your red-carpeted driveway, you have a series of world-class vehicles, including a Rolls, a Mercedes, a BMW, a Ferrari, and a chauffeured limousine to transport you to your equally opulent bungalow at the studio where you will be starring, directing, and producing your next award-winning feature film. You are the poster child for fame and fortune. Look up the words "world-renowned," and there's your ever-tanned face looking even younger than you did twenty years ago. Boy, what a life! Wow, what a dream!

The above image seems very much like a myth—and it *is* a myth. The only thing mythless about it is that some of it is actually true. There are people who do live like that, at least temporarily. Y'see, once any kind of success like this is achieved, those who have it spend the majority of their time trying to hold on to it so they don't become yesterday's star soufflé—y'see, this whole concept of glamor is fraught with insecurity. One day it's there; one day it's not, and the semblance of any real certainty is very difficult to pin down.

"One must accept that Hollywood is the land of make-believe and you are never sure of what is true or real," says actor **Eddie Applegate**, and yet the majority of the public insists on believing that Hollywood equals glamor, and glamor equals riches. Vast riches. The media emphasizes this in a concerted effort to further this fantasy. Well, I think the smog should be blown away on this subject.

ACCOUNTS:

Glamor? Riches? Are You Talking to Me?

I posed a few questions on the matter of glamor and riches, and here's what I got back.

Writer *Bob Schiller*: "Well, the actors and the etceteras lead glamorous lives, but the writers??? If you call working sometimes around the clock, eating take-out food because you don't have the time or the luxury of eating out glamorous, then it's glamorous. Writers don't get no respect."

Actress *Sondra Bennett*: "Glamor in Hollywood? The public has a great imagination."

Theatrical agent *Judy Coppage*: "Glamor? That's all they read about. *People* magazine doesn't do stories about the 99 percent of the people [in Hollywood] who are starving. It's not newsworthy. Why would people want to read about people like themselves?"

Director/producer *Tom Cherones*: "Glamorous? I don't think so. Most of us work hard. Writers, in particular, work way too many hours. When I was both producing and directing *Seinfeld*, I worked seventy-five to eighty hours a week."

Writer/producer *Arnold Margolin*: "We don't all lead glamorous lives. Having a house with a pool and two newer cars in the garage and your kid in private school could be considered glamorous by a counter clerk at KFC. But it's not the glamor of the business, it's the fun of doing the work that I would envy if I were on the outside looking in."

Writer/producer *Lloyd Garver*: "I don't have time to answer this question because I have to scold my chauffeur."

Writer/actress *Jewel Jaffe Ross*: "The 'glamorous lives' thing is what gets people hot enough to turn their lives upside down in pursuit of the impossible dream. . . . Are the Oscars even more boring than they are on the tube?

Sure, but so what? Even once you find out that it's not really glamorous, knowing that other people think it is . . . helps."

Actor/writer *Robert Hegyes*: "Well, the average mean salary in the Screen Actors' Guild is what, $9,000 a year? That's below the poverty level . . . and that's factoring in Jack Nicholson's fees."

Writer *Coslough Johnson*: "The perception that TV and film writers are all rich is a figment of the press that somehow always appears during strike negotiations. I wonder why?"

Writer/producer *Peter Lefcourt*: "The median income of all Writers' Guild of America members is about the top pay for a veteran school teacher."

Actor *Lou Wagner*: "Rich? It's a perception of Hollywood actors, but the truth is only one-half of one percent of actors make the millions that you hear about."

Actor *Hank Jones*: "One day at the North Hollywood unemployment office, I saw [movie star] Dana Andrews looking tired and worn out, being paged over a loudspeaker to go to the desk of a clerk so they could investigate his claim for payment. It was sad to see him have to do this. He was formerly the president of the Screen Actors Guild."

During my years in Hollywood, I've learned one important lesson: You manufacture your *own* glamor. All the allure and enchantment of your profession is strictly up to you and what speed you set your heart on.

L.A. LIVING: A GEOGRAPHY

Anyone seeking the show business grail will be required to live in or around the Los Angeles area. It is important to understand that L.A. is an enormous, over-sprawled city—and the Hollywood within it is basically a factory town with studio soundstages fabricating entertainment for an all too insatiable public. A factory churning out tractors would be just as important to the world as Hollywood, if tractor factories received the same kind of hype and publicity that TV and movies do. If, instead of *Entertainment Tonight*, there was a show called *Tractors Tonight*, the farm industry would very likely achieve its own glamor status, and John Deere would receive the same adulation as George Clooney.

The first thing that anyone aspiring to the entertainment business will notice about the city of Hollywood itself is that it looks a little worn, frayed at the edges, bunching a little at the seams, showing only flashes of former greatness, like the shiny seat of your grandfather's pants now on sale at Goodwill. Hollywood is just a small part of a suburban casserole made up of all kinds of interconnected burgs and hamlets. The only major movie studio in Hollywood is Paramount. Twentieth Century Fox is in Century City, MGM is in Culver City, Universal is in Universal City and Warner Brothers and Disney are in Burbank. A drive from MGM to Disney would take you well over an hour (that is, if the traffic isn't at a bumper-to-bumper standstill).

Millions of people live in the Los Angeles area, and everyone has at least one vehicle, which will inevitably be on the freeway the same time you are. This freeway system was designed in the late Forties and early Fifties by Mister Magoo–like urban planners who failed to foresee the traffic demands of the twenty-first century, resulting in exhaust-in-your-face frustration all day, every day.

There is public transportation (called Rapid Transit), consisting entirely of buses, which you will generally find poking along in freeway traffic behind other oversized gas-guzzlers. There is a recently built underground subway from downtown Los Angeles to the San Fernando Valley, but as a traffic solution it's like planting a peanut in hopes of feeding Bangladesh. And with all the earthquake fault lines, underground transportation is, in my opinion, a risky endeavor, but I guess to all of L.A.'s authority types, it's worth a shot just to keep all those people moving.

Fact is, L.A.'s early city planners quite obviously underestimated the capability of human reproduction and immigration raids from the South, East, and everywhere else. There is hope on the horizon, however, because many Angelinos are moving up to Oregon, Idaho, and Washington State—which may eventually give all of those places the very same problems Los Angeles has.

For the original New York City moviemakers, the lure of L.A. was, and still is, the weather. The sun appears constantly (often hazily through the smog) and the temperatures are rather pleasant year round. There's a short rainy season, usually in January, but the temperatures seldom approach wintery proportions. And if it's winter you're after, it's only a couple of hours' drive to the ski slopes, where you are free to break an ankle while continuing to improve your tan.

ACCOUNTS:

Fun in the Smog

Opinions on living in Los Angeles itself are as diverse as the people who live there, as noted by the impressions of these Hollywood professionals.

Writer/producer *Dave Hackel*: "Living in Los Angeles has been, for the most part, extremely pleasant. I've enjoyed the contrast from the small Ohio town where I was raised. It's a very diverse community with much to offer both culturally and educationally. What I don't like about it can be summed up in one word—*earthquakes*."

Writer/producer *Ralph Gaby Wilson*: "L.A. is the greatest place to live. Minutes from the mountains. Minutes from the ocean. No snow. Of course, I may be prejudiced, I lived in Kansas and Illinois first."

Writer/producer *Charlie Hauck*: "L.A.'s size, ethnic diversity, cultural opportunities, restaurants, and weather make it a very exciting place to live. People complain about the increasing traffic, but have you ever tried to drive around Paris, Rome, or London?"

Actor *Jed Allan*: "It used to be beautiful. Now I hate it. There's traffic, it's overcast, there are no stars at night, expensive, not pretty anymore."

Writer *Coslough Johnson*: "I love living in Los Angeles. After being raised in Chicago and having lived in New York, Los Angeles is heaven. The weather is marvelous. If one wants the theater, it's here; the museums are here; and I don't need earmuffs in the winter."

Actor *Eddie Applegate*: "Living under the warm sunny-skied Los Angeles basin has been very good. So close yet so far away from many places and things. But it's no longer as friendly—it's more dangerous, like other large cities. You must drive everywhere—the car is the thing—and the telephone."

Actor/writer *Robert Hegyes*: "I love the weather. But, as for the actual city, it's a rough place. Especially if you have children. I'm on the freeway all the time now. My nerves are shattered driving a hundred miles a day."

Writer/TV executive *Laurie Scheer*: "I love L.A. I have lived here a total of fifteen years and left once only to be completely miserable living in Chicago and New York City. L.A. is never dull or boring. It's a place where dreams do in fact come true and you never have to scrape ice off your car in the winter. You couldn't pay me to live anywhere else."

For some years now, there has been an ever-increasing trend toward living completely outside the L.A. area. Many artists and craftspeople in the industry have relocated out of the hectic Hollywood scene to live in a somewhat grand fashion at a fraction of the cost. And, thanks to technology, these people are able to conduct much of their business without having to commute to L.A. Even though actors can't e-mail their talent, I know several who are willing to drive hours to auditions just to enjoy what they see as a better quality of life.

STANDARDS OF LIVING: HOW SMALL IS YOUR APARTMENT?

It's important to come to Hollywood with a few dollars in your pocket. TV- and movie-job magic seldom strikes immediately, so it's always wise to have some kind of a financial cushion. Though it seldom rains in sunny L.A., there can be plenty of rainy days.

Now, unless your name is Getty and Daddy has financially set you up, you'll need to find a room or apartment that is, somehow, affordable. Staying with friends while you scout the area for a place to call home is a good idea. If paying rent requires a roommate, there are services listed in the Hollywood Yellow Pages that can set you up with a partner. (Just avoid anyone with tattoos and a multip-ierced body who goes by the alias of Jimmy The Snitch.)

There are nice and fairly affordable sections of town, such as Los Feliz, West Hollywood, Studio City, Sherman Oaks, Tarzana, and other widespread areas of the San Fernando Valley, and there are sections to avoid, which shall remain nameless to avoid sue-happy politicians seeking campaign funds. Newspaper classifieds come in handy when seeking a place to hang your hat—or whatever you wish to hang. The *Los Angeles Times* is most prominent in this area—especially the Sunday edition, which lists all kinds of rooms for rent and contains a San Fernando Valley section. The paper covers the entire Los Angeles basin, so it's a good idea to invest in a map (you don't want to end up renting a shack in the middle of the Mojave Desert). As maps go, the best aid is a *Thomas Guide*, which details all areas of the city, the afore-mentioned areas being the most popular with anyone new to the area. The trade papers (*Daily Variety*, *The Hollywood Reporter*) also have classified sections, and are worth checking out. Friday issues usually contain the most comprehensive list.

ACCOUNTS:

A Room of One's Own _____

Here's what a few of the professionals have to say about their standards of living when they first burst onto the Hollywood scene.

Writer/producer *Peter Lefcourt*: "I lived in a furnished one-bedroom apart-ment in Venice ($140 a month, utilities included), and I ate a lot of Kraft macaroni and cheese."

Actor *Hank Jones*: "I lived with the family of my college roommate in nearby La Canada. I would do chores and odd jobs to earn my keep there. Without their generosity and kindness I never would have made it. Later on, I had small apartments in Studio City and Hollywood. I never really econo-mized, per se, but I was never extravagant, either. Just semi-sensible."

Actress/writer *Candace Howerton*: "I rented an apartment on Pico Boulevard in Santa Monica. The rent was $125 for a furnished one-bedroom with pool. That was a lot for me. I economized after my first two weeks, when my Studebaker blew a gasket and I only had four dollars to my name."

Writer/TV executive *Laurie Scheer*: "I lived with two roommates in a two-bedroom townhouse on Riverside Drive in North Hollywood. Times were lean. I drove my five-year-old Mustang, and did very little socializing other than hanging out at house parties with college friends. Meals consisted of tuna fish and ramen noodles."

Writer/producer *Charlie Hauck*: "I came out to Hollywood while my wife remained in Pittsburgh with the children. I rented a one-room efficiency apartment with a kitchenette in West Hollywood. The heater didn't work, but I thought, 'Hey, this is Los Angeles, you don't need heat.' I spent the winter shivering under blankets at night because I persisted in insisting to myself that you don't need heat in Los Angeles."

Actor *Lou Wagner*: "When I got to Hollywood, I studied acting at the ANTA Academy. The Academy owned a house (the old William S. Hart place) that they needed a caretaker for so they could tell their insurance company someone was living there. I stayed there for nothing. Soon after, the Actors Studio took over the house, put a theater in the garage, and they allowed me to stay on, and I became a member of the Actors Studio. . . . As you can see, there was an angel standing over me at every turn."

Besides a roof over your head, there are other *essential items* that you will require—certain investments that the business demands:

1. **A Car!** Maybe you'll drive your vehicle to California like many do.
2. **A Phone.** Show business is a phone business. If you're obsessive about your career, a cell phone is not a bad idea.
3. **An Answering Machine or Voice Mail Service.** You wouldn't want to miss that call from Spike Lee.
4. **Internet Access.** Not always feasible at the start, but something that is being used more and more everyday in the conduct of show business. Most importantly, you must keep an e-mail account.

I've seen many interviews with Hollywood stars-of-the-moment who talked about the abject poverty they endured while starting out on their road to nirvana. These tales suggest that the starving-artist lifestyle is a necessary route to success. Well, let me set this whole thing straight. It is not necessary to live on Spam and potatoes with no phone while wearing ragged clothes with holes in the elbows. This is not a pre-star requirement, nor is it an image to be cultivated. Maybe in the Sixties, but not now.

There is a difference between humble beginnings and living like a poor slob. You will need certain necessities, like those listed above. You will have to be easily reached by phone or e-mail and will have to be responsible for your own mode of transportation. Modest living does require some necessary spending. These are investments in survival, not wasteful excess. So, think these things through, and be smart—if you simply cannot afford a car, get a motorbike (but stay off the freeways). As long as you address your needs and approach your business in a practical way, you'll be just fine. If you have any rich relatives, drop them a line now and then.

ROOKIE UPDATE

Rachel Lawrence writes that she hasn't found it easy setting up housekeeping in Hollywood:

> My parents arranged for me to room with my cousin, Abby, who works for an Internet business that just went belly-up, so she got real depressed, and that's when I found out she was gay, and I'm afraid to tell Mom and Daddy, who I'm sure don't have a clue. Anyways, I found this tiny studio apartment in North Hollywood, which would be pretty expensive if Mom and Daddy weren't helping out. . . . My Honda civic ("Daisy") performed beautifully all the way out here and it's been real reliable. . . . I went for an open audition for a play that I read about in *The Hollywood Reporter*. They call it a cattle call and all of L.A. was there! I never knew there were so many actresses, and I've always been told I have above average looks, but it seems that so do a lot of other girls. I waited over three hours and they were very rude, and I would never work with them even if they had given me the part, which they didn't. . . . And now, the big news! Ta-Da!! I have an appointment with an honest-to-goodness agent next week. Wish me luck! . . . Rachel.

Kyle Kramer e-mails:

> I've been living here in Burbank for about a week and a half. My parents have a two-bedroom they use as a 'getaway,' but I use it as a home. I saved up about $5,000, so I have a little freedom for the time being. I have a car, since it's almost impossible to survive in this city without one. It's a '95 Ford Contour with just over a hundred thousand miles on it, and the air conditioning keeps breaking, but I'll live with it. . . . I met with this manager and she's interested in helping me get a commercial

agent, and a commercial agent (if I'm lucky enough) will get me a Screen Actors Guild card. I also registered at the Cenex Casting Network for extra work and they gave me a hotline to call every day that gives the current job openings. . . . I'm also putting the finishing touches on my third movie script. . . . Talk to you soon, Kyle.

Chapter 3

CREATING A GAME PLAN

Bite off more than you can chew,
Then chew it.
Plan more than you can do,
Then do it.
Point your arrow at a star,
Take your aim, and there you are,
Arrange more time than you can spare,
Then spare it.
Take on more than you can bear,
Then bear it.
Plan your castle in the air,
Then build a ship to take you there.
—Anonymous

So, here you are, an official Hollywoodian with a roof over your head and a pot of indescribable stew on your hot plate. Your fantasies are suddenly a step closer to reality as you imagine your face on the cover of *TV Guide*, and your very own cubicle on *Hollywood Squares*. You'd even imagine an Academy Award on your mantel if you had a mantel. But all of this starry-eyed daydreaming indicates that it's time to start planting roots for your career growth—to stake your claim on a new life as you embark upon your journey through Hollywood. At this point, it is important to realize that this can only be accomplished by rendering yourself fit for the trip. It truly is an unknown jungle out there, and only the fit survive. Having talent is good. Incredible luck is better, but since you have decided to follow the lure of the brass ring and enter the realm of fantasy, it's up to you to equip yourself for the journey. You're the only one you can depend on here—it's an "inside" job. Actor Robert Duvall expressed it this way: "If you don't daydream and kind of plan things out in your imagination, you never get there. So you have to start someplace."

DEFINING YOUR GOAL

Survival in Hollywood requires that you develop a systematic *plan* to play the game while keeping your goal plainly in sight. Stick to that plan—it's good business. And, as you will soon find out, show business is a lot more business than show. A good way to get a clear picture of that goal is to form for yourself a mental motion picture.

Noted theater/film director/acting teacher Milton Katselas has written an excellent book called *Dreams into Action*, in which he advises show business folk with these words: "In truth, it's your movie the whole way. You're the writer, producer, director, and lead actor, and it's all based on your original story and idea." So, based on Katselas's premise, this is certainly no time to be dreaming in a modest way. Modesty is for wusses and wimps. This calls for an extension of vision, and a truthful admission of hidden desires. Those who dream beyond their wildest dreams leave themselves open for an incredible future.

You're on a life's mission. A personal quest. Be specific. Know what that quest is. *Visualize* your object, your ambition, your destiny. Those with unclouded vision open themselves up to *living* that vision, so fearlessly allow yourself to be led by optimism. Think big. Far too many people think it's wise to dream in realistic terms—with constraint. The feeling is that if they limit their thinking, failure won't hurt as much. . . . Well, wait a Hollywood minute, who's talking about failure here? Those who think small get small, and where's the big future in that?

Arnold Schwarzenegger once described his method of career visualization in this way: "It's the same process I used in body-building. What you do is create a vision of what you want to be, and then live into that picture as if it were absolutely true."

Once you've visualized your huge, unclouded goal, write it down. You may write: "I want to have a successful show business career." That's it? That's all you wrote? Well, curb that modest dreaming, buckaroo (or buckarette)—release your imagination from its politically correct cage and play with it—decorate your thoughts, adorn them with your most secret of all wishes. This is your success story—make it phenomenal because only big dreams yield extraordinary results.

PUTTING YOUR BEST FACE FORWARD

The best face is an honest face. You will only achieve your wildest dreams by approaching them with a realistic understanding of yourself. Hollywood demands that you be honest about who you are and view yourself from a practical perspective. You may be able to sing a killer aria, but do you have the catchy face and sprightly step required for the part?

"Singing was my primary talent," recalls **Jim Begg**, though singing wouldn't quite do the trick for him:

I quickly learned that having a good voice was only part of it. For the most part you had to have leading man good looks, so singing was a long shot. A very long shot. I feel you have to be honest with yourself about what you have to offer. Fortunately, character actors can do very well in Hollywood. That's how I saw myself.

As Jim did, you must see your talented self as a product, fully aware of exactly what it is you are marketing. Sure, you may be versatile—you can act, you can write, direct, do a Britney Spears impression through your nose—but you can't be everything to everybody. It's best to initially focus on what it is you do best and to be specific about what you are marketing to the wonderful world of entertainment.

People come in all shapes and sizes, but movie-star looks are a rarity. Accept yourself for what you are (at face value, so to speak). Be creative in using what you have—and I don't mean surgery. Too many people in Hollywood rely on plastic surgery, only to end up looking like they had plastic surgery. Woody Allen once commented that a certain actress looked like her face had been lifted by a golf pro. So, look at it this way. Imperfections can be used to your advantage. If your ears are uneven or your nose veers to the left on windy days, it may be what sells you, sets you apart from the rest, and makes you mysteriously enchanting.

Lou Wagner approached his career in this manner:

At 5'2" everyone said I'd never make it as an actor because of my size, so I signed with a children's agent and was playing thirteen-year-olds at the age of twenty-five. I guess you could say that I turned my shortage into an asset.

In contrast, I believe that I stunted my acting potential by limiting myself. Even though I possessed a young Jack Lemmon quality, I saw myself as a character actor, not a leading man. I was good at quirky characterizations, and played a lot of offbeat roles. Now, I don't mean to put down those sorts of opportunities; it's just that (though devilishly handsome) I refused to think of myself in terms of a leading man, and that was a shame. I could have gone on to win my very own Blockbuster Award. Knowing *who* you are and *believing* in yourself: These two elements are essential to success and survival in Hollywood.

THE AGENT GAME

Remember, success in show business is a lot about planning, and about marketing a product. The product is *you*—your talent, your skills, your face, the way your lip curls like Elvis when you snarl. You must tackle three universal elements that are essential to anyone's plan of action:

1. An understanding of the basic mechanics of Hollywood: how things work.
2. A gathering of necessary show business intelligence: information.
3. An organization of the necessary tools to get your career underway.

In a closer analysis of number 1, any show business wannabe will quickly discover the necessity of having an *agent*. An agent is the person who will represent you to the industry. No doors will open for you unless you are represented by an agent with some reputable visibility in the Hollywood scene. Agents rule the world of show business and any individual with skill and talent needs to have one. This goes for actors, writers, directors, producers—even cinematographers have agents. Most production designers, makeup artists, costumers, and people who specialize in funny voices have agents. The agent is to Hollywood what a nut is to a bolt, or a screw to a driver. You'll never get so much as a glimpse without one.

This brings us to element number 2: the gathering of *information*. And since your first target is the acquisition of career representation, you will find yourself asking the following questions:

1. Where do I find these agents?
2. How do I know who the good agents are?
3. How do I get a meeting with an agent?
4. Would it be best (as an actor) to start with an agent who specializes in commercials?
5. Would a personal manager be a good idea?
6. Should I be represented by an entertainment attorney?

These were the kinds of questions I considered when I began my career, and it took me far too long to find the answers, so just count yourself lucky that you have this book to help you through this list.

First: Where do you find these agents? Lists are available from the various Guilds: Screen Actors Guild (SAG), American Federation of Television and Radio Artists (AFTRA), Writers' Guild of America west (WGAw), and the Directors Guild of America (DGA). You do not have to be a guild member to obtain a list, but a small fee may be required. Go to the public library and check out an actors, writers, or directors directory; find out what agents represent the people who work all the time. These directories can usually be found at Hollywood bookstores like Samuel French and Larry Edmunds. Information can also be accessed online from the Hollywood Creative Directory. (See appendix B for details.)

This brings us to the next question: How do you know who the good agents are? You don't. This requires a bit of investigation. You will have to talk to people in the business who have been around a little longer and have had a touch more savvy knocked into them than you have. Names of the good agents will surface, and these are the people you should initially focus on. As for my two-cents' worth,

I believe that the best agent is the one who shows an interest in taking you on as a client; and, if you're a good client, you'll get work that will make your agent the best agent there ever was. Never forget, though, that the very best agent can only point you toward the job. Landing that sucker is up to you.

How do you get a meeting with an agent? Well, if you're an actor, get on the phone and call these movers and shakers. Doggedly pursue the short-term goal of getting a meeting. You'll find that many of the larger agencies are simply not interested in seeing new people, but there are a number of smaller (boutique) agencies that may agree to meet with you. And if they don't, just keep on plugging. Theatrical agent **Judy Coppage** notes, "You have to have a thick skin and not really care what other people think."

Commercial agents are always a good idea for actors. If you have an average appearance, a kooky look, a pleasant voice, or the ability to do "character" voices, by all means seek out a commercial agent. (Many of them supply talent to animated cartoon shows.) Commercial agent **Kim Muir** goes on to explain the accessibility of getting an agent.

> In finding an agent in Hollywood, it is usually easier to get a commercial agent than a theatrical (film and TV) agent. Commercially, we can have a larger client list. Also, theatrical agencies prefer actors with a few more credits and who are members of the Screen Actors Guild (SAG).

Kim continues, pointing out that securing agency representation is no easy task because of the changing business climate.

> When I started, there were no more than twenty top commercial agencies—and, perhaps, the same number of top commercial casting directors, so you really knew each other and could cast over the phone. I would have twenty of my actors in on one job. Now there are over two hundred commercial agencies—some representing about two hundred actors—and there are others who represent up to two thousand. And, now, with fifty or sixty casting people, and the same amount of jobs, I'm lucky if I get three clients in for an audition.

I had an excellent commercial agent when I was an actor, and I supported myself for years acting in national commercials for major products like Dentyne Gum, Crest Toothpaste, Canada Dry, Scotch Tape, and Hallmark Cards. Those residual payments got me through many a rocky valley of unemployment. The commercial market is highly competitive and the auditions are conducted impersonally on videotape, but it's worth a shot since there can be a whole bunch'a boodle in hawking constipation relief on the tube.

If you're a writer, send out a sample (spec) script to agents who specialize in writers. These names will also surface in the course of your intelligence gathering. It's always a good idea to call these agents before mailing to determine whether they accept unsolicited material. Smaller agencies usually will, so send your script to whoever is accepting, along with a self-addressed, stamped script-mailing envelope, and hope like hell they won't make the mistake of rejecting your genius.

ACCOUNTS:

Agents' Notes

Here's more of the inside scoop on what agents are looking for.

Writers' agent *Gary Cosay*: "Talent. It's on the page. If they have a positive presence and, most importantly, if they can write, that gets my heart going, that makes me passionate. I read a lot of scripts from recommendations, executives, other clients (which can be a great resource). I generally don't accept unsolicited manuscripts. When I was a young agent I did, but now that I've been in the business for a long time, it's harder for me to relate to a twenty-one-year-old because I am . . . well, over twenty-one."

Commercial agent *Kim Muir*: "*Never* sign with an agency that wants money up front. Again, the best way to find an agent is through other actors who are happy with their representation—or contact SAG and ask for a list of franchised agents.

We find our talent by going to showcases, workshops, plays, referrals from managers, and other actors—rarely from a picture submission. From hundreds of pictures and resumes submitted weekly, we *may* bring in four to six in an entire year."

MANAGERS

"A manager is someone who is supposed to know what the 'next big thing' is," says writer/producer/personal manager **Greg Strangis**, "and, consequently, can help his writer-client develop his next spec script. A manager should be able to read an outline, a treatment, or script and offer meaningful suggestions for shaping, trimming, or expanding the material. As long as the goals are clear, any writer can potentially benefit from having a manager."

A few facts (courtesy of **Greg Strangis**) that you should know about managers and agents:

1. Managers usually charge 15 percent to the agents' 10 percent.
2. Agents are regulated by the state; managers are not.
3. While both agents and managers put packages together (project, writer, director, top cast members), only managers are allowed to also play the role of producer.
4. Unlike agents, managers are not supposed to solicit employment for their clients. (Neither New York State or California law supports such activity.)
5. Managers usually have fewer clients than agents.
6. While agents seek employment for their clients, managers develop careers.
7. Anyone can have a manager or an agent, or both.

ACCOUNTS:

Managerial Opinions _____

Here's what managers have to say about management, along with an agent's perspective on the subject.

Writer/producer/personal manager *Greg Strangis* (on writers): "Sure, managers are a good idea, if you have a career to manage. Or a career in desperate need of a jump-start. Writers need to treat themselves the way actors and directors treat themselves. They need to be more forward-thinking, looking beyond their current job toward the future to shape their careers into something long-term. They need publicity so that they can become a 'brand' much the way directors and actors (and novelists) do. Managers can help a writer get their first agent or get a better agent. Managers can find and hire the writer a publicist. Managers can help put additional elements (an actor, director, etc.) into a project the writer is creating to make that project irresistible to potential buyers."

Personal manager (for actors) *Brooke Bundy*: "I like to think of myself as another arm for the agents, working in conjunction with them. . . . And, when an agent gets an audition, I always tell the client that the audition came from the agent. . . . Times are hard, though, and a lot of agencies are closing—it's just too difficult."

Writers' agent *Gary Cosay*: "The day of agent as 'protector' is quickly disappearing. Writers now have managers who, to their credit, have gone out and started the writers when they had no agents. . . . In the big agency business, where many clients feel lost, they feel a manager gives them a day-to-day person to talk to—who will protect them. In the Seventies and the

Eighties, the protector was the agent. Today, it's different, but, for me, my first priority will always be the client and the client's welfare."

ENTERTAINMENT ATTORNEYS—AN ALTERNATIVE?

Finally, as for being represented by an entertainment attorney, no reputable attorney will be interested unless you are working steadily in TV or motion pictures and your name has achieved a certain currency in the business. Agents are quite capable of handling the legal aspects of contracts, so I wouldn't recommend you be concerned with an entertainment lawyer when your career is just getting underway.

GET TO KNOW YOUR BUSINESS

Any aspiring Hollywood talent should make it a point to know the business, which means gathering any splinters of information that might prove helpful. You do this by simply scoping out the territory. Get informed. There are any number of ways that this can be accomplished.

Drop by the union offices of SAG, AFTRA, WGAw, DGA, and IATSE (International Association of Theatrical Stage Employees), bring donuts, explain who you are, and request any information that they might have that will help you get started. They are not likely to recommend specific agents or acting schools, but you never know what bubbles of information will surface. The Writers' Guild may provide you with a list of writing seminars because they realize that you're a future dues-paying member of their organization, and they'd be foolish not to help.

Question everyone you meet about anything you want to know—tips and bits of information that might help. You will quickly see that the favorite topic of conversation among people in the business is the business.

Constantly read the trade papers (*The Hollywood Reporter*, *Daily Variety*, *Backstage West*) for useful information. There are always stories about what studios and networks are planning—along with who the studio and network muckymucks happen to be at the moment. A typical story will reveal that Al Schmendrick has been appointed vice president of development at Spectacular Pictures, where he will report to president Sid Veemer. Months later, a story will appear telling you that Al Schmendrick has resigned as vice president of development for Spectacular Pictures to produce his own independent projects for the studio. Taking over Schmendrick's job is Casey Creeper. (In show business terms, this means that Schmendrick was fired; it's just that the word "fired" is never used.)

Personnel rotate pretty fast in Hollywood. An actor I knew kept a scrapbook of all the hirings and firings so that he would know who was who and where they were at the moment. A writer friend of mine keeps tabs on Web sites, since all the studios and trade papers have Web sites. (See appendix B.)

TOOLS OF THE ACTING TRADE

Any effective, professionally prepared actor's marketing plan must contain the necessary "tools" of the trade. In general, an actor needs enormous powers of observation in order to develop a sense of what makes people tick. It helps to observe, with frequency, the work of other actors in good performance—not to copy, but to *learn* from the best. There are several very practical items that no actor can do without.

HEADSHOTS. It's essential to have a huge stack of 8″x10″ headshots, showing your nose in its best light. I would not recommend snapshots taken by your Cousin Dud at the Labor Day family picnic; your headshots should be taken by a professional Hollywood photographer. These people advertise everywhere and are not difficult to locate. I always found out who the best ones were by asking around and, better yet, noticing good photographs and who shot them.

In regards to actors' photos, personal manager **Brooke Bundy** recommends that you:

Don't go cheap on pictures—or on the photographer. Good makeup, the right clothes. And when you duplicate the photos, don't try to save money. People spend like $500 on the photographer, get a $200 makeup job, great clothes, then they go to some hole-in-the-wall to get the photos duplicated. . . . You must have good photos—they're a major part of your business. The important thing is that you look like your picture. Casting directors go bananas if you don't. I just interviewed a girl and her pictures looked so unlike her. . . . And don't try to be glamorous if you're not: You will never work; you are going to be competing against people who are truly gorgeous. If you're plain, be plain. There are lots of parts for plain people—in fact, probably more of them."

Commercial agent **Kim Muir** offers this experienced view:

Good pictures are *vital*. Your picture is your calling card, and a good picture can get you in the door. Shop around—look at other actors' shots. Also, you can usually find samples of photographers' work posted in acting studios and workshops. . . . Meet the photographer and look at his or her work. Not only their books, but ask to look at proof sheets. (Naturally, their books will have only their best work.) Also important is the chemistry between you. In terms of cost, you *can* find excellent photographers who are moderately priced. . . . Although you may come to an agency with recent pictures, be prepared to shoot again. Your new agent may want new and different shots.

Now, these two professional representatives are in full agreement that you should have at least one good photo headshot. This means you'll have to find a reasonably priced photographer so you'll have something to send out to agents. (Yes, you'll have to shell out for envelopes and postage.) You likely will have new photographs taken when you get an agent, so don't blow a wad of money on pictures as soon as you hit town.

ACTION VIDEO. Where, in the past, your 8″x10″ glossy was enough, today's actors' market demands an additional tool—a performance video. Many producers don't audition in person anymore; they just want to see you in action in the privacy of their own mansion. If you have your performance on film, get the film transferred to tape. If you've appeared on TV, in even a small role, get it on video. If they taped your high school play where you played the lead, the quality probably stinks, so forget it. (If it was Shakespeare, I recommend you move to London.)

In recent years, VHS has been replaced by CD-ROM or DVD. But sooner than you think, some newer technology will take over, and you'll be forced to keep up with whatever is "hot" in Hollywood at the moment. For now, let's just say a good VHS tape will suffice.

If you're without a videotape, you'll be completely out of the loop and will have to have one made. There are businesses that do this. Also, you can take acting classes where scenes are taped. Which are the best? Ask around and you'll find the answer.

Brooke Bundy, who's an expert at these sorts of things, points out that:

An actor must have a performance tape that shows as much variety as possible. I think one of the dangers actors fall into is they want to make it entertaining, so they add all this stuff to it. . . . But the people who watch it—producers, directors, whoever—are not going to watch it to be entertained. They want two and a half minutes, five minutes maximum—boom, boom—in and out—they want to see what you can do, how you photograph, how you relate.

This videotape (film to video) can also be an effective tool for any aspiring director wishing to show a sample of his or her work. This is an absolute necessity. Producers have this quirk where they insist on knowing whether you have any talent before they let you direct. Well . . . most of the time.

If you're an actor pursuing the TV-commercial route, your agent may request that you also have a voice tape—lots of duplicate voice tapes for them to send out, in fact, so you can become the next voice of an animated bratwurst.

ACTING CLASSES. A good, conscientious actor hones his or her craft. This goes for newcomers to the profession, as well as New York actors schooled in stage technique, who need to learn the subtleties of acting before a camera. There is certainly no shortage of acting classes in the L.A. area. In a recent issue of *Backstage West*, I counted sixty-five ads for acting classes.

Actress/acting teacher **Helaine Lembeck** stresses the need for adequate training:

> These days, actors are trying to do whatever they can to be seen, but the biggest danger is being seen before you are ready. I have a friend who was a dancer—a beautiful girl who, when she stopped dancing, decided to become an actress. She had several interviews with casting directors and producers and didn't do very well. She decided to get trained, studied hard, and when she tried to see those people again, they didn't want to see her, because they remembered her. She had to fight very hard to get back in that door.

When I was producing TV shows, I was often involved in casting sessions where a series of actors would parade through my office in hopes that their script reading would knock me for a loop, and the loop-knockers were invariably those actors who studied and practiced their craft on a regular basis.

As a story editor on various series, I would take story pitches from writers and sit there in eager anticipation hoping that some writer would knock me for a literary loop. I could always distinguish the wheat writers from the chaff writers. The wheaters knew the show and its characters; they brought something new into the room, and presented a well-crafted professional storyline. The chaffers appeared not to have seen the show and rarely had any connection with TV reality. (For example, a sitcom with three standing sets is not likely to have exterior scene at the Hoover Dam.) Suffice it to say, the wheaters always won.

ACCOUNTS:

Strutting Your Stuff _____

Judging from **Helaine Lembeck**'s advice above, I'd say it's important for actors to make a good first impression because that's the one that will last. Here is some more advice on making that impression.

Brooke Bundy: "Come to Hollywood with some money in your pocket so you can take care of rent, you can get into class, you can have pictures taken. Enough money for at least six months. . . . Get into class, and a good class, not the cheapest class. Don't go to the one closest to home. That's like going to a cheap brain surgeon. Go to the best. It's an investment."

Helaine Lembeck: "It's not easy to know which workshop is reputable. You open up a paper like *Backstage West*, and there are a lot of ads, but which are the good ones? Well, the best piece of advice I could give is, ask around. Ask people whose work you respect—find out where they studied and who they studied with. If you ask around a lot, the same names are going to pop up more than once."

Kim Muir: "If you're new in town, the first move is to get involved in the acting community. Get in plays, do workshops, get in scene study and cold reading classes. Meet other actors. I have found actors to be very generous with each other—and they'll submit a picture and résumé of their friend. . . .The most important thing that I can tell anybody who wants to become an actor—whether it's in New York, Los Angeles, Dallas, Chicago—you must love auditioning, because that is what you do for a living. If you don't love the art of auditioning, don't do it."

TOOLS OF THE WRITING TRADE

A writer (like an actor) needs to be an observer—a people-watcher, sucking up the various traits that make up human nature. Writers should read the work of good writers and allow for at least a few hours of concentrated writing effort on a daily basis, something that takes enormous discipline. A computer (or typewriter) is a necessity, as well as a fax machine and access to a copier. The most basic tool is a writing sample—a script written on "spec," meaning you write for no money in the interests of grossing a bundle down the road (a recurring prospect for all writers). This can be a spec TV episode (either comedy or drama), as long as it's a series that is current and bears the mark of a hit. (A spec *My Favorite Martian*, despite its historical value, will not do the trick.) You'll have to have a good number of copies of your spec script to send out, so be prepared to make friends with the entire staff at your local Kinko's. If you're in doubt about the script format requirements for TV and motion pictures, bookstores like Samuel French and Larry Edmunds sell script copies that can be used to guide you.

As an adjunct to your spec script you should be equipped with several ideas for the show you are aiming at. However, things have a way of not working out as planned, and your script may get you in the door of a completely different show (for example, you might spec a *That '70s Show* and they want to see you over at *Frasier*). This happens, so always be ready to fortify yourself with ideas for that show. If a spec engages the interest of the biggies, the biggies will insist you "pitch" your story ideas verbally. Sure, they're engaging in a sadistic rite, but they want to see how spontaneously creative you are. They love writers who can quickly whip out fresh ideas for their shows. Fresh ideas keep shows on the air. In my own case, spec scripts and subsequent ideas often led me to staff writing jobs.

One of the finest sales tools in the Hollywood writing business is a completed screenplay (on spec, of course, and definitely more than one.). Studios are in a constant clamor for good screenwriting. Many writing, directing, producing, and acting careers have been launched by a solid screenplay.

Writing a spec screenplay and writing a spec teleplay involve two completely different businesses. The motion picture business is covered in amazing detail in the book *Adventures in the Screen Trade*, by William Goldman. Terrific information can also be found in Garry Marshall's fine book, *Wake Me When It's Funny* (with Lori Marshall), as well as in my own book, *Writing Television Comedy*.

ACCOUNTS:
Suggestions for Scribblers _____

Pay close attention to the following morsels of wisdom from these writing professionals.

Writer/producer *Arnold Margolin*: "Make contacts and use any you can find: alumni of schools you attended; people from the same hometown; fraternity brothers or sorority sisters; mom's high school sweetheart (who turned out to be gay, but now runs a studio)."

Writer/producer *John Furia, Jr.*: "I wrote a spec script and had an agent I respected read it. He promptly offered to represent me. I quit my job and gave myself a year to sell something. I wrote and submitted dozens of stories, outlines, and scripts, which were well received, but never sold. By Christmas, I decided I had failed and began to pester anyone I knew for a job in the production side, any job. Between Christmas and New Years—a bleak time in the industry, when most people are on vacation—I had a call from my agent. He had just sold my first story. It was never produced, but it somehow changed my luck and I began selling briskly right after the first of the year."

Charlie Hauck: "I have learned that when you go into a pitch meeting, a bad opening line is, 'Have you gained weight?'"

BOTTOM LINE

Okay, photos, videos, CD-ROMs, DVDs, voice tapes, tape duplication, computers, faxes, script copies, disks, postage—all these things cost money, which is why it's so important to have some financial cushion upon your arrival in Hollywood. These are necessary investments in your career. (But hurry while they're still tax deductible.)

Survival in Hollywood begins the very first day you arrive—and with the right steps backed by an effective, well-thought-out plan of action, you are well on your way to surviving your journey.

ROOKIE UPDATE

Rachel Lawrence writes with a career update:

> I met with that agent and she was totally discouraging. She went on and on about how tough it is and how being pretty and acting in high school plays aren't enough. She actually yelled at me for not being in an acting class and learning my craft—which was good advice, and I intend to do it. But you'd think that important people like her could be a little nicer. I kept feeling that she was blaming me because she never made it as an actress. . . . I heard about a class from this other actress and I'm going to check on it. She told me some agents actually come to the class and talk to the students, so who knows?? Maybe I'll be discovered or something. . . . Now for the big bummer—"Daisy" (my car) needs new brakes. Daddy just flipped, but he's sending me a check anyhow. In the meantime, just like Scarlett O'Hara, I'll never give up, or never starve, or whatever that line was! . . . Bye for now, Rachel.

Kyle Kramer e-mails:

> I've been hearing from other actors all about showcases for agents and casting directors. They usually cost between $200 and $300 and consist of someone standing in front of six uninterested agents/casting directors/someone's assistant and doing a monologue. This girl tried to rope me into paying $250 to do a scene with her at an agent showcase, but I respectfully declined. She said that the key to going into something like that is to go into it knowing you're going to get screwed and hope for the best. That didn't make a whole lot of sense to me, though. I'd rather just hope for the best. Anyway she went and did her scene from *Magnolia* where Julianne Moore cries and screams at the pharmacist for calling her "lady." I've seen her do the scene and she's really good at it. . . . So,

when she was done, one of the agents looked up and said (with a straight face), "Okay, do you do drama too?" The rest of the agents had a good chuckle and she left. So for the mere price of a DVD player she got humiliated and shoved out the door. Now, I'm sure that some people go to showcases where there are very professional, well-mannered, respectful agents/casting directors/assistants, but right now I think they're all bullshit and wouldn't be caught dead in one. . . . Keep smiling, Kyle.

Chapter 4

SELLING YOURSELF

To survive in Hollywood you need the ambition of a Latin American revolutionary, the ego of a grand opera tenor, and the physical stamina of a cow pony.
—actress Billie Burke (the Good Witch in *The Wizard of Oz*)

Judging from the above quote, it's obvious that Ms. Burke had her wand firmly in touch with the survival realities of 1930s Hollywood—realities that are pretty much the same today. It might be a good idea to take a moment to sum up what we've talked about so far.

You are on a career mission with an unshakable sense of purpose and a clear vision of your goal. Your high hopes are now even higher hopes because you know full well that optimism works. You possess an unwavering will to win. You're prepared (you have your plan in place, and now it's time to sell your talents to Hollywood) to let them know that there's a new kid on the block and nothing can stop the kid now. Of course, you've got to get yourself noticed first.

AGENT RELATIONS

Earlier I discussed the importance of having a plan—a set of short-term goals that *sell* you and lead directly to the big whamoo. The first goal was to get an agent, so I'll assume that you have managed to secure agency representation. If you have not, and you feel discouraged, and you are convinced that it's hopeless, forget the whole thing, okay?! You have no guts and will soon be back home shoveling slag in your family's lead factory! . . . Sorry, I got carried away. But, hey, all negativity aside—I have complete confidence that you will land yourself that coveted agent so, like I said, let's just assume that you have that agent. Congratulations, I never had a doubt in the world that you could do it. You are now ready to take the field and knock 'em dead.

Now, once you land this agent, the *relationship* you will choose to have with him or her is pretty much up to you. It is imperative to understand that your agent is not your surrogate father or mother, maybe not even your friend. I've had agents whom I considered friends and would see socially; I've also had agents I'd never want to be seen with in public because they were creeps—but they were terrific agents.

Far too many times, clients will view agents as their employers, with the false perception that they are working for the agents who represent them. It comes with the insecurities of the business, but it is totally false. Certainly, any client-agent relationship must be viewed as a ninety-ten partnership. You may get 90 percent, and your agent may get 10 percent, but it's a collaborative effort, with your success as the only goal. Clients who sit around waiting for their agents to find them a job could make a better living selling Jell-O in the jungle.

Any artist in his or her right mind is seldom in his or her right mind when it comes to dealing with an agent. A lot of agents aren't in their right minds, either, so call this one a draw. One thing, though: Never forget that your agent does not work exclusively for you. Your agent does have other clients, y'know. You are not at the top of the list. Other clients may be moving more quickly than you. This is a business. So, when it comes to your career, your agent can only be considered as part-time help. You, on the other hand, get the 90 percent, so yours is a full-time, independently self-indulgent commitment to get out there and hustle your little tush off. And if your tush ain't little, it soon will be.

Any client who sits around waiting for his or her agent to call is on a slow boat to nowhere. You call them. Agents must be reminded every few weeks that you are there. Be witty, be bright—in Hollywood, it's an asset to give good phone. You may even send little notes reminding your agent that you've ordered your star for the Hollywood Walk of Fame. Nudging is necessary, but don't fail to realize that your agent is indeed making efforts on your behalf. The entire situation requires teamwork, with your 90 percent of the team putting a 100 percent effort into furthering your own career.

How you choose to perform your 90 percent is up to you, but I do have a few suggestions for keeping close contact with your agent.

1. A birthday card is always a nice sentiment. It makes your agent think a little more fondly of you—hey, it makes your agent think of you, period!
2. A little holiday gift, perhaps? A tin of cookies? A small basket of fruit? Nothing ostentatious or expensive. Just a little token. (It's mucho important to know whether your agent celebrates Christmas or Chanukah.)
3. Maybe once a month, a short e-mailed update, filling your agent in on the efforts you've been making on your own behalf, contacts you may have made, classes you are taking, plays you will be doing, scripts you're working on. If you have nothing to report, boo on you—you should be ashamed.

ACCOUNTS:

Agents and Their Clients _____

Relations with agents vary. Client-agent relationships are as unique as the people who comprise them. Here are some opinions from both sides.

Writer/TV executive *Laurie Scheer*: "Agents are the scum of the earth. That's all, the scum of the earth. When you pick up a phone and you are greeted with '$#%* you!' instead of a nice 'good morning' for no reason, you know it's not going to be a pleasant phone conversation."

Writer *Franklin Thompson*: "The agent too often becomes the whipping boy, the handy target for the client's desperation and fear of failure. The agent must execute the client's worst, greediest impulses, leaving him or her free to play the 'nice' person."

Writer/producer *Del Reisman*: "I was never one to switch agents a lot. I stayed with one office for many years. Agents are extremely important and motion picture and television writers need their help. One thing is very basic—the agent can get around to more places than the individual without representation. Whether it's a theatrical attorney or an agent—representation is needed."

Commercial agent *Kim Muir*: "One common mistake clients make is just sitting around waiting for their agents to do everything. Waiting for that phone to ring. . . . That's a big one. The people who seem to work the most are the ones who have that energy—the ones who are taking classes, the ones that are always current with their pictures and resumes, who call once a month to see if we need more pictures, who get their faces out there with good stage work—or they take casting director workshops. The casting directors from successful prime time TV shows may show up and will look at new talent doing scenes. I know a lot of actors who have been called in because of casting director workshops."

Writers' agent *Gary Cosay*: "My agency, United Talent, is the fourth-largest agency in the world with eighty agents and two hundred employees. In the business today, agencies look at their buyer relationships and their internal relationships coming ahead of the client, so the clients are taking a lesser position, and I do have a problem with that. . . . I view my job as representing the client first—fighting for the client, and having a fiduciary relationship and the trust of the client. I love my agency, and I love parts of my work as long as I don't have to compromise my relationships with those I represent."

Theatrical agent *Judy Coppage*: "We all have unfortunate relationships. That's the nature of the business. Nothing stays the same. People also evolve at different rates. Most people don't realize how hard you have to work. If I hear one more 'Get me a job!' I'll scream. No one is going to do anything for you in this town. I tell people to take their power and do things for themselves. Don't expect others to take care of you—people only want you because you have something they want. You are not special."

GETTING NOTICED

A crucial aspect of Hollywood survival is an overabundance of positive mental energy. Putting yourself out there with a boldness of purpose, and an enthusiasm that proclaims: "Hey, Hollywood, looky here—it's *me!*" Now, this doesn't mean you should yell this on the corner of Hollywood and Vine (that would be difficult to do since all the good spots are already taken).

The positive mental energy I am referring to is an external expression of internal feelings—projecting an exciting aura to those with the power to hire you. These people are certainly not going to be banging on your door, so you have to go out and bang on their door. You must act with . . . well, the word *flair* comes to mind. And I see flair as a way of packaging the energy you will need to advertise yourself. You are a salesperson peddling a product and that product is *you*, and the best salesperson operates with verve, nerve, and a huge dash of gusto. To a good salesperson, pluck equals luck, and luck comes with guts, and all this clever wordplay is getting monotonous, but I think you catch the drift.

Market your creativity wisely and use each day as effectively as you can. Invest in a day planner so you can plan to make at least one career move each day. Get into a routine that will supply a foundation to your uncertain life. Work at your career, act diligently, and by all means, love what you're working on.

There is no magic. You open your own doors. There is being in the right place at the right time, but only because you have cleared the path to put yourself in the right place. The right place can sometimes be accidental. Once, while visiting with a friend at Paramount Studios, I was spotted by producer Hugh Benson, who was casting a movie called *For Those Who Think Young*. A week later, I found myself on a Paramount soundstage doing a featured role in a beach movie with James Darren, Pamela Tiffin, Nancy Sinatra, and Bob Denver.

Notice something about the personal experience I have just related? I said I was visiting a friend at Paramount Studios. This is always a good idea if you happen to know people who work at a studio, in any capacity. Arrange to visit them—have lunch in the commissary. Hopefully, you'll be introduced to someone important, or, at least, semi-important (there are a lot of semi-importants in Hollywood). Don't be pushy when you meet people—but avoid wallflowerism by all means. These kinds of introductions can often blossom into friendships—and who knows what from there?

"When you go to the market," says **Brooke Bundy**, "look good—you can wear your sweats, your jeans, stuff like that, but look cute. In this town, producers, directors, everybody lives everywhere and they all shop at two in the morning. . . . So, if you go out looking like a ghoul, you're shooting yourself in the foot."

It's always wise to pay close attention to your professional behavior. Don't bad-mouth people—it has a way of getting back to them. It's simply bad politics. Hollywood is a very political town, so everyone likes to appear in their best light, even those who may actually be devious, underhanded skunks. I guess what I'm saying is keep your big mouth shut.

"Door of opportunity often opens by pushing," said a fortune cookie I once opened. Good advice. You'll do well to heed what this fortune-cookie writer has to say. Don't be afraid to be pushy. In Hollywood, pushiness is an admirable trait—a downright art—and you must live by the code of push or be pushed—and I don't mean push like being pushy, but with a deft hand, so people don't notice they're being pushed.

Earlier, I mentioned the importance of giving good phone to your agent. Well, extend your mastery of the telephone beyond your agent to producers, casting people, studio people, network people. Call Mel Melman at Mammoth Movies (if he still has the job). You'll probably never get through, but then again, who knows? It happens.

Greg Strangis reports that, as a fledgling writer, he boldly called a prestigious Hollywood production company and the president of the company actually answered the phone! Greg found himself working as a writer/producer for that company shortly thereafter.

TECHNO-NECESSITY

You can't place a business call anymore without a person answering who isn't a person but a voice impersonating a person. We live in a maze of technology and are expected to adjust our lives accordingly. This is also true of show business, where technology is expected to be employed. Computer literacy, or at least a working knowledge—like knowing how to turn on your computer—is essential.

"I couldn't live without technology," says writer/producer **Ralph Gaby Wilson**. "I have been writing on a computer since 1978. My first printer came out of an Apple garage. I e-mailed in my last script."

These are words to live by, that's for sure. More and more business is done through faxes, e-mails, and Web sites. If you're not up to snuff on this stuff, you're in great danger of falling through a Hollywood crack. Don't live in the past in your thinking. Continued attempts to hold on to the old ways are counterproductive to your survival.

Actor **Eddie Applegate** claims that he uses his computer for printing photo postcards, which seems like a very good idea to me. What's that? You say you don't have a computer? You say you can't afford one? Okay, I'll tell you what you can do. Buy a used computer. It will provide you with Internet access, which will keep you in contact with the outside world. What's that? You can't afford to pay an Internet service? Very well, here's what you do, and read closely, because I'm not going to repeat this. You skip along down to your public library and use one of its computers. If all the library computers are being used by individuals seeking pornographic thrills, try visiting your local cyber-café, where for only the price of a $4.50 cup of decaf lava java latte, you can access the Internet on one of its computers.

Go to *www.hotmail.com* or *www.yahoo.com* and follow the directions for setting up a free e-mail account. Then you can return any time, and for a $5 cup of the same coffee (price hike), you can access your e-mail by typing in *www.hotmail.com* or *www.yahoo.com* (whichever you have chosen). You then type in your user name and password, and you are in personal e-mail heaven. E-mail is equally important for actors, who can put an e-mail address on mailed résumés, and for writers, who can add an e-mail address to the title page of their spec script.

There are all kinds of technological tools available to writers nowadays. You've probably heard that there's writing software out there that will make your job easier—products like Final Draft, ScriptThing, Movie Magic Screenwriter. These are programs that will help you develop a professional-looking script format. Contrary to some of the things you hear, there is no software available that thinks up stories—certainly not anything original. Software does not replace creativity, and if it ever does, we're all in big trouble. I sometimes wonder if the networks already have something like this and are using it to develop their new shows. Those bombs had to come from somewhere.

As a Hollywood neophyte, my home-office technology consisted of a phone and a typewriter, because at that time computers were the size of a city block. When personal computers burst onto the scene, I stuck with my typewriter until fellow writer **Ralph Gaby Wilson** insisted I accept his used computer and printer, and the tutoring that went with it. I'm forever grateful to him for doing that. He brought me into the twenty-first century.

ACCOUNTS:

Tech-Views _____

Opinions on the use of technology in show business range from avid support to not-so-avid support.

Peter Lefcourt: "How much a part does technology play? Very little. If you can write well with a computer, you can write well on a yellow legal pad. The computer has merely put a lot of script typists out of business."

Actor/production executive *Jim Begg*: "Technology is taking over our business. You have to jump in with both feet or you will be left behind."

Jewel Jaffe Ross: "A good script is a good script on a yellow legal pad, and drek is drek no matter how fast you can e-mail it to your agent."

Judy Coppage: "I use technology quite a bit. Faxes were a whole new era and now e-mail has replaced that. When you e-mail someone, you only get to them and they can choose to either answer or ignore you. They don't have to return a call, etc. I happen to really like it and it's cost effective."

YOUR OWN HOLLYWOOD WEB

Show business, like any other business, relies on contacts. It most definitely is who you know. One method of intelligence gathering that I have found to be extremely useful is to network with others in show business. In managing whatever plan or system you devise for whatever area of show business you are pursuing, it is essential to get to know people and get people to know you. Whenever possible, become chummy with the "little people"—those who work as secretaries, production assistants, gofers—many of these individuals have a way of moving up the show biz ladder and a few may even remember who was nice to them and when.

If your Hollywood goals lie in areas like cinematography, or jobs in various other areas of production, you will also find the information you need by asking around. I cannot emphasize the value of networking too strongly. I'll even guarantee that people in the business will lead you to other people in the business who will finally put you in contact with someone in the business who has the information (or even the job) you've been looking for. There's no assurance of a job, of course, but you're bound to get the leads you need to move your career forward.

Jim Begg is a great believer in networking:

I approach the business like it's a business. I never thought of it as an art form. There is good and bad in that type of thinking, and it doesn't work for everyone. You must do self-promotion. Networking is very important. And the most important factor is, people must like you. Many times people are successful because they are liked. Unfortunately, talent is secondary.

The best networker I've ever known is an actor-friend of mine. He had a wife and three young children to support, so he approached acting strictly as a daily job; he planned to be seen every day, because visibility is essential. He would schedule his week visiting and schmoozing with producers, directors, casting people—whoever would open their door to him. When doors didn't open, he found other ways. He was bold and not afraid to walk up and introduce himself to total strangers. He would even have himself paged at restaurants, hotels, and airports (which I thought a bit excessive), and he ended up rising to daytime stardom on a soap opera.

There are several show business networking hangouts in the L.A. area. One particular hangout I have visited is Residuals, a bar on Ventura Boulevard in Studio City, where show biz types get together to bitch, moan, celebrate landing a part, selling a script, and sometimes share tips on all kinds of stuff that might be happening in the business. You even learn who the good acting teachers are and where the writing or directing seminars are happening. One actor I met there told me, "I got my agent when I hit it off with this guy I met and he arranged for me to meet his agent. When you're not the same type, actors will usually help each other. Actors are congenial to a point . . . it's a pretty competitive profession."

Another form of networking for aspiring actors, writers, directors, producers, and agents is attending social events. When you're invited to an industry party—go!!! (More about the Hollywood social scene in chapter 9.)

I used to find out where the popular eating places were for producers and studio/network honchos and (when my budget could withstand the squeeze) have lunch at one of these places. I've never been afraid to have lunch alone. I would just sit there, looking fantastic, my nose engrossed in a copy of the aforementioned William Goldman's *Adventures in the Screen Trade*, hoping that some finger would point in my direction with a job attached. The finger thing never happened, but I did have some very tasty lunches, and was putting myself out there to be seen.

Hollywood big-wigs are a fickle bunch and they seem to change hot places every few months. In Hollywood, "hot" is a synonym for "it's pretty much over," but if you network and ask around you'll find out where the new places are. They're usually near the major studios. (By the way, William Goldman's superb book can be found at better bookstores everywhere. Buy a copy—the man's gotta eat.)

One especially good place to be seen is the Polo Lounge at the Beverly Hills Hotel. As I recall, they serve free snacks with their expensive drinks (which proves that the best things in life are never free) but the joint is usually buzzing with moguls, mogulettes, and other inflated Hollywood personages. Once, I met Dean Martin and even got to join his table. I didn't get a job out of it, however—just a lot of laughs.

BE A PERFORMER

Let's talk about *auditions*. If the word is not familiar to you, it is defined as a way to test talent. An audition can also be defined as a trial, which is often the feeling a person gets when walking into a room only to be confronted with a group of sour faces who look like heads of the five families in *The Godfather*.

Hey, face it, anyone out to sell their Hollywood dream as an actor, writer, director, producer, cameraperson, designer—whatever—is frequently going to go through episodes of being judged. TV writers face this constantly when they are expected to verbally pitch their stories—the reason for this being that a lot of producers can't read.

At the beginning of my acting career, I feared auditions. When I turned to writing, I was terrified of pitching. I was a nervous wreck when I had to tell a story, read, sing, or dance for a part. Performing under pressure like that seemed so uncivilized—like some brutal device invented by Vlad the Impaler. These realities are simply old show business rituals, so you're going to have to get used to them. And the faster you get used to the judging process, the sooner you'll stop being your own worst enemy. There will be plenty of adversaries in your career without adding your own name to the list.

A bad attitude is a bad habit, but habits can be changed. One bad habit is to obsess negatively on what might happen. It's a grand waste of time, so letting your overheated imagination run amok is not recommended. You'll never make it if you're intent on screwing yourself up before the fact. What you're doing here is acting out of the fear that you will fail. Well, in show biz, you fail a lot— it's part of the game. Just don't go around expecting the worst to happen. Heed the words of the mighty Babe Ruth: "Never let the fear of striking out get in your way."

Let's look at a few performance tips on presenting yourself as an actor, writer, director, and craftsperson at auditions, meetings, or interviews. Although the emphasis is on acting auditions, these tips apply to all areas of show business—any business, for that matter.

PERFORMANCE TIP #1. Practice smiling, shaking hands, moving with confidence. See yourself as a winning personality. Write yourself an act. If you can't write, just improvise something. Rehearse with a friend who doesn't think you're a numbskull. At first it may seem awkward, but with practice you will find your real self and your proposed self beginning to meld into a single self that works for you. Heck, you may even start to relax and settle into a more confident you. One thing is certain: You won't be nearly as boring as you used to be.

PERFORMANCE TIP #2. Keep in mind that image of yourself as an extremely talented individual. You would not be putting yourself in this position if you hadn't committed to that belief.

PERFORMANCE TIP #3. You have prepared for this moment—studied acting, performed in plays, written scripts, directed, designed, worked at whatever craft you are aspiring to enter. Everyone has to start out at the beginning, so preparation and experience will fuel your confidence. According to actress/acting teacher **Helaine Lembeck**:

> The most important thing about making it or not making it in Hollywood is to make sure you are good enough to go on auditions to begin with. Get yourself trained. Get yourself educated. I think that learning your craft is the most beneficial thing you can do for yourself.

PERFORMANCE TIP #4. Be sober, aware, receptive, conscious of every moment. I recommend consciousness as an excellent way of living. Any stimulants before any performance will likely have you screwing up somewhere along the line. I once puffed on a joint before performing in a play. After the play, I thought I was fabulous, until the cast approached me en masse and said, "What the hell were you doing out there?" It goes without saying that I never repeated that experiment. With regard to the supposed Hollywood high life, personal manager **Brooke Bundy** says,

> You have to show up at an audition prepared. Be on time—in fact, be early, and know where you are going. You don't go out on a date the night before or party with your friends. That audition is worth gold. I have an actress that I am furious with because she had an audition for a major, major show, and she didn't do a good job, because she was hungover and she was in la-la-land. Just because you are in Hollywood doesn't mean you are in la-la-land. You've got to be responsible. Careers are ruined that way—that kind of reputation is a killer.

Hollywood survival depends a great deal on reputation. Granted, it's difficult to spread the word around town that you're a show business bright light, but step out of line and all kinds of people who never heard of you will know about it.

PERFORMANCE TIP #5. Relax. Calm your nerves. It happens to everyone. We all get the jitters when we are about to face a judgment call. Butterflies aren't always such a bad thing—they are the tummy's way of telling us to get a hold of ourselves. Focus on breathing—deep—no, deeper—long, deep breaths. Concentrate on your breathing. Clear your mind . . . then use your imagination to visualize a best-case scenario and the wonderful feelings the future holds.

PERFORMANCE TIP #6. Prime the courage of your convictions. Don't just sit in the waiting room, reading an article called "30 Days to a Firmer Butt" in last April's *Good Housekeeping*. Put the magazine down, go into the restroom and study your face in the mirror. Talk to that face. Admit to your nervousness and vow to overcome. Review all the good things about yourself—how skilled and consistently good you are at what you do. Complete sentences like: "I'm really good at. . . . People like me because. . . ." (Do the whole Al Franken/Stuart Smalley number on yourself.) What you're doing is very healthy. You're sorting through your emotions, renewing your confidence, giving a boost to your self-perception. . . . So, make that restroom a routine location for preparation. Just try to talk louder than the guy at the sink next to you so you can hear yourself think.

PERFORMANCE TIP #7. When your name is called, spring out of your chair, take the deepest of breaths, and tell yourself you refuse to be denied. This job is yours. Focus on the moment. Put on your game face.

PERFORMANCE TIP #8. Enter the audition with "zing." By "zing" I mean a brightness in your smile and a vitality in your step. When you shake hands with the honchos and honchettes, make immediate eye contact and repeat their names when you tell them what a pleasure it is to meet them, even if it's not. Zing excites and draws interest. Any successful salesperson will vouch for this.

Asked what she looks for in a prospective client, commercial agent **Kim Muir** says,

> Complete personality. Coming in and just intriguing me. A sense of fun, of confidence. A sense of self. Agents are turned off if someone walks into a room and is uptight, nervous, quiet. You want somebody who comes into your office and is having a blast—loves auditioning, loves the interview process.

The key here is the first impression, the love of your work that you convey at the door, on your way to shake up the world of those who are about to discover you.

PERFORMANCE TIP #9. If you still can't seem to shake the nervousness, simply tell those you're auditioning for how nervous you are. Tell them you're scared to death. Show them how your hands are trembling, and exaggerate the tremble. This may get a laugh, or at least put them in the position of trying to calm you, which could make this a much more relaxed situation, although I can't guarantee it.

PERFORMANCE TIP #10. It takes practice and experience to overcome the fear of failing. Just remind yourself that, if this opportunity doesn't pan out, there will be another opportunity just around the corner. A theater director friend of mine always tells his auditionees that plays are like streetcars; if you don't catch this one, another one will soon come along. (The fact that there are no longer any streetcars doesn't seem to matter to my friend.)

PERFORMANCE TIP #11. Important advice for an actor: Never, ever agonize over what you think the auditioners are looking for. They don't have the foggiest idea what they're looking for. They're waiting for you to *show* them. When reading a part, don't try to be what you're not—be the best "you" you can be and project your personality into the role. Trust your instincts. Bill Cosby hit it right when he said, "I don't know the key to success, but the key to failure is trying to please everyone."

PERFORMANCE TIP #12. One Hollywood reality actors and even writers have to face is being "typed." This is frustrating because you know that you are possessed of an amazing range, but the auditioners don't care about your range; they just want to cast the stupid part and get it over with. The best advice I can give is to showcase yourself in stage roles that stretch you in another dimension, and hope that some influential mucky-muck shows up to see you.

Hank Jones has his own personal take on being typed:

Due to my slight build and character face, I had to face the fact that I would never get the girl in anything I ever did. I would always be somebody's "best friend" or cast as "weird cousin Norman." One producer gave me a back-handed compliment, typically Hollywood, when he said, "Hank, you have the no-look look."

PERFORMANCE TIP #13. One thing you have total control over is your appearance, so dress for success. I don't mean in a suit and tie or cocktail dress: I mean neatly casual, reflecting you. Don't listen when friends tell you to dress for the part. If you're reading for the part of a bum, do not dress like a bum. This will only project a negative perception to those in judgment, and they'll think, "This guy's a bum—we can't hire some bum to play a bum."

PERFORMANCE TIP #14. The competition in Hollywood is fierce. The town draws talent like the sponge that sucked Cleveland. Others will always be there who want the same job you do, but that's no reason to despise them or secretly wish them bad luck. Competition should be viewed as a healthy situation. Competing with the best stretches you and causes you to perform at your maximum potential. I often used to find myself competing with an actor named Richard Dreyfuss. In watching this guy in action, I was observing a real pro at work. He exuded confidence with enormous zing! Competing with him made me reach to do better and I gave some of my best auditions. I was using the competition to my advantage. Well, not to my complete advantage. Dreyfuss always got the part, always out-zung me, but I grew in the process.

PERFORMANCE TIP #15. There is no one way to move your career up the Hollywood ladder. There is entirely too much competition on that ladder with you, so it's going to take a lot more than just reading lines or submitting a spec script. You have to be super-imaginative in figuring out how to sell yourself and land the job.

My favorite audition story comes from actor **Jed Allan**, who relates how he tried out for the part of the forest ranger on the *Lassie* TV series:

> Lassie was a male dog. I went to a friend's house and ran around with their dog, who was in heat. It was a female dog, and I wanted the smell on me so that when I met Lassie, he would like me. Lassie really liked me. On the plane, the dog sat in first class, right next to me.

The above tips (including the anecdote on Lassie) apply equally to any artistic individual out to show their wares in the Hollywood market. One audition tip I've omitted is a familiar one that I'm sure you've heard: "Picture them in their underwear." (I tried that once at an audition, screamed with laughter, and was asked to leave the room, so I don't recommend it as a reliable tip.)

Now, the aftermath of any audition, meeting, interview, or similar tribunal consists of a period of *waiting* to see how you did. This waiting period comes with a certain amount of fall-out where you will seldom convince yourself that you nailed it and the job is yours, but instead your head will be littered with feelings of doubt and worthlessness. "I blew it! I stink!" Then you replay the scene with, "I could've. . . . I should've. . . ." My advice? Let it go. Forget it. Move on. Another streetcar will be coming along any minute now.

WORDS FOR SALE

An actor auditions and whatever the outcome, that's that. A writer, however, can travel a longer, bumpier road in his or her quest to sell his or her talent to the industry. My friend, writer/producer **Rich Eustis**'s story is a good example. It is the saga of a writer's place in 1960s comedy television. Today's hiring practices may differ, but, as for the process of selling and writing a script, it's a situation that's as real today as it was at that time.

"Many new series were so ill-conceived that established pros weren't interested in doing scripts for them. As a result, there would be 'cattle calls' for writers. The producers would organize a screening of their pilot episode, usually attended by twenty or thirty hungry writers. When the lights came up, the producer would make a little speech saying what kinds of stories they were looking for, etc., and 'if you've got any ideas, here's the phone number.' The writers would then put together a half-dozen story spitballs and go see the guy. If he liked one, you had a job. If not, you moved on to the next cattle call.

"Which is how [Al] Rogers and I found ourselves watching the pilot of a midseason replacement series starring Red Buttons (*The Secret Life Of Henry Phyffe*). It was a spy spoof intended to capitalize on the success of *Get Smart*, about a guy with a humdrum life who happens also to be a secret agent. We had some thoughts. Our agent made the call, and we were invited to see Sid Dorfman at Filmways Television.

"We told Sid a few of our ideas for *Henry Phyffe* stories. One that he thought had a chance was a story about Henry missing connections on a $100,000 cash payoff to a turncoat, then stashing the cash at home overnight only to have his fiancée discover it and become convinced he's embezzling from the office where he's employed at his 'cover' job.

"Sid liked it, and took us in to meet the producer, Luther Davis. Luther greeted us warmly, apologized for the fact that he was naked from the waist up and, dipping an applicator into a bottle of something called 'Heet,' he explained that he was treating his upper back and neck for muscle spasms brought on by his position as show-runner on a comedy with no supporting cast, no scripts, and going on the air in two weeks.

"We sat down and discussed our story. He said he liked it. 'Do you play golf?' he asked. We thought about the social side of being Hollywood writers. Since neither one of us had ever played, we wondered if we should accept a golf date and ruin Luther's afternoon, or turn him down and blow a chance to do a script for him. The hell with it. We said, 'Sure.' We'd have time to go to a driving range and figure it out. How hard could it be? 'Good,' he said, 'I have a story in the back of my mind that involves Henry learning golf in order to carry out a spy mission. Think about it and I'll get back to you.'

"Three weeks later, we heard from Sid Dorfman. He apologized for the delay, and explained that there had been considerable upheaval on *Henry Phyffe*. The air date had been pushed back. The show had been rethought and reshuffled and rewritten and refilmed into a 'much better show.' And just in time because the new premiere was one week away. 'Bring in some more stories,' he said.

"We took in some more stories. Sid wasn't too crazy about any of them. 'But I'm not the final judge—Nat Perrin is.' Sid told us Luther Davis was 'out' and that Nat Perrin was now 'in.' But just in case Nat doesn't like any of these stories,' said Sid, 'do you have anything else you might like to ad lib? Just off the top?' On a hunch, we pitched Sid our original idea about the $100,000. He didn't comment, but promised to pitch Nat all of our story ideas.

"Fifteen minutes later, as we walked into our little office on Sunset Boulevard, the phone was ringing. 'Nat didn't like any of them,' said Sid. But he had an idea that he wants you to work on. It goes like this: Henry gets this $100,000 in cash, see, and. . . .' We said it sounded great, if a little familiar. We worked it out and phoned Sid. He liked it, and made an appointment for us to discuss it with Nat the next day.

"I walked into the dark, heavily paneled office of Nat Perrin, a short, fiftyish man in glasses, with a sour demeanor. 'Tell me your story,' he quietly commanded. I told him the story. 'I hate to piss all over your story,' he said, 'but there's no story there.' He made suggestions. I made notes and got ready to take the whole thing back to the drawing board.

"On the way out I met Sid Dorfman and told him my sad little story. Sid was irate. 'Don't worry about it,' he said. 'After the meeting I just had, we won't have to worry about Mister Perrin anymore.'

"On Monday, I phoned Perrin to tell him how I had repaired the story. He told me to mail it in. He didn't want to discuss it over the phone. Right away, I put in a call to Sid Dorfman to ask him if I was wasting my time, and see if he thought I should wait until Perrin was 'out,' as he'd predicted, before delivering the story in any form. The Filmways Studio switchboard operator had no idea of the impact her words had on my life. 'Sid Dorfman no longer works here,' she said.

"I mailed Perrin the story. A week passed. I phoned him. 'The story still has a lotta holes in it,' he said, 'but I'm gonna plug them, then turn it over to you to write the teleplay.' Two more days passed. Perrin called me. 'I've been calling you all morning,' he said. 'You gotta start on the teleplay right now—today! I want a finished script on my desk Monday morning,' he said. 'We start filming it a week from today.'

"As Al and I were working late Saturday, Nat Perrin phones us. 'Where's the first act,' he demanded. 'Noon, Sunday, like you said,' I replied. 'Deliver it to Luther Davis at his home. I'm out. I've quit the show.'

"On Sunday afternoon we handed the first act over to Luther Davis at his home in Beverly Hills, and I made a mental note to buy a place like it someday. . . . With Luther back in, it was fun again as he kidded us about being the 'Chicken Delight' of TV writers with our home delivery service. We returned to the office to work on act two, and within minutes Luther called to say he was delighted with the first act. Life was getting more and more bearable by the hour.

"Late Monday, we finished the second act. We delivered it to Luther back in his office on the Filmways lot. 'If this is anything like the first act,' he said, 'and I'm sure it will be, I'm going to ask for you two to join the staff and do rewrites for me.' Ohmigod. A steady job. I could feel a tremendous weight beginning to lift from my shoulders. . . . The second act? Luther was ecstatic. 'Great job,' he said, 'we're filming it Wednesday.' We'd heard that promise before, from Nat Perrin, and somehow the magic Wednesday had never arrived. But this time, maybe it was actually going to happen. 'One more thing,' said Luther, 'the suits have to sign off on it, but that's just a formality. This one's a keeper.'

"When I got home that night, my wife gave me a telephone message. 'Call Nat Perrin.' Shit. I called him. The thin, unpleasant voice brought back the pain. 'Luther Davis is out. I'm back in. I hate your script, what there is of it. How come you never wrote a second act? And why did you put in the scene about the pool hall?' 'What pool hall?' I asked. 'The pool hall where he meets the guy to give him the hundred thousand.' 'Luther must have changed it,' I said. 'Luther is out now. I'm rewriting your script.' We phoned Luther Davis to see what he knew. 'I thought it was a damn good script,' he said.

"The next day, Nat Perrin called, demanding our second act. We had given it, of course, to Luther Davis, and there should have been a few copies of it lying around at Filmways, but they couldn't find any. I took a Xerox of it over to Perrin. He was in his office, frantically rewriting our first act prior to the start of filming the next day. I handed him act two. He looked it over quickly and said, 'Shit.' I left.

"Two days later, we received, per guild regulations, Perrin's final draft of our script. It was unrecognizable. . . . The day after that, we received another draft of Nat's draft of our script, done by a third writer hired to 'save' it. He had thrown out Nat's script, gone back to the script we had given Luther Davis, added a slight polish, but left our teleplay more or less word for word as it was originally. Our credit was uncompromised and, for better or worse, our script was filmed as written—by us. Not Luther, not Nat Perrin, not the staff rewrite guy. Us. We got our first credit and a scale half-hour episode fee of $2,750. After taxes, social security, agent's commission, and the split with Al, I had a check for $831.34 in my hot little hand. The rent was paid, and my wife and kids fed and clothed for another month. After a shaky start, we were on our way."

Some story, huh? So ridiculous, yet so Hollywood in its content. Why, I'll bet the same kind of thing is going on at this very moment behind some of the most important doors in town. **Rich Eustis** and Al Rogers survived a Hollywood experience that has sent lesser individuals packing for home. They persisted through idiocy and saw their vision through to completion. There are millions of nutso stories like this in Tinseltown. This is only one of them.

ROOKIE UPDATE

Kyle Kramer e-mails:

I auditioned for and joined a workshop that's considered the best by everyone I talked to. I bought a package of thirteen workshops for $300 (a savings of $64 off the cover price!!!) and have found them to be both fun and valuable. These sessions take the place of a general interview and a lot of casting directors come to them. . . . I talked with a manager who agreed to aid my career from an (unofficial) advisory standpoint for the time being, so at least I have some kind of representation. She set up a meeting for me with a theatrical agent. So, I go into the office and read a scene while her dog licked my feet, which was only mildly distracting. Then, the next day, I found out that the agent had passed on me for the reason that I was "normal" and could play a wide variety of roles and would be a hard sell because I am difficult to "place." The manager had some very comforting words. She said that it was important to find not just an agent, but an agent that 'gets' me, and I think that's an important thing to know. Just because someone isn't impressed with you doesn't mean you are bad. If an agent isn't passionate about you—if they don't "get" you, you will be doing yourself a disservice by signing with them. The better they "get" you, the harder they will work for you. That's the bottom line. . . . More to come, Kyle.

Chapter 5

LIVING WITH REJECTION

I'm telling you if you want to realize your dreams, you'd better know how tough it is. You'd better know that opinions exist in direct opposition to our dreams. Surprisingly, some of these opinions can be found within ourselves.
—Milton Katselas, *Dreams into Action*

The Yellow Brick Road through Hollywood is paved with grease, sullied with potholes, and all too often slopes downward toward a sheer cliff or two. As carefully as your career plan may be crafted, things don't always turn out as neatly as your map to success says it should. In psychological terms, setbacks have a way of mucking up your path while getting your sense of purpose all screwed up.

This sort of thing happens all over America, and more frequently in recent years. Individuals are downsized—let go from their jobs—and aren't needed anymore. This happens to people in show business on a regular basis, with one exception: There isn't usually a job to be let go from because there isn't usually a job to be had. Day after day, Hollywood hopefuls as well as veterans put themselves out there only to find that their efforts are for naught. More than often, those in power will fail to display the simple intelligence and good taste of hiring you. But, if they turn out to be bright and tasteful, and you do land that role or a writing gig, hooray for you! . . . But hold off on the party. It's only temporary. A whole new series of rebuffs may be waiting in the wings to brush off your future.

Welcome to the cruel and irrational world of *rejection*—the most devastatingly destructive element in a show business career. It's like getting mugged on a regular basis, only instead of snatching your purse, they bite off a chunk of your spirit. With actors, the rejection is usually of your physical appearance—your face or body. For writers and other artists, the rejection is of your creative efforts—your mind and imagination.

A supremely self-confident person will let a rejection roll right off his or her back, while continuing to press forward... but even the most together, head-on-straight individual can begin to frazzle a little around the emotional edges after being dumped time after time. How you process these rejections is vital to your survival in Hollywood. "I always said that not getting a part really didn't bother me," says actor **Hank Jones**, "but it did. However, reality dictates that if they are hiring veal chops that day, you can be the greatest lamb chop in the universe, but you still won't get the job!" Now, Hank displays a calm, realistic point of view here, but notice that he doesn't so much say it but exclaims it ("!"), which is a very good indication that he is a tad or two prickled by the whole situation. Meanwhile, writer/actress **Jewel Jaffe Ross** demurely recalls, "There weren't that many genuine rejections, mainly things just faded into an ever-darkening miasma of nothingness. The big rejections I did have, I took badly, but kept well." And from another standpoint, writer **Franklin Thompson** reveals, "I have never coped well with failure and rejection and still find them crippling. I've never been able to accept myself and my work at my own valuation rather than that of others in the business. My rage takes the form of unproductive depression."

Reactions to rejection vary, but more often than not, they result in negative thoughts toward those who rejected us, the business in general, but mostly toward ourselves. This is not surprising, since we live in a society in which we are force-fed negativity on a daily basis. The media wallows in horrible events—they're called good news days. TV dramas focus on crime, rage, divorce, disease, basically whatever tragedy is hot at the moment. We seek shelter in comedies, only to wonder what the laugh track finds so funny, leaving us stuck in a pretty grim atmosphere. If I sound jaded, keep in mind that I call 'em like I see 'em.

In a stressfully skewed environment like this, it should come as no surprise that people are flying off the handle in record numbers. Emotional storms are now a perfectly acceptable part of our daily landscape. Anger is "in"—it's the way you're supposed to react, right?

Wrong. You don't have to react in anger. Displays of anger should be avoided like slick car salesmen in checkered suits. I understand the drill here. You get rejected, feel enormous disappointment, are nettled at those who spurned you. Often that disappointment breeds a secret desire for revenge, to get even: It's payback time. And off you go on imaginary flights of terror that involve weapons of destruction leading to pillaging and basic unpleasantness. But that's perfectly okay. It's never good to repress your emotions, so go ahead, feel those feelings, imagine those carnage-filled fantasies—as long as they're just fantasies. Get it out of your system, and be quick about it. Rejection begets stress and stress begets all manner of problems.

Once I was hired to play a huge supporting role in an independent motion picture. It was a drama; I was the comic relief. It was a great part, and I got huzzahs from the entire company for the laughs I provided. Flash forward: The movie opens. I go to see it and nearly choke on my popcorn when it dawns on me that I'm not in the movie anymore. Oh, there are a few long shots where I could be Harpo Marx and nobody would know because me and my comic relief are on the cutting-room floor. I was told the reason was that the leading man felt I was coming across too strongly in scenes, and he wanted me out. The leading man had also put up the money to make the picture, so I was as out as a bridesmaid at a divorce hearing. I had been victimized, kicked in the teeth, thrown to the dogs, left in the lurch, and whatever other clichés I could think of. The life I had elected to lead had been vetoed, so it came as no surprise that what followed was not pleasant. I moped for days—never leaving the house in fear that the "loser" brand on my face would give me away. I was pretty new to the business. I had yet to realize that I wasn't the only one this had ever happened to. I was in good cutting-room floor company: Try to find Kevin Costner's scenes in *The Big Chill*. Of course, a fact like this had little effect on me at the time, since I was too busy wallowing in wretchedness while upwardly progressing on the old self-alienation scale.

During my first year as a professional TV writer, I was on the staff of the wildly successful *Love, American Style*, which was run by a producing staff of finely talented, supportive people. I was in writer heaven, and receiving all that positive feedback from my peers spurred me on to do even better work. The following year, the finely talented, supportive peers left the show to be replaced by mean-spirited, no-talent oafs, and for the first time I began to feel the whip of repulsion. I—who had been spoiled by so much acceptance—began to have material rejected, causing me to feel a lot less talented and to be pretty hard on myself. It wasn't that I couldn't take criticism, I just had a lot to learn about show business. I would have stories turned down and sulk like a world-class sulker. My equilibrium was shaken, defeated—my confidence at an all-time low. Nothing could empty a room faster than my walking into it.

Rejection occurs with maddening frequency in show business; therefore, dealing with those rejections is a full-time job. As an actor, you'll go to more than fifty auditions until there's even the possibility of landing one job. These rejections are never explained, and the only feedback you'll get is that you weren't the right type, so you'll agonize over when your type will be the type they're looking for—and whatever happened to talent?!

As a writer, you may write ten or twelve spec scripts—and the rejections will be slathered over a period of years during which absolutely no interest is shown in what you have to offer. You never hear these rejections—they just manifest themselves in silence, often resulting in deep hurt and depression.

An actress friend, Amanda St. John, once told me, "Sometimes we just have to get over ourselves." So, as my career trudged on, I made every effort to get over me. I began to view these rejections as less of a loss and more of a very opinionated business run by idiots. And, despite the idiot part, I grew in my ability to rebound from what I now see as simply an inconvenience.

Okay, so what do you do when you've gotten over yourself? Actor **Lawrence-Hilton Jacobs** points out that you must keep working—you mustn't decrease your efforts over your disappointment at being sent out the door:

Things happen because you put the work in. You plant a flower, it will grow. You cultivate it in a certain way, it will grow a certain way. That's how I believe life, that's how I believe show business. That is the thrust for me. When it is dim, I don't like sitting around and feeling sorry for myself; it's counter-productive and not going to get me anywhere. I go through a few moments of depression and then I say, "Okay, cat, let's go again. It's round number two."

See? What you have to do is separate yourself from your career obsession. It's not easy, but with the recognition that you have a problem, you can begin to remove your ego from the sphere, pick up, pack up, kick in, and try again. Even the Milwaukee Brewers will win the World Series . . . eventually.

STRESS CHESS

Rejection and stress go together like pressure and cooker. Stress can be compared to a game of chess, with every move against you being countered with an urgency to panic, act irritable, and never get invited to parties again. Asked about her ability to bounce back from rejection, actress **Sondra Bennett** responds, "I don't know that I ever did. I just pretended. I used emotions like anger or resentment, harboring under the delusion that hardness was needed to hang on. Chicken soup always provided great substance in times of need." Anytime we are confronted by changes or increased demands, we experience The Five Stress Brothers: Fear, Anger, Tension, Guilt, and sometimes Zeppo. See? That's the kind of healthy silliness that pricks holes in stress, but most of us are too crab-ridden to see the humor, and the fall-out can be damaging. Stress eats away at your spirit and beats up on your resolve as you continue to make the same moves in the wrong direction. You form emotional habits that will not serve you well and will rule you until you checkmate yourself and remove the thorn from your mental paw. In other words, *Whooooaa, there!*

Now, I'm not suggesting that you can simply erase stress overnight, but that it can be reduced through *management*. In fact, your ability to actively manage the road through disappointing times is the key to your career endurance. You begin to manage by recognizing the underlying causes that are destroying what is meaningful in your life. Actions and reactions that are intended to lessen the pain can often have the opposite effect.

In *The Six Pillars of Self-Esteem*, Dr. Nathaniel Branden points out:

When we are young we may experience a good deal of hurt and rejection and develop a policy, in "self-protection," to reject others first. This policy does not make for a happy life. And yet its intention is not to cause suffering, but to reduce it. Survival strategies that do not serve our interests but in fact hurt us, but to which we nonetheless cling like life preservers in a stormy sea, are the ones psychologists label "neurotic." The ones that serve our interests we properly label "good adaptations."

Okay, now that we've identified the chance of being labeled neurotic, we're getting somewhere. Next, we realize that what we're doing is packaging our reactions by forming negative avoidance tactics, and this sort of behavior has us habitually responding to stress in self-protective ways. We spend entirely too much time trying to sidestep our chances of getting hurt again, and wind up hurting ourselves anyhow. The whole process is like squashing your head in a vice—it's gonna feel so good when you stop . . . . Now, if you could only stop.

Stress affects us because we don't grow up learning that it can be managed, so we just hide behind absurdly destructive behavior for protection. As a result, stress can make us become a person we're not, and does anybody really want to live with a drip like that?

Stress creates *pessimism*, and when anything bad occurs, a pessimist is certain it will last forever and destroy everything that's good, that it's all his or her fault. Oscar Wilde defined a pessimist as one who, given the choice of two evils, chooses both. We all experience self-doubts about our talent, even about our chosen career. That's a normal reaction, but when it leads to pessimism, it will trash all signs of positive mental energy. Listen closely to the hushed words of Clint Eastwood: "I don't believe in pessimism. If something doesn't come up the way you want, forge ahead. If you think it's going to rain, it will." The man knows what he's talking about. Don't mess with him.

The times I have quit the business can be counted on the fingers of The Mormon Tabernacle Choir, but I never actually quit—I stuck with it and stayed in there. Despite a good writing reputation I often failed to sell my stories. TV comedy pilots were the toughest. Seven produced (a feat in itself) and seven pilots shot down (par for the course). But I got over these things. You fail now and then—that's a given. That failure should lead to ulcers and brain damage is strictly a made-up routine. And if you're into making up routines, how about making up a conscious effort to feel your loss? You can't help but do that. Just don't wallow in the bad vibes. Take the time you need to feel crappy, and then determine that you will rise above the crap to clearly see that there are new opportunities on the horizon.

Optimism is a natural emotional state. To an optimist, rejection is a temporary reality that is ripe for overcoming. The sooner the better. Optimists live longer than pessimists, because optimism renews life, and pessimism is self-defeating. This only goes to prove the old adage that if you take life too seriously, you'll never get out of it alive, so why bother torturing yourself? You *do* have a choice, y'know.

CHARACTER, ONCE AGAIN

It's no simple task to overcome strong emotions, to choose the positive over the negative. All we can do is try. A feeling of optimism takes enormous effort at times, but then again, so does pessimism, or finding underwear that fits perfectly. It's downright labor intensive to continually soak in grief.

This is where *strength of character* once again means the difference between surviving and not—where qualities like persistence, perseverance, and fortitude bolster, both mentally and physically, your quest for success. It's been proven many times that, if you're willing to take the knocks and stay in the game, you will find yourself ever-so-certainly ascending the show business ladder. Sometimes it's more of a creep up, but at least it's up. Success happens overnight for very few, the rest continue on, knowing they've got what it takes, and it's only a matter of time before lady luck smacks them with a golden whammy. Seeing the glass as half full . . . that's character.

In this discussion of rejection, three components of character are especially worthy of mention:

COMPONENT #1: WILL. It must be firmly in place. Our minds can will things to happen. Positive energy works amazingly well. I'm not inferring that you can levitate your brother-in-law Buster high over the punch bowl. I am only pointing out that, though it may take some effort to renew your allegiance to yourself, it's well worth the determination it yields.

Will is strength, purpose, determination. It's choice, decision, and responsible action—to do what is in your heart. Without exercise, will turns to wilt, with a noticeable droop in your resolve, and you wouldn't want to go around with a droopy resolve, would you?

COMPONENT #2: COURAGE. This is paramount. Problems must be confronted with our close pal *fortitude*, along with its cousins *pluck* and *spirit*. *Patience* is definitely a part of this family—as is *tolerance*, the ability to grin and bear it. To know in your heart what's right.

Courage is nerve; it's heroic, a quality of fearlessness. It's boldly going out there alone to face the Dalton Gang, the Capone mob, and Quick Draw McGraw all by yourself, armed only with unflinching self-reliance. You're cool, composed, all's under control. They used to call it moxie—I call it guts.

COMPONENT #3: CONFIDENCE. Confidence must be there to motivate you—to add reason to your actions. Confidence is closely partnered with courage—and can be simply defined as a trusting relationship within yourself, with all your mental parts in synch. This attribute is nicely illustrated by writer/producer **Ed Scharlach**:

In show business, you have to be thick-skinned, more so for an actor than a writer, but definitely for a writer, too. You can't take every negative criticism to heart, otherwise you will have to quit the first day. Every time you write something and somebody says that they don't like it, you think you are the worst writer in the world; then the next day somebody says they love the exact same script, and you think you're the best writer in the world. You can be influenced by other people's opinions. But to really survive, you have to trust your own opinions. If you know something is good, then you have to trust that it's good and trust that you're good."

For actors, confidence is not to be confused with ego. Confidence is not an in-your-face kind of attribute, but the silently self-possessed assurance that you are absolutely the best you can be. Confident actors work all the time.

ACCENTUATE THE POSITIVE

Positive thought is at the very heart of conscious living. It provides a form of therapy that must be experienced in the privacy of your own mind. It's self-therapy—an inside job—it has to be. As Nathaniel Branden emphasizes in *The Six Pillars of Self-Esteem*, "No one is coming. No one is coming to save me, no one is coming to make life right for me; no one is coming to solve my problems. If I don't do something, nothing is going to get better."

We all fail at one time or another, but there is never a need to lose hope. Failure is not there to close doors, but to open other ones. Thomas Edison failed repeatedly, but if he hadn't tried, there wouldn't be a Hollywood, and the movie stars would have to give us all our money back.

In my case, I kept myself going through a process of education—only to learn that there isn't a problem in the world that can't be solved . . . except maybe how to refold a road map.

ACCOUNTS:

Pluggin' Right Along _____

By now it should be obvious that a Hollywood career has more than its share of rejections. If this comes as a surprise, go back to page one and start reading again, because how you process these rejections is what will keep you in the survival derby. Check out the following comments from those who are certainly in the know.

Production executive/writer *Paul Mason*: "Sure, you'll get your head whacked a few times, but one of the most important lessons of our industry—for writers, directors, actors, for everyone—is never to take rejection personally. It is only disappointment from someone who doesn't know any more than you do. And never let people deter you from what you believe in. You've got to have a passion to continue in this business—never let people dilute that passion."

Actress/Teacher *Helaine Lembeck*: "No one can prepare you for rejection, and I think you've got to be willing to go through the hard times to get to the better times. There are always going to be highs and lows in someone's career—rejection comes in waves."

Writer/Producer/Personal Manager *Greg Strangis*: "I viewed even minor successes as huge wins. They didn't buy my script, but they liked some of it. That's a win. Getting a meeting with someone important. Hey, they didn't buy my pitch, but they said I could come back anytime. I figured that eventually the odds would work in my favor, that I'd sell a project and life would be grand. Each interview puts you closer to your goal."

Producer/Writer *Alan Sacks*: "My skin is thick from rejection. I get rejected, on to the next thing. I have so many things going on at once I can't just rely on one thing. There have been disappointments, but I've conditioned myself over the years to take it, and my attitude is I'm bringing in something that is so good—and if they don't go for it, they're making a mistake."

Writer/producer *Del Reisman*: "I was working on a series called *The Man and the City* with actor Anthony Quinn. One day, at the studio, I had to go down to his trailer dressing room, and I said, 'Can I talk to you for a moment?' He said, 'Sure,' and I was trying to find a way to say it, so I just said, 'Tony, ABC has canceled the show.' Tony stood up; he was a tall man and I could see that he was getting angry. He didn't say a word—not a word. He started to shake a little. I could see his face was flushed and I thought that, at any moment, this man was going to hit me over the head. Finally, he calmed down and the first thing he said was, 'Let's go steal some stationery.'"

RESILIENCE AND TENACITY

So, now you're beginning to see how this works—you get hit, take a moment to recover, and then come right back for more, knowing that this time you're a winner. Stealing stationery is always an option—in fact, it's sort of a Hollywood ritual when one is let go from a studio job.

In the following excerpt from *Dreams into Action*, Milton Katselas lays out a clear pattern for survival when he says:

> Get ready to be knocked down, because if you're out there chasing a dream, you're bound to bite the dust.... You have to get up, dust yourself off, straighten out your chops, get your ass in gear, gas up your tank, and jump back into the fray. Getting up once is tough. Getting up a hundred times is ridiculous. Be well prepared, because that's the way it might be.

Earlier, I mentioned the danger of forming negative emotional habits. Why did I say that? Because positive emotional habits will serve you far better—the two most important of these being *resilience* and *tenacity*. These two are a dynamic duo—and major antidotes to rejection.

A few definitions of resilience that I have gleaned from an assortment of dictionaries include:

> 1. The ability to recover readily from adversity. 2. To spring back. 3. To rebound. 4. To return to original form or position after being compressed or stretched (Ouch!).

All of these definitions combine to tell us that the exquisite quality of resilience is a basic refusal to quit. It's a mental flexibility—a buoyancy—a set of emotional water wings that keep you afloat and enable you to rise again after being declared dead. When in the possession of a certain buoyancy, a resilient person is not easily underfloated, and simply refuses to take "no" for an answer.

"Whenever I received rejection regarding a job I'd applied for," says **Laurie Scheer**, "I would seek out three more jobs and knock on those doors." Or, in the words of **Jim Begg**, "When you fall down, get back up again. No matter how many times you're knocked down, bounce back up. Remember, you are going to deal with a lot of egotistical idiots who will do their best to bring you down to their level. Ignore them. . . . You are your own best friend."

I can't say too much about the importance of being resilient. Actually, I could say too much, but why labor the point? Just know that, once you've resiliently bounced back, it's time to move on—to persist—to steadfastly stick to your guns. This is called *tenacity*. Gleaned from the very same dictionaries, tenacity is most often described as:

> 1. The ability to keep going; to forge ahead. 2. Keeping a firm hold. 3. Not easily pulled apart. 4. Tough, rugged, indestructible.

In my own words, I would characterize tenacity as good, old-fashioned stick-to-itiveness. It's purpose, resolve, perseverance, strength, determination, all in one amazing package. *Patience* is an essential asset here (as it is with courage)—it's life's great shock absorber. It renews strength and keeps the faith through thick or thin, rain or shine, and enough with the clichés already!

Tenacity was best exemplified by TV and motion picture writer/producer Norman Lear when he tried to get his series, *All in the Family*, on the air. He was repeatedly rejected, censored, insulted, and generally vilified for attempting to introduce a breakthrough comedy concept to network television. He was determined to succeed. When the first pilot failed to make the network schedule, he produced a second pilot, then a third. Finally, his tenacity paid off when the show was finally scheduled, and went on to become one of TV's biggest award-winning hits.

Another excellent example of tenacity in action is revealed in this reminiscence from **Lawrence-Hilton Jacobs**:

> As an actor over the years, I have been told many times that I was not getting the part for one reason or another. I was told by Steven Bochco (on a show he executive produced called *Paris*, starring James Earl Jones). He told me, "I cannot cast you off *Welcome Back, Kotter* to come on this show." And I said, "You know something? This character you wrote, you want him to be optimistic, arrogant, and forceful, a hard-edged guy with a glow in his heart. Well, there is not one scene in your entire script that even displays any of this and you expect that energy to walk through the door. . . . Well, guess what, Steven. I am displaying that energy right now in front of your face, and you don't even see it." . . . I called his bluff and said, "Thank you for the meeting." Five minutes later, I got a call and I got the gig.

GUIDANCE FOR THE BUMMED OUT

Quick review. Rejection is a major presence in the emotional Hollywood chess game. It can bring you to your knees, making you grovel and appear absurdly small. I think the following survival tips should reach you just in time.

SURVIVAL TIP #1. Head for the bathroom. Not a public convenience, your own bathroom where you can talk to yourself in the privacy of your own mirror. Review all of the positive things in your life. Congratulate yourself for the things you've done well—take pride in your accomplishments. Smile at yourself. Grin. Lean in close and give yourself a big, wet kiss. Go ahead, mess up the mirror. Do it again. Now make a face. Another, even sillier one. *That's* the one! Now, you're laughing, right? At least a giggle. This is so silly!

SURVIVAL TIP #2. Boys are wrongly brought up not to show vulnerability. A real man never lets anyone see him cry. A lot of women feel pressure not to demonstrate their emotions, either. Therefore, a majority of the U.S. population staunchly maintains a resistance to tears. It's uncool to vent with wetness. These people may be quaffing Maalox by the case, but they're not weak—no, sir, not them. This is such bullcrap! Sadness is a true emotion—tears are a natural reaction. Cry! Do it in private if you must, but just *do* it. Let the tears flow, bawl your head off—you'll get happier a lot sooner.

SURVIVAL TIP #3. Any time you're rejected, don't take it personally. You've got company. **Jim Begg** points out that "there is a great deal of rejection and disappointment in this business. You just can't take it personal. That was very difficult for me. But just look around, it is happening to all of your peers."

Always remember that the "no's" Hollywood regularly distributes are based strictly on business decisions—or on basic stupidity. Just keep in mind that rejection is not a condemnation of your talent. The fact that you were thought good enough to be considered is a minor success or, as **Greg Strangis** sees it, "a huge win."

SURVIVAL TIP #4. While you're at the mirror making faces and breaking yourself up, be reminded that humor is a wonder drug for the blues. Humor energizes. Laughter heals. Just note what actress Goldie Hawn has to say: "Once you laugh . . . you can move forward. Comedy breaks down walls. It opens up people. If you're good, you can fill up those openings with something positive. Maybe you can combat some of the ugliness in the world."

REJECTION COLLECTION

There are rejections in your future—there's no getting away from them. A positive management of these rejections will give you strength and a strong reminder that rejection is only a temporary setback on the road to success. So, just feel it, forget it, and get on with it, a whole lot smarter than when you started. Or, as Carol Burnett put it, "I have always grown from my problems and challenges, from the things that don't work out, that's when I've really learned."

I've had more than my share of rejections during my thirty-year Hollywood career. Some hurt deeply, but I overcame them. I persisted and endured. I survived. I always knew my goals were right within reach. If not today, tomorrow. I'd be back. Constant faith and strength of spirit—these worked for a character like me, and they can work for you.

Chapter 6

HOLLYWOOD BLUNDERS

If I had it to do all over again, I'd make the same mistakes,
only sooner.
—Actress Tallulah Bankhead

Hollywood is often referred to as a place where the inmates are running the asylum, and there's a lot of truth to that—even for the most mentally stable person. Mistakes are a matter of course as evidenced by the high ratio of bad movies and TV shows, all brought to you by the decisions of executive bunglers or swift accountants looking for tax write-offs. The emphasis here is personal, however, about the blunderings we all make in coming to terms with the harsh realities of a "let's pretend" business.

IT'S YOUR DEAL

You pilot your way through show business by making personal choices. This is your story—you're the author, the star—so you try to create the results that you desire. It's all about decisions. You have power over what you will or will not do in your career. You can stop yourself from moving in the wrong direction. You can give the green light to what seems right for you. You've already shown yourself to be decisive by beginning this Hollywood expedition in the first place, now you'll have to keep those decisions coming. Right and wrong are subjective here—personal truth is what's important. Naturally, your gut will fail you at times; nobody bats a thousand percent. The last person to do that is reported to have risen from the dead, spawning a rash of religions, each with opposing right answers that seem to serve them all just dandy.

Wisdom can play a factor here. But, then, if I were wise and all-knowing, I would've won the lottery and you'd be reading a blank page. When it comes to wisdom, we summon the best within us, which brings us back to whatever our gut feels is right for us at the time.

Never let the fear of making mistakes affect your decisions. Fear will unfailingly have you engaging in a process of self-manipulation, which will put you in danger of wavering from your plan with the grave possibility of abandoning your quest before you really get started. Have confidence in your abilities; you are a definite asset to yourself.

In Hollywood reality, however, all the confidence in the world is not going to assure that your judgment is infallible. Sometimes it may simply be a wrong call that works against you. There will also be times when you will encounter circumstances you have no control over. Whatever the source, those circumstances can feed into your insecurities—and insecurity has a way of resulting in self-defeating behavior.

GOOFY CHOICES

Bad business decisions are a fact of life. My all-knowing gut has failed me on many occasions. Guts are like that. I often think that guts are like airliners, with all the parts provided by the lowest bidder.

I was once approached to join the writing staff of *M*A*S*H*. The show was in its eighth year, and word around town was that this would be their final season. In the meantime, I was offered the chance to help on the writing of a new pilot, and being partial to things new, where I would have the chance to shape the show, I chose the pilot. My gut said, "Go," and I went. Well, the pilot crashed, and *M*A*S*H* sailed happily through its eleventh year. But, hey, do I have any regrets? . . . Let's move along, shall we?

Stupid damn gut.

Now, any actor who hasn't worked for a while does not hesitate to accept a role when offered. Most actors will be anything, wear anything, say anything, as long as anything means a checky-poo. "I once made a movie called *Village of the Giants*," recalls **Hank Jones**. "It's been voted one of the worst movies ever made." I never had the luxury of turning down some witless role—I always had this insistent craving for food. This being a fact of my acting life, decisions were sometimes made out of desperation.

One dilly of a career choice I made was accepting a co-starring role in a very independent movie called *The Wizard of Mars*. The film mirrored the "Oz" story with astronauts following a yellow brick road in search of a good script. I should've known better, but I needed cash fast, so I took the job figuring that the movie would quickly disappear without a trace. No such luck. To this day, that sucker is on the shelves at Blockbuster and not a year goes by without several well-meaning clowns telling me they saw it, and asking: "How could you be in such a dumb movie?" Geez, I feel like I'm being haunted by this young imbecile who used to be me. And you know what the kicker is? The producer of that epic still owes me five hundred bucks. He knows I'd never take him to court. I'd have to testify that it was really *me* on the screen, and the judge would ask, "How could you be in such a dumb movie?"

Movie stars are really at risk in the stupid-choice game. Much more at risk than lesser-known actors. A star makes a rotten movie that makes no money, and it's a black mark against that star. (Not the rotten part, the no money part.) Two box-office stinkers and a star's career is el dumpo. Three and it's whatever happened to . . . ? on *E! The True Hollywood Story*. Think back to the hot young stars of, let's say, ten years ago. Young stars in loser flicks. Where are they now?

Instances of personal blunderism are all a part of the Hollywood survival trip. You can accept the right job, reject the right job, accept the wrong job and be miserable as hell. Your gut can fool you, but you must take full responsibility for whatever decisions you make. Like I've said before, it's an inside job.

ACCOUNTS:

Assorted Regrets

No matter how professional we are in our approach to show business, we all make mistakes and have our regrets.

Producer/Writer *Alan Sacks*: "I left *Welcome Back, Kotter* for a pretty lucrative deal at Warner Brothers. They asked me to write and produce a rip-off of *Kotter*. It was called *Best Friends* and it never aired. They asked me for *Kotter*, but *Kotter* was lightning in a bottle. . . . You should never rip yourself off."

***Gary Cosay*:** "I was a little naïve and thought the grass was greener. The grass is *not* always greener. It just sounds that way when people try to paint it. I guess if I had to do it all over again I probably would have grown [my smaller agency] Leading Artists into a big agency as opposed to merging various cultures, which I feel is difficult and not as fulfilling a process."

***Arnold Margolin*:** "My partner [Jim Parker] and I left *Love, American Style*, after the fourth season, just when we had figured out how to do the show in the most creative and efficient manner, and had put together an excellent staff. Had we stayed with the show, I am convinced that it would have gone on far longer than the one season more it lasted, and that we could have used it as a platform to launch other series, as we did with *Happy Days*. Looking back, it was a horrible blunder and one we made more in anger at the studio for perceived wrongs, than with thoughtfulness. Unfortunately, we lacked the foresight to realize what we were giving up."

REPRESENTATIVE BOO-BOOISM

Okay, times get hard. Pressure and anxiety take center stage. You feel as if your whole career quest is going the way of the eight-track and Windows 3.1, so it's natural to lash out at someone for your failure to succeed.

It's not whether you win or lose, it's where you place the blame. And I would say that the most popular Hollywood blame-ee is your agent. You may even consider getting a different agent and take steps to do just that. Hey, the urge is always there, as you begin to think that the person who is supposed to be representing you is off having a fun vacation on the money you haven't made him. This is a sign that your thinking gear is out of whack, so take a few minutes and get over it: Careers take time.

Several years ago, I gave one particular agent, who was very supportive of me, the old heave-o-rino when my career went through a period of inactivity (during which I was bordering on insanity). He was not only my agent, he was my friend, but I yielded to the madness and told him I was signing with another agent. The man was cut to the quick, but I felt I was doing the right thing. Well, I did not do the right thing, and I have lived to regret it ever since. I acted rashly, emotionally, and blamed my career problems on my agent. I was relying too heavily on the man to get me work. I had yet to realize that a show business talent—any talent—has to take control of his or her own career. I don't harbor many career regrets, but I've never gotten over the irrational, headstrong actions that resulted in losing a fine agent and friend.

Be aware that irrational behavior is always waiting to be put into play when insecurity strikes—especially after extended periods of relative security. **Eddie Applegate** was a featured star on a hit TV comedy series, but, unfortunately, good things do come to an end:

> After *The Patty Duke Show* shot its final (112th) episode, three months went by with no job or even an interview. My friends kept telling me I should be working, which fed my actor's anxieties, so when one of the junior agents split to form his own agency, he asked me to join, promising big things, and like a fool I did. Six months later, my new agent told me he was closing the agency to go back into the import-export business. . . . Not too smart on my part.

No one has ever had a Hollywood career without the help of an agent, but there's another side to this issue that I think you should be aware of. It's called sticking around too long, also known as beating a dead horse. Actor **Lou Wagner** found himself in this predicament early in his career:

> One mistake I made was being too loyal to an agent when I should have moved up to a stronger agency. I have never really had a powerful agent

on my side, and there was a point where I was really left behind. Looking at my career, that was probably the main problem I had. I was loyal to an agent that didn't want to grow, wanted to stay small. When it came time to move up to the great stuff, I wasn't represented.

So, listen to the voices of regret. Talk with your agent when things are slow. Reexamine your relationship. Get your feelings out in the open. Whatever you do, don't act out of the emotions of the moment. This is a business that requires loads of communication and a blind eye to negativity. Any display of knee-jerk, and emotional decisions will, more often than not, lead to regrets and setbacks to survival. Patience and loyalty can be rewarding.

PERSONAL CONSIDERATIONS: YOUR LOVE LIFE

The way the general public sees it, the term "Hollywood marriage" is an illogical, contradictory pairing of words and people, which has resulted in far too many legal eagles' spreading their wings over the polluted Los Angeles skies. I actually heard there's a store on Hollywood Boulevard that rents wedding rings. The marital fall-out in Hollywood does seem somewhat excessive, but it's probably not any more frequent than in the rest of the country. Hollywood star marriages just get way too much hype—and then we sit in awe as these little king and queen bees flit from flower to flower, entertaining us with their romantic insecurities. Icon split-ups titillate us. We get off on seeing Tom Cruise jilt and be jilted.

Now, this may come as a surprise (or possibly a disappointment) to you, but there are a great number of successful Hollywood marriages or significant pairings in Hollywood. You seldom hear about these people, but many of them have been hitched for thirty, forty, fifty years or more. And I like to think that these individuals are happy and not just waiting around to see who dies first so the survivor can sell the house and make a bundle.

In Hollywood, a fifteen-year marriage is considered a success. And I would say that the majority of the divorces are due not to adultery or devil worship, but to "the business." Show business begets disappointment, which begets behavioral blunders, causing emotional structures to weaken and collapse. Simply put, stress can strain, destroy and leave harmful, long-lasting effects on people's lives. Or, as **Peter Lefcourt** states, "Erratic finances put a strain on marriages."

The kind of mate you choose to cohabitate with is all-important to the survival of any Hollywood marriage. An actor will often marry another actor, figuring they have so much in common they'll make an ideal pair. Well, that ain't necessarily so. Actor spouses will mutually commiserate over one or the other's failure to land a job, but when one gets a job, there is often a kind of professional jealousy—call it resentment. It's childish, but true, as the unemployed spouse murmurs, "Why not me?"

It takes enormous effort to make a Hollywood marriage work. A great deal of overtime has to be put into a relationship. By overtime I mean effort and attention. You promised to share your life with one another, so don't ignore, or blame, or deny your spouse the love he or she deserves. Stay aware—don't be blinded by career. Of course, this is a two-way street. Spouses (or "non-pros," as *Daily Variety* calls them) have an equal responsibility to be supportive to a mate with dreams.

Gary Cosay attributes his marital happiness to the generosity of his spouse—and the collaborative role she played in his career decisions. "I've had good support from my loving and beautiful wife, Healy. I relied on her and was able to go to her, discuss things, and make certain choices that were of major importance to my success." Similarly, **Greg Strangis** notes, "Now I have a very supportive, very successful wife (Pam) who contributes more than her share to my career."

You'll see examples of spousal support among a great number of show business professionals. I know a stockbroker who supports a writer; a caterer who supports an actor; and, in certain instances where support was lacking, I saw the marriage fall apart, and the lawyers move in to make things even worse.

I must confess to having had two divorces that were heavily attributable to the vagaries of a Hollywood career, a career that all too often swung the doors open to stress, resulting in certain errors in judgment. Therefore, I think a few Hollywood marriage survival tips are in order here.

HOLLYWOOD MARRIAGE SURVIVAL TIP #1. "I don't wanna talk about it." This is the most widely used destructive phrase in any marriage. Relationships fail in silence. Talking out your problems and openly expressing your feelings is imperative to the longevity of any marital relationship. A silent partner is no partner at all. So, make a habit of sharing your feelings with your spouse—tell him or her the way you feel and why you feel that way. Believe me, your marital partner feels your silent pressure.

HOLLYWOOD MARRIAGE SURVIVAL TIP #2. Do *not* take out your frustrations on the person standing opposite you; it could be dangerous—your spouse may be holding an iron skillet. Try to be calm in expressing any anger or frustration. There's no written rule that says you have to blow up and act like a fool. Try biting an old shoe and not your tongue. There is no reason for you to fly off the handle. You don't have to follow through on those negative impulses. If you have kids, by all means, level with them. They will surprise you with their capacity for understanding. I realize that trying to explain Hollywood show business to others is no easy task, but talking it through may very well have you reaffirming your goals and desires. (And if none of this works, go chop wood or something.)

HOLLYWOOD MARRIAGE SURVIVAL TIP #3. Take a break from yourself now and then. It's easy to be consumed by your profession, so ease up, for cryin' out loud! Stop going around being self-centered all the time. Engage in activities that have nothing to do with show business. Go to the zoo, the park, a museum. There's a whole reality beyond Hollywood beckoning you to join in. (Movies and TV are definite no-no's.)

HOLLYWOOD MARRIAGE SURVIVAL TIP #4. Cultivate friendships with individuals who are *not* in show business. If all your friends are in the business, the only thing that will ever be discussed is Hollywood, and how misunderstood everyone is. This can get pretty boring to a civilian spouse. I know this because I was married to one.

HOLLYWOOD MARRIAGE SURVIVAL TIP #5. A lot of good-looking people populate the world of Tinseltown. Some of them are even funny and smart. Any number of spouses may experience feelings of jealousy. For example, let's say you're an actor shooting a scene where you have to kiss Uma Thurman. Well, you can stave off any jealousy your wife may be feeling by explaining that it's necessary to the story. . . just two actors doing their job . . . nothing emotional. It's business, and if the production didn't go forward, hundreds of people would be thrown out of work! If this gets you nowhere, go back to the part about it being necessary to the story. By now, you should really be in deep, so introduce your wife to Uma Thurman and hope they'll get along famously. If this doesn't work, a little professional counseling may be in order.

As a sidebar to this issue, a writer friend of mine once had a female agent who was as stunning as a model. When his wife expressed jealousy, he pointed out that whatever fantasies might be, his agent was only entitled to 10 percent. This humorous approach actually cleared the air and those two kids are still married today. He even has a new female agent who looks like Peewee Herman.

HOLLYWOOD MARRIAGE SURVIVAL TIP #6. Play a never-ending game of show and tell with your spouse, the object being to express the words "I love you." Do this on a daily basis. Any marriage that survives under the influence of Hollywood show business is entirely due to character and communication. Mutual traits such as faith, patience, tolerance, and loyalty must be present constantly.

KEEPING THE FAITH

The most monumental blunder of all is letting others run your life. When you lose faith, you lose everything, and you will go through life agonizing over what could have been. So, buck up and remain vigilant as your faith is constantly tested. Each day will demand adjustment, revision, fortification and, most importantly, renewal.

ROOKIE UPDATE

Rachel Lawrence writes:

I met this other actress in the building. Her name is Melanie. She's been in Hollywood for years, so she knows all the "ins and outs" of the business. She even sent me to this photographer who took some great shots, and I plan to send my picture to every agent in town. Melanie introduced me to these guys who are doing this independent movie, and huge news! I read for them and they cast me in a leading role!! We start shooting as soon as they get all the financing set. I play this girl who gets strung out on drugs and kills her boyfriend—and it's even got some comedy in it. This is the kind of part that could really do it for me, and my dreams are a lot closer to becoming real. Keep your fingers crossed. . . . I have to admit that ever since I got here I've been feeling pretty unsure of myself, but now things are starting to happen and I'm even starting to write my Oscar speech. This may seem like I'm counting my chickens, but you have to be a little pushy and act positive in this town or it will eat you alive. But I don't want to be negative, great things are in my future! . . . Bye, bye, Rachel.

Chapter 7

NAVIGATING THE TOUGH TIMES

The way I see it, if you want the rainbow,
you gotta put up with the rain.
—Dolly Parton

Anyone who has chosen a career in Hollywood, or in any of the arts, will likely face difficult periods during which life is tough and you are forced to dig deep for the straps you need to pull up your boots. It may seem like your career is nothing but a continuous struggle where you wake each morning with shades of moody uncertainty that can oh-so-gently rip at your insides, giving a rigorous workout to both your body and your mind.

There is no such thing as security in Hollywood. The industry is fickle and in a constant process of reinvention. People come and go, and those who stick it out can never live with the assurance that they really have it made. Actress/writer **Candace Howerton** recalls the moment she learned that no amount of previous success can ensure a stable future:

> I once played opposite Jack Lemmon in a fifteen-minute spot for United Way. . . . While we were filming at Ralph's Market in the Valley I noticed Jack had a funny look on his face. He asked me, "Have you been working?" I answered "Yes, I have." And he said, "I haven't worked in ten weeks." . . . That brought it home for me.

According to the wise and witty Dorothy Parker, "Hollywood money isn't money. It's congealed snow, melts in your hand, and there you are." While money plays an important role in show business success, the lack of it plays an even more important role. If you are independently wealthy, skip this chapter, but please donate generously to show business charities.

Y'see, most Hollywood professionals do not rake in the bazillions squandered on star writers, star directors, and movie stars. In fact, Hollywood can sweep even the most balanced star-in-waiting into a highly illogical, handball sort of existence, bouncing around from emotion to commotion, wallet deflated, ego bruised, left with the urgent feeling that action must be taken.

WAYS AND MEANS

In taking action it's not a bad idea to employ the concept of *frugality*—a word that means "why buy a new car when the old one runs pretty well all the time?" Frugality has a special place as a Hollywood survival device. We all can learn from individuals with financial sensibility.

Frugality is a good thing despite its stingy reputation. A person who is frugal is displaying a realistic sensibility, thereby extending her chance for survival. Wise money management is an asset to any actor or writer, and if there's any money to manage, a savings account is always a good idea. Funds should only be allocated for what is absolutely necessary, including that occasional business lunch where you need to cultivate contacts and be seen. Splurging is a definite no-no, and will only result in . . . well, why bring it up? A budget is an excellent survival device for handling tough times—as long as it doesn't blow out of proportion during the good times. (There are fascinating details on budgeting in chapter 8. Betcha can't wait, huh?)

ACCOUNTS:
Rainy Day Maneuvers _____

There have been altogether too many times in my career where I have sensed the need for more money in my pot, but the funny thing is, I don't ever remember living the life of a starving artist. I was always determined to find a way to get through. The methods vary, of course, as you will see by the following.

Jim Begg: "I have always been interested in business and money; I have always lived below my means and tried to keep money in reserve for the bad times. If I made a thousand dollars, five hundred went into the bank. . . . So, when things got slow, I was prepared."

Hank Jones: "I budgeted well, and yet enjoyed some of the frills, too. But I never was one to go out and buy a boat or something like that. That's the danger when the money comes in too fast and too much. Acting is a profession that, when the show is over, you are immediately among the unemployed. No guarantees about anything. And everyone is replaceable!"

Greg Strangis: "Hey, hard times are hard. You cut back on expenses, borrow money, rely on your friends, consider alternative careers, ask your enemies for help—and all the while you hit the typewriter and try to write your way out of trouble."

Now, an ever-popular mechanism for survival is to marry a person with money—or at least be kept by them (forever if at all possible). A beautiful actress, for example, will cozy up to and marry the gawky, ill-mannered son of the guy who invented a better mousetrap, and she'll reside grandly in a Bel Air mansion. This nouveaux-riche actress will take on lovers, serve on boards of directors, and live unhappily ever after as the heiress to a rodent-squashing fortune. This happens a lot in Hollywood . . . honest, for men as much as women. If you don't believe me, invent an even better mousetrap, move to Bel Air, and watch the desperate opportunists beat a path to your doorstep.

Also be aware that, in opportunistic instances like the above, love seldom reigns supreme, often resulting in divorce, palimony suits, and property settlements, which (excepting any pre-nup deals) can make a formerly starving artist extremely rich and the ideal target for a whole new generation of starving artists.

A writer friend of mine (who prefers to remain anonymous, and why I will never know) is the author of more than a dozen screenplays but has yet to get a film actually made. Still, he doesn't worry about money.

My wife works as a chef for a restaurant in Beverly Hills, so we don't have to be concerned about making ends meet. . . . 'Course, I've taken odd jobs just out of guilt. One time I modeled nude at an art school and almost caught pneumonia. I hadn't told my wife what I was doing so she got pretty mad when she found out. Some day the tables'll turn though, even though my wife has no problem with the [current] situation. She's positive I'll win an Academy Award. . . . I'm a lucky guy.

This writer's relationship with his spouse is not unusual in Hollywood. Another (anonymous) friend of mine who, at age thirty-eight, is still looking for his acting break, privately admits that he and his wife are responsible partners in their everyday lives. "My wife works in real estate where we live in the San Fernando Valley. She doesn't make the kind of money they do in Beverly Hills, but she's good at it and does okay. I pick up occasional acting jobs—just did a couple of lines as a reporter on *The Practice* and made some good contacts on the set." He went on to admit that he's "at liberty" a lot, so he works two part-time jobs, tending bar and working construction as a carpenter. "Harrison Ford supported himself as a carpenter for years before he became a movie star," he glowingly observed, "so maybe I can hit the nail on the head too. Y'never know. Meantime, me and my wife share the responsibility and have put together a pretty good life."

SURVIVAL-JOBBING

Early on, while pursuing my acting career, periods of no money usually meant a phone call to my in-laws for help. Nothing big, just a small loan . . . lots and lots of small loans. And bless their kind hearts, Ben and Pearl Jaffe were always there, showing a compassion that had them close to being broke themselves, which was not a good sign since they were the richest people I knew.

It had become apparent that I couldn't keep up this scrounging routine. A creatively unemployed person like myself could no longer afford to hitch a ride on the wings of fancy. It was time to pick up a newspaper and look for a job in the real world.

Now, making a living in show business can be extremely difficult until you're somewhat established. Often, the best you can hope for is a hand-to-mouth existence, or as **Jewel Jaffe Ross** says, "I've been hand-to-mouth poor and hand-to-mouth rich, but it's always been hand to mouth."

You will have to seek out ways to support yourself with employment outside of show business—to have what is called a "day job" that keeps the bills paid while you craft your artistic bent. There are many kinds of these jobs, ranging from the menial to the skilled.

No matter how much your mind may be twisted by the Hollywood media, famous people do not start out famous. In his book, *The Road to Success Is Paved with Failure*, Joey Green reveals that Jerry Seinfeld sold light bulbs over the phone, Madonna worked behind the counter at a donut shop, and Jay Leno failed the employment test at Woolworth's. To this, allow me to add that Martin Sheen was a janitor, Billy Bob Thornton worked for a caterer, and Jane Leeves (*Frasier*) admits to having "one job where I think I made four or five dollars an hour packing those hideous nail gems that people used to wear on their fingernails."

Of course, the jobs most appropriate to show business are those that allow you time off to attend auditions, pitch meetings, whatever. So, how do you find these jobs? One reliable method is to scour the classifieds section of the daily newspaper and pursue a job hunt with the same zeal as you do your career. It's all a part of the resourcefulness that is indispensable to your survival.

Many of the jobs that you find in the classifieds will give you the opportunity to maintain a flexible schedule. The following is a partial list of these jobs, many of which allow you to work evenings and weekends. But first, here's an old Hollywood joke: Someone asks what you do for a living and you tell them that you're an actor . . . and they ask what restaurant you work at. Therefore, topping the list is:

Waiter/Waitress

• Ad copywriter	• Ad salesperson (TV, radio, newspaper)
• Art school model	• Automobile salesperson
• Caregiver	• Cashier

- Catalog model
- Childcare giver (baby-sitter)
- Collection agent
- Courier
- Deejay
- Hotel desk clerk
- Limo driver
- Paper route driver
- Promoter (demonstrator)
- Retail salesperson
- Taxi driver
- UPS or FedEx worker

- Caterer (server, bartender)
- Cleaning person
- Cook
- Delivery driver
- Food deliverer
- Insurance salesperson
- Maintenance person
- Pool maintenance person
- Proofreader
- Security guard
- Telemarketer
- Yard worker

Then there's that recurring ad—"Earn between $500–$2,000 a week! Be your own boss with your own hours stuffing envelopes at home!" I never answered an ad like this for the simple reason that you wouldn't see these ads all the time if you really *could* make $2,000 a week . . . or even $500 . . . do I hear $250?

Employment opportunities can also be found in the classifieds sections of trade papers like *Daily Variety*, *The Hollywood Reporter*, or *Backstage West*. In a recent issue of *The Hollywood Reporter*, following a real estate ad for a fixer-upper in Malibu slashed to only $6,800,000, I found these "Help Wanted" listings:

1. Part-time bookkeeper needed for L.A. production company.
2. *Backstage West* (the actors trade weekly) seeks sales assistant for the marketing/advertising department.
3. Radio announcers/Deejays to do music/talk/interview shows for radio station. No experience necessary.
4. *Crew Net*—The #1 film/TV professional online career resource—New jobs posted daily—*www.crewnet.com*.
5. Researcher for L.A.–based media company.
6. Secretary/Assistant for personal management company.
7. Production company seeks highly motivated part-time intern for script development. Excellent opportunity for future writer/producer.
8. Junior Accountant for post-production service company. Part-time, excellent pay.
9. Receptionist needed for large talent agency.
10. Telemarketers needed immediately. Base, bonuses, great hours.

TEMPING FOR DOLLARS

Landing the right sort of job that will support your show business habit is no easy task. You certainly don't want a job that smacks of permanence or requires you to wear a uniform or sit in a cubicle and make change. You're an artist, for crumb sakes, you deserve a position with dignity.

I used to register at temporary employment agencies where I was (as you may have guessed) temporarily employed. In case you're wondering how I found these temporary agencies, they found me. Temporary agencies that are particularly friendly to show business folk will generally advertise in the classifieds of the previously mentioned trade papers, so by constantly monitoring these classifieds, I was able to find a number of temporary openings that suited my lifestyle—which, at that time, had very little life and no style. My temp jobs consisted of things like filing, unfiling, packing, unpacking, shipping, and cleaning up messes. (Lucky for me, there was no typing required because I flunked typing in high school. Boring, repetitive, you keep hitting the same keys, there's no sense of closure.)

Temporary jobs are generally of the office variety: secretary, bookkeeper, receptionist, clerk of some kind, so typing will likely be required. These jobs are lower on the pay scale, especially after the agency takes their cut, but if you have special computer skills, such as Word, Excel, PowerPoint, Outlook, Photoshop, and Quark, your value will most certainly increase.

PART-TIMING

If you possess special skills, a unique appearance, or special accreditation, you can find part-time work in a wide variety of areas. "I always had a job," recalls **Candace Howerton**, "because I could type and I knew the skills to work in production. At times, I answered fan mail for celebrities and worked on the Academy Awards for many years. It was fun, hard, exciting work." So, if you possess any of the above-mentioned skills, appearance, or accreditation, part-time work may be found in such occupations as:

- Celebrity look-alike
- Musician
- Seamstress/tailor

- Fitness instructor
- Paralegal
- Substitute teacher

Or, you could always employ a particular expertise to start your own part-time business as an:

- Accountant
- Interior decorator
- Landscaper
- Massage therapist
- Mime (just kidding)

- Computer tutor
- Internet trainer
- Language instructor
- Medical transcriptionist
- Script typist

Director/teacher Milton Katselas, in *Dreams into Action*, reveals that he worked for a moving company.

It was an all-day job, but the pay and tips were terrific . . . it perfectly solved my problem. People usually move at the beginning and end of the month. So for eight days a month I was busy on the moving truck, and then I was free for the other three weeks to push my career.

I found my own exciting work cooking hot dogs at Dodger Stadium, where they let me wear a chef's hat, which gave the illusion of dignity. My co-workers called me Wolfgang Weenie, and I certainly was. The job also had its perks because most games were at night, so I had my days free to pursue my show business career. How did I land this job? A "contact." I had done a play (for nothing) with another actor who moonlighted working for the Dodger concessions company and his good word got me in. It always pays to know people who know people.

ACCOUNTS:
Odd Jobs

Let's hear the professionals relate their various experiences as odd-jobbers.

Robert Hegyes: "I was always working jobs to get money up. I stacked shoes for Florsheim. I worked as a delivery boy for a stationery store. I was even a teller in a bank."

Sondra Bennett: "I didn't want to wait tables while waiting for a break, so I took a job selling cosmetics at Robinson's in Beverly Hills. I told everyone it was because I was preparing for a role and needed to 'feel' what it was like to be a salesgirl. . . . This began my career as a bullshitter."

Eddie Applegate: "I'm a responsible husband and father, so I worked at all kinds of jobs to stay afloat. . . . When I first started selling carpeting to home-owners, I would more often than not be greeted with: 'You're Richard from *The Patty Duke Show*, why are you here selling carpets?' . . . . I once sold Marlon Brando a portable whirlpool—he understood, a good man to do business with. When I sold a whirlpool to Forrest Tucker (*F-Troop*), he was so impressed that he wanted me to speak to his actor friends about saving their homes and cars by working outside of show business. . . . The meeting never took place."

Hank Jones: "In 1986, I auditioned for *Jeopardy!* This seemed the right show for me to try out for since my mind is filled with useless information and trivia. There were about two hundred people who took the tough exam and only three of us passed. . . . All those years in front of the camera really helped me because I didn't have any nervousness at all. I felt right at home on a soundstage again. However, since the public thinks all actors are filthy rich, they asked me not to say I was an actor during the interview, so I said I was a genealogist. When Alex Trebek asked, "Can you really make money at that?" I lied and said, "Oh, sure." The wild thing is that I got so much mail after the shows aired asking questions about family history research that my genealogy book sales tripled for the next six months! I lasted three days as 'champion' on the program and won $18,000. The consolation prize when I finally lost was an all-expense trip to the Bahamas, which (being single at the time) I took with a clinging blonde."

CYBER-JOBBING: SURFING THE WEB FOR LISTINGS

The Internet can be a very useful tool in your job search. You don't have to be a union member to access the following:

1. *www.sag.org* (Screen Actors Guild)
2. *www.aftra.org* (American Federation of Television and Radio Artists).
3. *www.actorsequity.org* (Actors Equity—theater actors, stage managers, dancers, singers)
4. *www.wga.org* (Writers Guild of America)
5. *www.dga.org* (Directors Guild of America)

The Screen Actors Guild, in particular, offers a Jobs Hotline, with listings of jobs available within the SAG organization itself. It may be worth looking into. It can also be accessed by phone at (323) 549–6023.

You can also access information from these trade paper Web sites:

1. *www.variety.com*
2. *www.thehollywoodreporter.com*
3. *www.backstage.com*

Information on employment related to the show business industry—jobs like tour guides or script readers at studios—can be found by asking around, or by calling the studios directly to get the real lowdown.

ATMOSPHERING AND STUNTING

In Hollywood, bodies are often needed to provide background "atmosphere" for film and TV productions. Many of my friends have worked as "extras," which are contracted through the Screen Actors Guild. As of this writing, extra pay for an average eight-hour day is $100, but this can often get into time and a half, double time, and even golden time. A certain number of union members are required on each production, but there are jobs for those who have yet to join SAG. Call the Cenex Casting Network at (818) 562-2700.

Robert Hegyes explains how extra work helped in moving his own career along.

> It's like whatever gets you inside, man, whatever gets you through the door. I worked as an extra on the movie *Dog Day Afternoon*. I would be there everyday, even when they didn't need extras, so they saw me around all the time and I became friends with the first assistant director. I was on the inside and it had an influence on me being that close to Al Pacino and watching them shoot all those wonderful scenes. This is the kind of dedication I have.

And yet another tip: If you're into risking your life (and the fact that you are in show business proves it) you might even try contacting the various stunt associations and companies in and around Hollywood. The best resource is *The Hollywood Creative Directory*, at *www.hcdonline.com*. There's a yearly subscription rate, but with such postings as a Hollywood Job Board and Hollywood Classifieds, it may be well worth the investment.

MOVE IT OR LOSE IT

During your continuing efforts to keep your head above the financial ooze, you have to ensure that your career survives as well. It is imperative that you keep your place in show business moving on an upward plane toward your goal. You must be tenacious in your quest for gaining the attention of those who hire. You do this by involving yourself in creative efforts that can move you a link or two up the Hollywood food chain.

This continuous questing means different things to different people. For actors or directors, it's a commitment to theater: working for nothing in an effort to get lucky and be discovered. Sitting on a stool in a coffee shop will not get you discovered anymore unless, of course, you're a stunning individual, fully in possession of whatever cosmetically surgical procedures are all the rage at the time. (Personally, I never liked those huge lip injections. What good can they do? There's not an actor in Hollywood who has a chance in hell of replacing Donald Duck. And that's a fact.)

Whatever method you use, it all boils down to some form of "showcasing" in hopes that some producer, casting director, or agent spots your genius and swings open the magic door to that sought-after break.

I found a wonderful acting showcase in the middle of Hollywood called The Masquers Club—the West Coast version of New York's Lambs Club, which has nothing to do with The Friars Club, which is a Jewish-Catholic order where ancient comics anoint each other with insults at a series of Last Suppers. The Masquers Club was a haven for many famous Hollywood character actors (Percy Helton, Alan Mowbray, Mousie Garner, Vince Barnett, Harry Antrim, Fred Clark, Frank Faylen). Look these guys up—their familiarity will ring happy and immediate cinematic bells.

These guys, who were in every other movie ever made, became my friends—mainly because they were always in desperate need of a young actor to fill the idiotic juvenile roles in their plays. I even got to be a "Stooge" in a sketch with Curley Joe. There was no paycheck at The Masquers, but the plays were well attended by industry people. Every time I did a play, I got a part in a movie or TV show. There's nothing like playing an idiotic stooge to get you noticed.

My old friends have since passed on, and The Masquers Club has been ripped down to make way for substandard housing. But Hollywood (in fact, all of L.A.) is dotted with theaters just waiting to let you show your stuff with a lot of new, past, and future pros you never ever dreamed you would work with. You may even get your play produced. There's generally no pay, but it's a real bump up the emotional survival curve.

THEATRICAL POSSIBILITIES

For those of you who think that Hollywood is a theatrical wasteland, think again. The arts organization, Theatre L.A. *(www.theatrela.org)*, boasts 190 member theaters—large and small, safe and risqué. That's a helluva truckload of theaters, so don't go asking me to list them. The L.A. area has large, well-known theaters like The Mark Taper Forum, The Ahmanson, The Shubert, The Pantages—all of which actually "pay" Equity actors and such. But the overwhelming number of theaters are the "Equity Waiver" theaters, which don't have to pay you if they have less than 99 seats. Most theaters have less than 99 seats, and just think of the money they save. However, even if you are performing or writing or teaching for free, it's a chance to hone your craft, make contacts, and possibly be considered for something that pays in TV or motion pictures.

The best theatrical guide in Hollywood is the weekly publication I've already mentioned, *Backstage West.* This thing is chockfull of great show biz gab and information on classes in

- Acting
- Auditioning
- Sketch comedy
- Commercial acting
- Vocal coaching
- Writing workshops

- Cold reading
- Improvisation
- Stand-up
- Voice-overs
- Private acting sessions

In the same issue, I discovered forty ads devoted to

• Photographers
• Photo and audio duplicators
• Videographers

Actor and writer Web sites are also featured, along with loads of casting information (including tech jobs), even a job opportunities section. There is no better source for information than *Backstage West* (and I don't even know these people). There are several comedy workshops around the L.A. area: The Groundlings, Second City, and Acme Comedy Theatre, just to name a few.

Actress **Helaine Lembeck** (along with her brother, Michael Lembeck) runs The Harvey Lembeck Comedy Workshop, which was started years ago by their father, noted film, TV, and stage actor Harvey Lembeck. When asked about herself and the workshop, Helaine explained,

> After majoring in theater arts at the University of Washington, I came back to L.A. and studied with Lee Strasberg for two years, and also took my father's class for eight years. Harv used improv as a tool for teaching comedy. He believed that the more you do it, the more you are going to get it. By using improv, everyone gets on stage at least three times in a class. We get agents sending us clients all the time who are good dramatic actors who have never done comedy. (A lot of big comedy writers have come from the workshop, too.) Some of our former students include: Robin Williams, Penny Marshall, John Ritter, Jenna Elfman, John Larroquette, Alan Rachins, Kim Cattrall, Scott Baio, Bryan Cranston, and Sharon Stone.

THE WRITE CONNECTION

Keeping a writing career alive takes continuous writing. Even if you're busy parking cars at the Beverly Hills Burger King, you must set aside time to write every day. That's what I did, and one of the first things I wrote was accepted by a magazine. It was a check for a year's subscription, but a person's allowed to dream, and writers are allowed to embellish, so it's on my résumé.

I wrote all kinds of things: TV scripts, screenplays, pilot concepts, even a cooking show, but I couldn't get anybody to bite. Then, in an act of desperation, I answered a "Writer Wanted" ad in *Variety*, and was hired at a slave wage to write a mail-order course on radio broadcasting. I got the job because I snowed the guy into believing that I knew all about radio broadcasting, which I didn't, but research did the trick, and I live with the satisfaction that I made the guy so rich he stopped returning my calls.

Four attributes all writers must possess:

1. Loads of ambition that never stops.
2. Abundance of nerve, to sell that ambition that never stops.
3. A "spec" script in the hopper. More than one.
4. A large drawer or shelf filled with writing samples. These samples will be invaluable in proving to an interested agent that you are indeed serious about your craft and are pretty much what God would be like if he was lucky enough to write, even though he prefers to direct.

There are several Web sites that offer aid and information to aspiring, even veteran writers out to display their wares. The old reliable *www.wga.org* offers several valuable resources: an online mentoring service on the craft of screenwriting; a Hot List of new media Web sites for writers; a list of literary agents; a TV market list (information on all current and new shows); articles; and interviews.

Another Web site, *elactheatre.edu*, is based at East Los Angeles College, which features a theater library and a section where you can publish your own plays or read plays by other aspiring playwrights.

If you're a screenwriter working on a spec feature script, you can track up-to-date information about projects in development, what's sold, and open writing assignments by accessing *www.4filmmakers.com*, *scriptsales.com*, and *holly-woodlitsales.com*. These three sites are all central repositories of screenwriter information, allowing you to bone up on marketing facts without flying blind. *Scriptsales.com* and *4filmmakers.com* are *free*. *Hollywoodlitsales.com* is by subscription at a reasonable monthly fee. (They allow you a free peek.)

ROLLING WITH THE PUNCHES

Show business is closely related to the sport of prizefighting. You have to learn how to weave, to duck, and when punched to quickly get off the mat and take whatever measures are necessary to keep your chances alive.

Always bear in mind that luck is just around the corner and you will survive the hard knocks through patience, diligence, and an unconquerable vision of yourself as a winner.

ROOKIE UPDATE

Rachel Lawrence writes:

After Daisy's brakes were fixed, she was running fantastically until something happened with some kind of alternator thing and Daddy is not happy, but Mom has her own account and I should be getting a check any time now—but I'm stranded until my car is healthy again. Not that it matters because nothing at all is happening, and I'm still waiting for my movie to start. Still trying to raise the money they say. . . . Looking for an acting teacher is turning into a real project. I sat in on one class just to check it out and the teacher didn't seem to know what he was doing. All he did was criticize, and he wasn't really very helpful, so I don't think he's the teacher for me—but I'll keep looking (when I have a car). This one cute boy in the class asked me out and took me to this party where there were loads of other actors and this one casting director who some of the girls were coming on to even though he looked kind of old. My date was getting drunk, so I hitched a ride home with this other girl. My, isn't Hollywood glamorous! I'll write again soon when I (hopefully) have something fabulous to report. . . . That's all for now, Rachel.

Kyle Kramer e-mails:

Greetings from Burbank, the Paris of L.A. I got three writer/agent names from a writer who lives in the building. I sent them query letters and received two responses saying they were not accepting new clients and the other one is MIA. . . . At this particular juncture, I would say that most of my time is devoted to writing. While acting is my main purpose for being here, I have learned that it requires a great deal of start-up time. Since I got here, my acting-related activities have been sparse. The manager who has been helping me recommended a photographer so I can get my pictures. An actor is nowhere without pictures. A good picture is like a passport to fame and fortune, or so I like to think. . . . I was expecting to do some extra work, but every time I've called their hotline, they either want someone ethnic or someone thirty-five who has three business suits. I just don't fit any of the things they want. That's one of the things I was hoping would help me out, but that hasn't worked out. The pursuit is mostly waiting and hoping at this point, but as soon as I have all the pieces in place, I know I can begin to take a more active role. . . . More fortunate things to come. . . . Kyle.

Chapter 8

BUDGETARY MATTERS

In show business, you can make a killing,
but you can't make a living.
—George S. Kaufman

I talked earlier about planning—putting together a blueprint for your career. Having an idea of where you want to go gives you a decided advantage because the first couple of years are especially unpredictable. Having a direction will come in even handier later on down the line, when panic lurks because you're not achieving your goals as quickly as you would like. Hollywood show business is a landscape filled with hills and valleys: the hills being the high times, the valleys the pits. It all amounts to "paying your dues." It's also continuing to pay those dues, and exactly how much those dues may amount to no one knows because, as I've said earlier, nobody in Hollywood ever has it made.

Show business people lead a gypsy-like existence, rarely of their own choosing. They go from job to job on show to show, picture to picture. Everything ends requiring new beginnings, which are often hard to come by, resulting in long, drawn-out periods of unemployment. At times like these it is best to turn your attention to *budgetary matters*. Think long and hard about what you will need to get through the initial stages, in order to keep moving ahead and survive. Budgetary matters fall into two categories: (1) *mental budgeting*—what's in your head; and (2) *physical budgeting*—what must be done to survive.

With periods of unemployment come money pressures, which can be all-consuming and lead you to go on automatic pilot so you can constantly *worry* about it. That's what you're supposed to do. Everybody does it. Your parents worry (especially about you). Your siblings, relatives, friends—they all worry. Even that teacher who told you she was worried that you were going to flunk out, making *you* crazy with worry—she's still worried about you now.

Worry is nothing to worry about. It's a habitual form of mental budgeting passed down to us through generations of worriers. Most of these worriers (the majority of whom likely worried themselves to death) have left us with the impression that the natural and proper reaction to disappointment and the frustrations of having no money is to worry. We are expected to anticipate the worst, and then worry that we might be right.

Well, to this I say, "Piffle!" Yes, piffle. I know the word may offend, but that's the way I feel. To worry about a problem is not to solve it. Worry never changes anything; it merely clouds the issue and renders it insufferable. And yet, there you stand—uptight, nervous, anxious, stressed, totally burned-out because it's the way to act, the thing to do. You've become this Frankenstein of your own making on a path to self-destruction. And the only person responsible for this monsterism is you. Nobody else made you that way; it's all an inside job. You made the decision to worry, so you have to take all the crap that goes with it.

Something to mull over, isn't it? How much mental budgeting we devote to useless behavior. You can change this way of thinking and acting, y'know, and it might not be a bad idea to give it a shot. It's just a matter of redecorating your thinking in order to exchange a negative habit for a more positive one. In his book, *Your Erroneous Zones*, Dr. Wayne Dyer advises: "There is nothing to worry about! Absolutely nothing. You can spend the rest of your life, beginning right now, worrying about the future, and no amount of your worry will change a thing."

ACCOUNTS:

Survivors' Stamina _____

There will be rough, tough times, not only at the beginning, but with some frequency after that. But don't fret—you're not alone in this. Even the most successful people have experienced their own bumpy ride.

Jewel Jaffe Ross: "I was collecting unemployment when I first hit town. Then it got tougher. Eight years of crappy jobs and too many potatoes."

Ralph Gaby Wilson: "My wife, Susan, and I lived in a converted chicken shack in Venice and I wrote in the garage. We lived on cheese and crackers and hot dogs. Six months later, we moved to a small, two-bedroom house in Hollywood (hooker heaven), and I wrote in a larger garage. We moved up to hamburgers and spaghetti."

Arnold Margolin: "When I first got to Hollywood, I had a wife and two kids, a rented house, one used car and generous loans from my parents until I got on my feet. Why they had faith that I would succeed I have no idea. My wife and I both worked at jobs we hated, but we believed it would lead to something better. It did, but there were no guarantees."

Lawrence-Hilton Jacobs: "I was living in a little studio apartment and I didn't know how I was going to pay the rent. My cash flow was majorly low, I was driving a rented Vega. I had a roommate, an actor friend from New York; we pooled our money together so we could have dinner and totaled fifty-seven cents. I bought a can of Hormel chili and the guy at the store wanted fifty-nine cents. Thank God he let me slide for the two cents. I was never downtrodden, but there were dim days when I didn't know how I was going to keep the lights on."

HOLLYWOOD ON A BUDGET

Budgeting is a necessity when you have to pick up pennies. Life must be pared down and simplified. You compare what you need with what you have in the hopes that you will get *some* of the things you need. You take the responsibility of putting some order into your life. You don't want to wind up like the legendary film star, Errol Flynn, who said, "My problem lies in reconciling my gross habits with my net income."

Everyone (especially the late Errol Flynn) needs to put together a budget. I'm not talking about something that's going to last for a lifetime; this is only an aid to keep you afloat. A monthly budget of living expenses is a practical survival device. It's a systematic way of living within your means, of balancing what you need with what you have, so you can learn to go without. It's telling your money where to go instead of wondering where it went.

You have to be imaginative in creating a budget, yet practical. Figure that 30 percent of your money goes to rent, 30 percent to food and clothing, 30 percent to car and insurance, 10 percent to doctor bills or a possible emergency, and if there's anything left, feel free to squander it any way you wish. An effective budget will serve you well and ensure that your ends are met, provided that nobody moves the ends.

BUDGETING TIPS MARTHA STEWART NEVER THOUGHT OF

If you were brought up (like me) in economic uncertainty, a budget should not be a difficult thing to work out. If you're accustomed to getting whatever you want, welcome to a bold, new adventure in budgeting tips.

BUDGETING TIP #1. First, sit down and figure out what you need to live on each month. Once you've done that, figure out what you can just scrape by with. Consider possible sources of income. Maybe a skill or hobby can earn you some bucks. You may take a part-time job, as I discussed in the previous chapter. If you qualify for unemployment insurance, by all means collect it.

Many a famous person has gone on to glory via the helpful hand of unemployment compensation.

BUDGETING TIP #2. Gross habits may have harmed the late Errol Flynn, and they can make a shambles of anyone's attempt at budgeting. If you smoke, quit. Okay, then try to quit. Okay, then smoke less. Cut your cigarettes in half, misplace your lighter, stop buying matches. If you like to drink, quit. Okay, then try to quit. Okay, then drink less. Buy inexpensive brands—vodka with a Russian name that's made in Kiln, Mississippi, or cheap tequila with a plastic worm. I used to buy this beer called Golden Grain, and the artificial beer flavoring made it actually taste like artificial beer.

BUDGETING TIP #3. Food is an important part of a balanced diet, so you must be scientific in your supermarket shopping. Save newspaper and magazine coupons. Choose a supermarket that "doubles" your coupons. You may have to do some comparison shopping to see where you can get the best deals. A store that actually displays prices is a good start. Never improvise—always make a list of what you need. And never, ever, go grocery shopping when you are hungry.

BUDGETING TIP #4. There are three basic food groups—canned, frozen, and junk. Many of these items are not high on the nutritional food chart, nor are they that inexpensive. (Have you seen the price of potato chips lately?) The best buys in any supermarket are in the produce area. Most fresh fruits and vegetables (with some exceptions) are quite reasonably priced (spaghetti squash among my favorites). Buy the generic brands of other foods whenever possible. Buy in bulk—bags of potatoes, sacks of rice, large boxes of pasta. Foods like these are expandable and, once cooked, can stretch to two or three meals.

BUDGETING TIP #5. Fast food can be expensive, and fries with everything can get pretty boring after a while, so why not be creative and devise your own recipes? I know we're not all Emeril in the kitchen, but we don't have to live on a diet of ketchup soup either. Give it a try—after all, practice makes perfect. There are plenty of cheap paperback cookbooks floating around that tell you how to eat healthy on a budget. All you have to do is devote some interest to food preparation and enjoy experimenting with recipes that you whip up for practically pennies a serving. Bon appétit!

BUDGETING TIP #6. Haunt garage sales. Rummaging can be a saving grace when looking for clothing, furniture, books, and assorted household items. I once found a Pierre Cardin sweater in great condition at Goodwill. At a rummage sale I found a metal vegetable steamer for only a buck. (They even threw in a free framed print of dogs playing poker.)

BUDGETING TIP #7. It's been said that one person's junk is another person's treasure, so get together with your friends and stage a joint garage sale. Everyone has junk they don't want and there are always suckers who will show up to buy it. Heck, people will buy anything if it's cheap enough, and this will give you a chance to unload all of that junk you've picked up at garage sales. I sold that framed photo of dogs playing poker for a buck. (He haggled me down from three.)

BUDGETING TIP #8. You don't need a large wardrobe for L.A. living, just the necessary shorts, tees, jeans, sneakers, a sweater, jacket, inexpensive underwear and socks. Men need one good suit, dress shirt, shoes, and a tie. Women need one good dress (or pants suit), blouse, shoes, and accessories. Your clothes will wear a lot longer if you keep them clean—and if the armpits to your suit start to smell like sardines, it may be time to go to the laundromat and try out the dry cleaning machine). Most clothing is washable—just follow the instructions on the label so your sweater doesn't go from large to shrimp. An iron and a can of spray starch are your friends. If you have an ironing board, great—if not, any hard, flat surface will do.

Always appear well groomed. Look like you bathe now and then. It will endear you to people. For men, I recommend finding a reasonable-priced barber, probably in a less-than-upscale neighborhood. For women, what can I say, beauty shops are expensive, but treat yourself now and then. And, when you do, ask a lot of questions so you can learn ways of doing for yourself. Using those hair-at-home kits is completely at your own risk, so don't come complaining when your hair falls out in clumps.

BUDGETING TIP #9. Be prepared to take care of needy little things (repairs, etc.) by yourself. Learn to darn your socks and sew on buttons. Get yourself a used copy of one of those "Helpful Household Hints" books and you'll discover amazing things, like using a crayon to fix the dings on your car, or making pantyhose last forever by using nail polish, or concocting a bit of baking soda and water to cure the heartburn caused by your own cooking.

BUDGETING TIP #10. Go over and over your budget as often as possible. Do it at night. By the time you're done, it'll be too late to go out and spend money.

THE CREDIT TRAP

At one point, I was overdue on my credit card payment and received a threatening missive instructing me to "Send the Amount Due *Now!*" So, I sent them a note that said: "The amount due is $849.12." They didn't think that was funny. Credit card companies have no sense of humor.

Okay, so it's time to give credit its due, and if you're a user of plastic, credit will *always* be due. It's been said that debt is the only thing a person can acquire without money. Amusing observation, but there is no such thing as a free, plastic lunch.

Granted, credit cards can provide temporary relief, but they can also be an eternal nemesis. There's an insidious danger, a kind of self-sabotage where you get locked into payment programs at exorbitant interest rates, paying only the minimum so that the balance never diminishes. Over the long haul, I think I've spent nearly twice as much for everything I ever bought on sale. If you're one of those people who shop to ease the pain of rejection, you're in for deeper pain.

Practically anyone with a halfway beating heart can get a credit card. They practically beg you with their mail offers. If you can lick a stamp and sign a monthly check, you can line your wallet with plastic. You'll only get turned down if you have a record of bankruptcy, and most personal bankruptcies are caused by credit cards.

If you're going to use credit cards, my advice is to try to pay off the balance every month. Not easy when you face seasons of joblessness. Some years ago, I had the good fortune of pulling myself out of the economic doldrums by becoming a well-paid story editor on a network comedy show called *Head of the Class*. This enabled me to pay off the huge credit-card balances I had accumulated during my doldrums. Later, when the gig ended, I found myself in doldrums again, and I was soon back to building up my credit card debt (which I hope to pay off when hell freezes over).

If you insist on using credit to get by, take this tip and use only department store cards. The interest is much lower and you'll find yourself being more selective in your spending, with a much lighter burden of debt. Agent **Judy Coppage** nails it when she says, "I learned from the get-go that smart people don't have much debt."

LABOR DAZE

A *union labor strike* can cause drawn-out intervals of no money coming in, because you're not allowed to work. Strikes are often necessary because show business management tends to want the whole monetary pie for themselves, so they occasionally have to be reminded of the fact that actors, writers, directors, grips, whoever, are entitled to a piece of the pie, too. During these times of work stoppage, it is imperative that you budget both your money and your mind.

I've been through three writers' strikes, all lasting longer than forever. These strikes eventually resulted in good monetary gains and still no respect, but you give up things to get things. For some quirky reason, these strikes always took place when I was gainfully employed on the staff of a TV show. It was difficult, but I had one thing in my favor—I could sit at home and write. (Many great feature films were written during strikes.) For actors, directors, agents, and production personnel, none of who work at home, strikes can be and have been disastrous. Problems of the labor variety are a major test of your talent for survival.

ACCOUNTS:

Struck Out _____

Here's what the professionals have to say about surviving labor strikes.

Bob Schiller: "During the strike of 1960, my partner (Bob Weiskopf) and I went to Detroit and wrote a presentation for the new Ford models. In other strikes, we just picketed and lived on our stored fat."

Ralph Gaby Wilson: "How does any working stiff survive a strike? You keep the bill of your baseball cap pulled down over your face when you enter the bank or convenience store."

Candace Howerton: "I was working in production at a studio during the writers' strike of '84 and I was scared. They were saying nasty things about writers. I got into an argument with one of my superiors (a director wannabe) who was against what the writers were striking for. I gave him a blank sheet of paper and said, "Can you direct that?""

Jewel Jaffe Ross: "By the time a strike made a difference in my life I was so accomplished at surviving bad times that it didn't make any real difference. Perhaps people prepare, I don't recall that I ever did."

Eddie Applegate: "In this past commercial strike (2000), I was able to work as a census enumerator with the flexibility of being able to work five of any seven-day period. It was made for an actor—meeting and talking with people from all walks and backgrounds. It gave me time to participate in the strike rallies and in the picket line. I was lucky to work through most of the strike."

Greg Strangis: "I've been a member of the WGA for thirty years, thirteen months of which have been spent on strike. I have no regrets about time spent out on strike. As a young writer, I wasn't prepared. I had no idea what a strike really was or how devastating it could be financially. But over time, anyone paying attention learns how to prepare for a strike. . . . Strikes can be good for writers. It gives a writer the time to write that spec script they've been putting off 'cause they're always too busy. Or write in another field, such as plays and novels."

CHARACTER REFRAIN

It's been said that everything comes to him who waits. It's the waiting that's tricky. Being "at liberty" for long interludes is the ultimate trial of a person's capacity for survival. It demands emotional budgeting of the mind, where you accentuate the positive and soft-pedal those negative creepies that weaken you. During these troubling times, any person's stamina is given the old once- or twice-over, but the stubborn, shatterproof certainty that you will overcome and succeed renders any idea of quitting unthinkable.

Allegiance to your commitment takes fortitude, and fortitude leads to the kind of endurance you need to withstand the pressures and stay in the race. This kind of stability of spirit is a clear demonstration, a personal acknowledgement, that you indeed do possess the qualities it takes to survive the Hollywood Derby. Quitters never win, and winners never quit, and the clown who said, "Quit while you're ahead," didn't know zip about show business.

ROOKIE UPDATE

Kyle Kramer e-mails:

Groceries are rather expensive here, though they might have been back home, too. I never did much grocery shopping. I have one box of macaroni and cheese and am saving it for a rainy day, determined not to be the stereotype I was in college. I find that tacos are a good, healthy source of nourishment. A pound of ground sirloin makes two big meals. I make smoothies for breakfast as much as I can, but peanut butter is probably my best friend. Even though I am trying to eat as healthy as possible, I'm having a hard time breaking the old Wisconsin habit of sitting down and eating cheese by the block. . . . My parents are basically supporting my habit right now and I am very fortunate to have them behind me. I had $5,000 of my own when I came out here, but due to pictures, workshops, and things like that, it is dwindling. It's very costly. I am going to get a job soon; I'm at the point where I need to start contributing a little more myself. I want to stay away from the food service industry because I really don't want to become a cliché—the actor/screenwriter/waiter. I have some administrative background working at companies and I would like to find something in the industry. Maybe something at Warner Bros. right down the street, maybe doing some office work to begin with. We'll see. . . . More later, Kyle.

Chapter 9

THE GRAND
HOLLYWOOD SOCIAL SCENE

*Look, I really don't want to wax philosophic, but I will say that if
you're alive, you got to flap your arms and legs, you got to jump
around a lot, you got to make a lot of noise, because life is the
very opposite of death. And, therefore, as I see it, if you're quiet,
you're not living. You've got to be noisy—and colorful and lively.*
—Mel Brooks

This cogent advice from Mel Brooks could very well apply to what outsiders
imagine the Hollywood social scene to be (at least I think that's what Mel was getting at). I'm specifically referring to the wild parties you hear about where everyone swaps mates, gets drunk and naked, and jumps into the Olympic-sized pool,
all to a south-of-the-border Mexican beat. Well, I'm sorry to have to bust your
bubble but, as lewd and bawdy as this all sounds, it's a fabricated fantasy. Today,
this kind of thing probably takes place more often in suburban Akron than it does
in Hollywood. I've attended many Hollywood social affairs and, except for an
occasional drunk falling into the pool to a south-of-the-border Mexican beat, I've
never actually witnessed this extreme sort of behavior.

PRESERVE WILD LIFE—THROW A PARTY! (a sign in a Hollywood liquor store).
As this sign indicates, the popular concept of Hollywood fun, frivolity, and devil-
may-care is still being promoted, an image that harkens back to the silent-movie
days when there was no income tax and multimillionaire movie personages felt
they had every privileged reason to act with reckless abandon and did, their antics
providing fodder for the Hollywood social whirl. In later years, gossip columnists
like Hedda Hopper and Louella Parsons effusively reported on the nightclub
sightings of Gable and Lombard at Mogambo, or Bogie and Bacall ringside at
Ciro's, all four never failing to use the right fork.

Today, there are gossipy columnists still reporting on the social goings-on,
but the reading of these columns is pretty much confined to the industry itself.

The function of the studio publicity machine is still alive and well, though it's been taken over by "fictional reality" shows like *Entertainment Tonight* and *Access Hollywood*. These shows spew out a constant stream of Hollywood social propaganda that's all a-glitter with stagey, overblown images aimed at getting viewers to believe that all Hollywood people ever do is attend parties, premieres, and shows where they give cute little gold awards to each other.

Now, don't get me wrong, socializing is a fact of Hollywood life. That much is true. It's considered a part of show business. However, even though the previously discussed glamor clamor has been laid on thick, it is hardly the life for the average Hollywood Joe or Jane. All of this attention on the social is just so much puffery and should not be considered the authentic Hollywood way of life.

ACCOUNTS:
The Real Social Scene _____

I posed this question to my group of Hollywood professionals: "Do you think the *social aspect* is important to a Hollywood career?" Here's what they had to say.

Eddie Applegate: "How important is social? *Social is the game!* Keeping your name and face in front of industry people is very important. The fact has been proven to me many, many times. Being prepared, on your toes, so when you are in the right place at the right time it rings the pay-off bell."

Sondra Bennett: "Most people feel the social aspect is paramount, but it never worked for me, though I always pursued it in the hopes that it would."

Production executive/writer *Paul Mason*: "In certain phases of your life, the social aspect is very important as it pertains to networking and gratification and a lot of people are motivated by all of it. But there's a point when the social aspect isn't important—and that's when you have a reputation and people hire you for your work rather than where you're seen."

Lawrence-Hilton Jacobs: "It definitely seems to be a business of, not so much who you know, but who knows you, and how they know you. You go to an audition, you do a play or a film and you'll always come across people you've worked with or wind up working with again. You create relationships."

Laurie Scheer: "The social aspect of Hollywood is pivotal. Remember that this is a town filled with overgrown children who like to play, therefore it's the social scene that provides the backdrop for the playing. I have to say that most of my connections have taken place at industry events on a very real level. There are people of integrity here and the others are just flakes and you can figure them out within minutes."

Writer/producer *Ed Scharlach*: "Socializing is going to help in any field, but ultimately no one is going to hire you because they met you at a party. They are going to hire the person who they feel has the ability. Someone is going to hire a writer off a really good script sooner than someone they had fun drinking with at a party because the quality of the project is at stake, as well as a lot of dollars."

Helaine Lembeck: "The social aspect? I think there is a certain amount of schmoozing done in Hollywood that's important and maybe even benefits some people. If I went to a party and someone said, 'Oh my God, she looks great, she would be right for something,' yes, then it does me some good. But to go out and look for the parties, it's just not part of my life."

Judy Coppage: "I hate the social Hollywood. Never have liked it. I don't think it helps. People here really don't care about you, they only care about themselves."

Candace Howerton: "I didn't get invited to many social events except when I was working, and you have to work more at them than actually working at the job. When I accompanied my first husband, John Bell (second in charge of new talent at Universal Studio), my dreams were crushed. The people were only talking to my husband because they thought he could do something for them. When he lost his job, his phone never rang."

Okay, we've pretty well established that, while normal civilians throw parties to release the tensions of the workaday world, Hollywood parties can serve to intensify a person's drive to work their way into the limelight by making themselves socially visible. Or is that the way it *really* is? Perhaps a closer analysis of the Hollywood party scene is in order.

"A" PARTIES

"A" parties are bashes for Hollywood motion picture nobility where the incredibly lucky go around appreciating each other's money, good looks, and the marvelous fact that they are not normal after all. "The business" is the prime focus of discussion, with the pronoun "I" dominating most conversations. Movie deals are often consummated as producers, directors, and agents with hot scripts neatly tucked away in their Armani money belts hob-nob with stars. Writers are seldom found at these parties. I'd like to say they're too busy writing, but they're simply not invited. After all, movies belong to stars and are a director's medium, and a writer can always be replaced. (But don't get me started.)

These "A" soirées are generally held in enormous homes, mansions, even estates in places like Beverly Hills, Bel Air, or Malibu, and their success is measured by how much money is wasted on lavish displays of exotic foods, separate margarita and champagne fountains, those musicians playing Mexican music I spoke of earlier, and an ice sculpture of the host or hostess capturing them in their finest screen moment. (Picture Streisand as a frozen yentl.) Nonaristocratic Hollywood is generally represented by serfs posing as waiters, waitresses, and the kids who park cars. Some of these parties are formal; at others guests wear their own clothes. These parties are often crashing bores.

Just a slight notch below these motion picture "A" parties are "A-minus" parties thrown by television royalty. Many of the homes are equally overabundant—as are the parties themselves—only on a smaller scale of importance according to the size of the screen the guests are involved with. (Yes, in Hollywood, size does matter and, on the Glitterville social scale, movies outrank television.)

"B" PARTIES

The "B" stands for " below" because the guests are not in the upper echelon of the Hollywood crust; they are of a somewhat lower pedigree. "B" partiers are the moderately successful—those who work but have yet to achieve their show business goals. They are actors, writers, directors, even a gaffer or best boy—all professionals who are going through the process of being employed, then not employed, but sticking it out while they work on their suntans. There is no particular division between movie and TV types, just people who are open to jobs and hope to make connections. Once again, the main topic of conversation is "the business."

These parties are usually California-casual home affairs at semi-affluent dwellings in places like Burbank, Tarzana, and assorted other communities in the San Fernando Valley. No valets. You get to dent your own vehicle. The food is not catered, but your host or hostess will lay out a spread of Kentucky Fried Chicken with all the trimmings. Many guests will contribute to the feast, bringing casseroles that defy description. The beer is brand name, there's wine, vodka, scotch, all the best deals that can be found at Trader Joe's. (When you move to L.A., you'll quickly learn all about Trader Joe's.) Music is on CDs, featuring the Mexican musicians who perform live at "A" parties.

In my position as a lifetime "B" partier, I've thrown a number of these get-togethers myself, in places like my house in the Hills of Beverly and, later, my condo in Hollywood. My "B" parties were a lot less pretentious than "A" parties—they were actually fun.

"C" PARTIES

Since these parties are for neither "A" nor "B" partiers, the "C" stands for " common," and the guests are of the lesser gentry—the heels on the lower crust of the Hollywood loaf. This group generally consists of young, struggling Hollywoodites just starting out. You tend to find the same cliquish group at every party, a gathering of professional dreamers out to make it, and banding together for mutual support. These are fun times, and no matter how far you rise in the business, these are the parties that you will always remember.

The majority of the "C" guests will be actors. They are also writers, musicians, directors, even future agents and producers. These weekly gatherings usually take place in modest apartments in the Valley, West Hollywood, or Hollywood itself. The socializing at these events is on a decidedly lavishless scale, with chips, dips, no-name salami, cheap cheese cubes with store-brand crackers, beer bargains and wine-in-a-box. No noticeable frills and never enough chairs. Many of the guests have parked cars at "A" parties so, to some extent, I suppose you could say there is valet parking. The host or hostess can't afford CDs, but a guest has brought along a guitar and will sing hit songs by the Mexican group who performs at the "A" parties. A whole lot of partiers will be crammed into the tiny kitchenette, where they will get a little tipsy and bitch about "the business." Everybody will likely be "up" for something. Up is good. Up gives you hope.

During my early years as a mostly unemployed actor in Hollywood, actor **Jed Allan** and his wife, Toby, frequently threw house parties that brought Hollywood people together. If it hadn't been for Jed and Toby, I never would have met producer Jim Parker, which led to my writing break as story editor on *Love, American Style*. I thought that what Jed and Toby did was one of the nicest things that ever happened to me, and to many others.

"D" PARTIES

"D" means "drugs," which is the purpose of the party.

Guests can range from the occasional "A," to " B" or "C," to the shady types who brought the drugs who should rightly be classified as "S"s—or sleazeballs. Warning: These parties can be habit-forming. (More about this in the next chapter, so, I'm sorry, you'll have to wait.)

MANUFACTURED GAIETY

Social fun is quite often fabricated by the denizens of Hollywood. Note all of the *awards shows* on TV, each one heralded as "special." Examples are the Oscars,

Emmys, Golden Globes, AFI Awards, Blockbuster Awards, People's Choice Awards, SAG Awards (and I would go on but it's a waste of paper, and I'm into forest conservation).

I've been to a few of these awards ceremonies and found them to be major snores. They always put the writers in bad seats, and if you're not nominated for anything, where's the thrill? If you like these things, the best seat is at home, watching it on TV.

Another Hollywood social function is the *wrap party*, which is usually held on a soundstage at the end of the final day of shooting a movie or a TV show. These are depressing affairs with a whole lot of about-to-be-unemployed people floating around zombielike, forcing themselves to have a good time, 'cause this could be the end of life as they know it.

One kind of party you don't see much of anymore is the *testimonial dinner*, where celebrities "roast" a fellow celebrity. The Friar's Club still carries on this tradition, and good for them. I mean, if you can manage to attend one of these roasts, you can steal some of the greatest jokes ever stolen. The Masquers Club (which I referred to earlier) used to throw testimonial dinners all the time. I can clearly remember sitting at a table between Bette Davis and Gypsy Rose Lee. I was a cute, young thing—Bette and Gypsy were enchanting—and each had a hand on one of my knees. I felt honored.

One final party example is one that you may not expect. A *child's birthday party*. This kind of party is a longtime Hollywood tradition that dates back to Alfalfa and Shirley Temple. The parents (actors, writers, the usual suspects) all gather in honor of one of their children, even though the kids usually haven't a clue about what's going on—they just want cake. These mini-galas give the parents a chance to be seen and to schmooze about "the business." There's a clown, a magician, and other jobs for the "C"s. I attended one of these parties on Halloween at the Santa Monica Pier Carousel, and I will never forget the proud actress-mother strutting around in a chicken suit. Her little daughter was dressed as an egg.

SOCIAL BEHAVIOR IN LA-LA LAND

Hollywood parties, no matter what letter of the alphabet, do provide the chance to meet others in the business. So, in the interest of furthering opportunity and self-fulfillment, here are a few Hollywood social tips.

HOLLYWOOD SOCIAL TIP #1. Good manners may be hard to find in Hollywood, so you'll have to bring your own to any social occasion. A person who displays good manners can impress many an ill-mannered Hollywood creep with connections.

HOLLYWOOD SOCIAL TIP #2. A sense of humor is always an asset in social situations. Besides brightening your own presence, humor can help you tolerate jerks and smile through the unbearable. If your idea of humor is to tell gay, racial, or ethnic jokes, avoid Hollywood parties.

HOLLYWOOD SOCIAL TIP #3. A good conversationalist is a plus at any party, so never open your mouth unless you have something to say. If you're not a good conversationalist, you can still impress as a good listener. Surprise people by not talking about yourself—they'll take care of that end. If you really want to impress, pretend not to know whatever another guest is telling you.

HOLLYWOOD SOCIAL TIP #4. You will inevitably run into people who never let ideas interrupt the flow of their conversation. These people give meaning to the word *boring*, as they ramble on, talking about themselves or their very dear friends who are people you've never heard of and couldn't care less about. Actors are always stereotyped as being egocentric and self-absorbed, but that's not so; the same can be said for writers, directors, producers, agents, the whole crazy gang. My favorite tactic for shooing away a bore is to look off and suddenly exclaim: "Look—over there—it's Steven Spielberg!" They will dash off in a plume of smoke.

HOLLYWOOD SOCIAL TIP #5. Stay sober. People stopped laughing at drunks years ago. How much alcohol you consume is the gauge of what kind of impression you will make (providing the other person is not a drunk). As poet Dylan Thomas once observed at a party: "Somebody's boring me and I think it's me." Discipline is a valuable resource in the Hollywood game. If you're out of control, so is your future.

HOLLYWOOD SOCIAL TIP #6. I don't think there's anything wrong with attending a party alone. There will be a lot of beautiful people there and, who knows, cupid may jam his little quiver right into your heart. Just be yourself when you meet someone. Drop all pretenses. If you say you're a producer and you're not, you'll never be able to leave the party with someone and go back to that crappy little dump you call home. If you feel you must bring a date to the party, try to pick someone who understands Hollywood and can put up with all the bullshit about the business. If you're married, hopefully you've attached yourself to a mate who is supportive of your career goals. If your mate is not supportive, hasta la veesta!

HOLLYWOOD SOCIAL TIP #7. I am not a big fan of "crashing" a party that I am not invited to. In fact, when I used to crash, I never had a good time; I couldn't feel comfortable knowing that I was a fraud. I was once questioned by man at a party I crashed: He asked me how I had come to be there, and I told him I was a friend of the host. Turned out he *was* the host. Now, I never leave the house unless I am invited.

EDDIE'S FIRST TIME OUT

When actor **Eddie Applegate** came to Hollywood he was already a bona fide TV comedy star on *The Patty Duke Show*, which had moved from New York to L.A. The show was produced by President John F. Kennedy's brother-in-law and close personal friend of Frank Sinatra, movie star Peter Lawford. Eddie explains his first crack at the Hollywood social whirl:

I was invited to Peter Lawford's beach house for a dinner party. I was greeted at the door by Mr. Lawford, "Come on in, Eddie, take your coat and tie off, loosen your white button-down shirt and I'll pour you a large drink." My mind absorbed the fact that the other male guests were dressed in khaki pants and T-shirts, and my plan of not drinking or drinking very little was suddenly going down the tubes. My fear of how to act in front of this small but celebrity-laden party grew and I realized how different from me they all were as they danced the twist and the watusi. Dinner was pleasant, and Lee Marvin comforted me with, "Of course we all want the same things, Eddie, fame and fortune," and everybody roared with laughter. Next, a round of poker in the hexagonal game room draped with photos of Frank Sinatra. During a round of poker, I leaned back in my chair and caused a framed photo of Sinatra to fall to the floor. *"Don't ever do that again!"* came the command from Mr. Lawford as I picked up the photo. Beginner's luck caused me to win the final hand of poker, but I was so embarrassed to win the largest pot of the evening that I suggested they use the pool winnings to start when they met for their next game. "I *do* think we can all afford to let you have the winnings, Eddie," came the universal response and more roars of laughter. My actor's insecurities and personal naïveté were definitely a problem that evening.

FRIENDSHIP IN HOLLYWOOD

One of the most important aspects of the Hollywood social scene is the opportunity to develop true and lasting friendships. When, as a young actor, I attended my first few "C" parties, I began to bond with certain people, usually fellow actors and actresses. These were individuals who shared my interests and were mutually supportive. We shared our opinions, doubts, and convictions. Our group optimism was energizing as we all pulled for each other's success. It was a lot cheaper than paying for group therapy sessions, and many of these people remain friends of mine today. In fact, several of their voices are heard in this book.

The idea of friends helping friends is a prominent issue in Hollywood. When I wasn't working in a job where I could hire my talented writer friends, I hoped my talented writer friends were working and thinking of hiring me. Friendship is tested here, and certain possibly unfair demands are put upon it.

ACCOUNTS:

Chums?

It's often said that Hollywood friendships are only examples of social opportunism and rarely of any true value. So, I pitched a few questions about Hollywood friendships to the professionals: Are friendships real, are they difficult, and do people rely on their friends to find them work? Here's what they had to say.

Bob Schiller: "If you have talent, you don't need friends. If you have talent, the friends will come. However, if your friend owns a studio or a network, you don't need talent."

Jim Begg: "Friendships can be very important in this town. Just don't expect them to last. It is an 'all about me' type of existence and friendships are for the most part based on what you can do for each other. When that need stops, so does the friendship. If this sounds very cynical, it is meant to be. It is a dog-eat-dog business, and if you know that going in, you can protect yourself."

Charlie Hauck: "Friendship? I don't think it's any different than anywhere else. People in Hollywood are the same as people everywhere else (except, of course, for stars). You tend to create the world you expect to find."

Lou Wagner: "It's difficult to maintain friendships where there's a lot of ego and sort of a hidden caste system. I have been in the Actors Studio with people who have gone on to super, super stardom, and as they move up, it's a whole different circle of friends for them and you obviously wouldn't feel comfortable even trying to get into that social scene. . . . When you get really high up, you know, Nicholson and Tom Cruise status, I am sure they wonder whether the people that are hanging with them are there because they like them, or because of the power and prestige that goes along with it."

Ralph Gaby Wilson: "Good friendships get you through the toughest times. A friend helped me get my first script sale. Another got me a job writing for a comedy series. One of my current (feature film) scripts in development is a result of two friends' help. Friends have probably been involved in 90 to 95 percent of my sales. You've got to have friends."

Writer/producer *Dave Hackel*: "Yes, friends have hired me, and I've hired friends. True friends, however, understand that friendship isn't the only criteria for whether or not a person is right for the job."

Writer/producer *Lloyd Garver*: "I would say that at least 99 percent of my jobs have come from friends, and I always try to help friends. In fact, I will help strangers, too. If anybody feels passionately about this business, I'm glad to help them. Why not? Somebody helped me."

Writer/producer *John Furia, Jr.*: "As a producer, I have employed many writers, some my friends, some strangers. I take pride in having helped a number of writers to get started or to take a step forward in their careers. I think every producer I know has done the same."

Robert Hegyes: "I would help my friends get jobs if I had jobs to give because I operate differently. I grew up in New Jersey, in a blue-collar situation, where blood is thicker than water—you help your family and friends. . . . If I produce something, everybody works. My friend, John Travolta, recently produced this movie on The Movie Channel called *Bar-Hopping*. I'm starring in it."

GREASING THE WHEELS

Many of your business contacts and associates may have surfaced as a result of social situations or even chance meetings, and these relationships need to be cultivated and "watered" regularly just as you would any potted plant. The social aspect is an ongoing part of the continuous networking process, and a major part of this networking is accomplished at the all-important show business luncheon ceremony. Most Hollywood commerce is done while masticating Cobb salads and linguine with God knows what vodka sauce, and this kind of socializing keeps your career on track.

An occasional breaking of luncheon bread with your agent is recommended—usually *your* treat. If he or she insists on paying, don't haggle—you are deductible. The same goes for any studio or network bigwig you have met and wish to build a relationship with. Often, breakfast meetings are appropriate, depending upon schedules. If your bread-breaking partner chooses the restaurant, be amenable to their suggestion, but raid your piggy bank because it will probably be expensive. If it's your choice, make sure it's a good restaurant on Sunset Boulevard or in and around Beverly Hills. Just don't look for food bargains at a place where the catch of the day is fish sticks. One of my favorite luncheon spots is this great Mexican place in Hollywood. Very authentic. You're not allowed to drink the water.

ROOKIE UPDATE

Rachel Lawrence writes:

My dear friend Melanie went to some big producer's house for Thanksgiving dinner, so I spent the day by myself. The first Thanksgiving I was ever alone. I called Mom and Daddy and they're all excited about my upcoming movie debut even though they don't like me playing a drugged-out murderer. . . . And then you'll never guess who called—my old boyfriend, Brian. He asked if I was going to a big Hollywood party, and I told him I was just having Matt Damon and Ben Affleck over for cocktails and sex. Brian didn't think that was funny. He told me he was still in love with me and I told him I was flattered (and I was), but my career came first. He couldn't understand how I could just up and leave, when he thought we had a future together. It's really sweet of him to think that way, and I do love him in my way, but I can't get "tied-down" to a man or marriage or kids or any of that stuff. All the famous film and TV stars had to be independent and committed or they'd never have the fame they have today. Anyways, it was sweet of him to call, I really like him a lot. He sells cars. He sold me Daisy. I should've asked him for my money back. (Ha, ha!) I'm serious—that car is (as Daddy would say) "nickel and diming" me to death. Little things are always going wrong, but at least it's running. I'd die without a car in L.A. . . . Bye for now, Rachel.

Kyle Kramer e-mails:

I'm used to a good Midwestern Thanksgiving at Grandma's house, so it was a new experience to go to my first Thanksgiving in Beverly Hills at the home of a woman who owns a gourmet restaurant. I was invited by a friend who is a waiter at her restaurant. Among the guests were the punk rock manager of the restaurant and her seemingly gay husband who brought along this random fat guy from San Francisco who never said a word all night. There was also a musician, and a guy who used to be on *Saved by the Bell* until he got all his teeth knocked out. The dinner was served in eight courses, amid original Dali's and Picasso's, and our gracious hostess took it upon herself to price out every dish for our benefit just in case we had thoughts of dropping it on the floor. The pumpkin and pecan pies were served with more margaritas and my fruit fluff was laughed at. I'm a good sport, so I laughed along, although inside I was hurt that my effort had been in vain. Everyone except me proceeded to get drunk and the gay couple had a tiff over a scratched Mercedes while our hostess bragged about her brief relationship with David E. Kelley before Michelle Pfeiffer stole him away. Finally, when the camera came out and the lovely fifty-plus hostess began posing rather tastelessly with her twenty-four-year-old waiters, I knew it was time to go. Next year, I will be at Grandma's without fail. . . . Best, Kyle.

Chapter 10

THE SEAMIER SIDE OF TINSELTOWN

Hollywood's a place where they'll pay you a thousand dollars for a kiss, and fifty cents for your soul.
—Marilyn Monroe

It's been said that Hollywood is a phoney, back-stabbing, pretentious, money-grubbing place, but that's only a vicious rumor started by the people who live there. Now, this is obviously a joke at the expense of the motion picture and television industry, but it reflects the absolute truth. "Like in any business," notes **Jim Begg**, "you have your share of jerks."

Knocking Hollywood has been a major sport since early on, when silent-movie producers flocked there from the East to escape patent laws, and if found out, they could be over the border and into Mexico at a moment's notice. Thus began the oft-repeated belief that Hollywood is the place where honesty and sincerity go on vacation.

Humorist S. J. Perelman deplored Hollywood as "a dreary industrial town controlled by hoodlums of enormous wealth, the ethical sense of a pack of jackals and taste so degraded that it befouls everything it touches." And if that's not enough, legendary actor John Barrymore (Drew's elder relative), called Hollywood "That dermoid cyst . . . The flatulent cave of the winds . . . This goddamned sinkhole of culture." After a trip out West, architect Frank Lloyd Wright observed, "Tip the world over on its side and everything loose will land in Los Angeles."

In Hollywood, B.T. (before television), wily studio movie moguls like Louis B. Mayer, Harry Cohn, Sam Goldwyn, and Jack Warner wielded tremendous power over everything and everyone while very neatly manipulating the tastes of the American public. Building careers and ruining lives were all a part of the daily business ritual of these crude, undereducated guys who drove large cars, lived in huge mansions, and smoked big fat cigars. They are true testimonials that absolute Hollywood power corrupts.

Today, there are a greater number of ethical people leading the motion picture and television industries, but chances are you will run into the seamier side more often than you would like. In fact, according to **Lawrence-Hilton Jacobs**, "etiquette in Hollywood is at an all-time low." Yes, Hollywood has more than an abundance of power-crazed weirdos—individuals in high places to which they ascended through hijinks and low values. They stand alone on their pedestals, high above convention. Power is all. Power makes them right. Power gets them expensive clothes and the best table at whichever restaurant is hot at the moment. Some are narcissistic, others are bullies, and far too many project the whiffy essence of megalomania.

Okay, okay, I hear you saying, "Boy, he's really coming down on these people. Why is he doing that? Do these kinds of individuals still exist today?" I'm glad you asked. Yes, they still exist today, and that's why I'm coming down on them, but perhaps a little more explanation is in order.

Y'see, Hollywood attracts a wild group of misfits from all over the world, and everybody is hustling something, someone, or, mostly, themselves. Some of these people try to succeed through integrity and civilized rules of conduct. Far too many maintain the belief that it's the survival of the slickest, so that there's a kind of Cannibal Lechter, eat-or-be-eaten mentality that controls their behavior. To them, the only way to accomplish their climb to the top is through machination and manipulation. In the words of **Ed Scharlach**, "It's often the ugly egos that wind up getting power. The people who have control over the creative people and diminish the quality of the work that goes out to the public."

In one of my more unpleasant career experiences with Hollywood's power elite, a certain producer (who shall remain nameless or he'll have me whacked) ordered me to make drastic changes in the "piece 'a shit" script I had written, which I thought was pretty good shit. When I tried to reach some compromise, there was no dealing with this guy. To him, there was his way and the wrong way. He was so sure he was always right, it was impossible to tell if he ever was. "If you don't write it my way," he said, "I'll get somebody who will!" Then, in a moment of superb (others may say idiotic) judgment, I told the bozo to do just that. The show was canceled shortly after, putting the bozo in the position of going on to ruin another show, which, of course, he went on to do.

And I'm certainly not the only one who has taken his share of unfounded abuse. Writer **Coslough Johnson** doesn't mince words when he's asked for an opinion about power-tripping execs:

> It's abhorrent to me that, in many cases, noncreative people are making, or dictating, creative decisions. It's disturbing when a producer buys your project, then wants so many changes that it completely changes the concept he bought in the first place. And then, to make things more painful, when you ask him about the changes, he says he read the script to his wife or maid or secretary and they made their suggestions.

Actor abuse is a common practice in Hollywood. This is because actors (unless they are stars) are viewed as the bottom of the Hollywood creative chain. This misperception is probably due to the fact that there are so many actors that they are seen as so many squashable bugs, to be re-formed and regenerated as necessary. A director can be an actor's worst nightmare, especially a dictatorial, anticollaborative schlemiel, who supposedly knows acting better than anyone—so why listen to some dumb actor? Then, there's the director who hasn't a clue about how to work with actors, and gives them absolutely no direction at all.

Another dangerous type for actors to beware of is the egotistical, newly minted TV star who must have it all, and who is so deeply insecure that he or she will see to it that any actor who poses a threat (like getting too many laughs) will find his or her part suddenly cut from, say, fifteen lines to "Hi!" This happens more than you may think. Fortunately, most TV-series stars act normally at least half of the time.

THE TINSELTOWN RUN-AROUND

The Hollywood scene is often referred to as a "rat race," and convention dictates that you have to enter the race if you ever want to get anywhere. Lily Tomlin had an interesting take on this when she said, "The trouble with the rat race is that even if you win, you're still a rat."

What makes it a rat race is the fact that there are a lot of ratlike people running. These are the kinds of people who believe in winning at all cost, the first casualty being *honesty*. So, to be perfectly honest, they lie a lot. Not all the time, only when they move their lips. Hollywood consists of three major groups of people:

1. People who can't tell a lie (small group)
2. People who can't tell the truth (big group)
3. People who can't tell the difference (huge group)

Group two we are familiar with, but beware group three. You must take everything these individuals say with great grains of salty suspicion. The weird and wild thing about these folks is they don't think there's anything wrong with "embellishing" the truth. They generally preface their opinions with phrases like, "To be quite honest...," or, "In my honest opinion...," and even if they are "on the level," it's difficult to understand how level their level is.

Hollywood's confirmed liars play fast and loose with the truth, and for only one reason: to gain (or hold on to) power. Here's an example: A producer I worked with on a show used to tell me in private that some of the other writers were saying unkind things about me. In the meantime, he was telling those other writers that I was saying crappy things about them. He was pitting us against each other so he could boldly step in and quell hostilities, thereby enhancing his power over us all. Pretty nifty trick. It made him indispensable as our leader... for a while.

Some chronic liars are subtle and get away with it most of the time. Others lack finesse and occasionally get caught in their lies, revealing them as phonies and making it impossible to believe any lie they tell unless they tell it very convincingly, which they usually do. Of course, the oddest thing about this truth-juggling is that I've never seen lying as a cause for anyone being fired. It just seems to be the accepted Hollywood way of doing business. Sick, but accepted. So watch that you don't become a prize skeptic with a complete unwillingness to believe anyone. Just keep a wary eye out for those who would stab you in the back and then tell the cops that you're carrying a concealed weapon.

VARIATIONS ON THE THEME OF LYING

You will hopefully be fortunate enough to have very positive career relationships in collaborations with people of good character. I've enjoyed several of these, but have also had to deal with more than my fair share of bamboozlers.

Hollywood is a land of opportunity, but, unfortunately, it's overpopulated with opportunists. This type of individual will be interested in you only if you have something they want. **Robert Hegyes** zeroes in on this when he says, "In this business, I don't know anyone who's willing to reach out and help you up if you can't do something for them. They'll do you a favor only if you do them a favor."

SWIPING FOR DOLLARS

A sculptor employs a chisel to render his or her art, but in Hollywood there are many for whom chiseling itself is the art. The town is rife with swindlers out to fleece the vulnerable. Good ideas are the major currency of Hollywood, and there are those who will stop at nothing to get their hands on those ideas and make them theirs. Writers are especially vulnerable and often the targets of larceny on a grand scale.

A partner and I once submitted a completed spec screenplay to a major movie star's production company. After months of waiting, the company turned it down. Less than a year later, an exact replica of our screenplay was put into production by the same movie star's production company. So, what did my partner and I do? Nothing. What could we have done? Sue a studio? Sue some filching movie star? Look, we're all familiar with the expressive warning, "You'll never work in this town again!" Well, sue a studio or a network or a filching movie star and you'll never work in this town again. The blacklist did not end when Senator Joe McCarthy died; it just changed its way of operating.

But, then again, there's the story of James Garner, who once sued a studio to get his fair share of the profits from *The Rockford Files*. It was considered professional suicide, but he did it anyway. After he won, it didn't seem to hurt his career a bit; he even went on to work for the studio he sued because they needed him. This is an example of another standard business practice in Hollywood. It's a sort of "come and get us" approach, where major money (i.e. percentage of profits) is withheld from people who are rightfully entitled to it for as long as possible without getting caught. James Garner caught them. I really respect the guy.

In another sticky-fingered episode from my checkered Hollywood past, I joined with a partner to write a "Movie of the Week." (I'm not going to say which network, but I'll give you a hint: It has three letters in its name.) Anyhow, our perfectly wonderful script was taken away from us and given to another writer to rewrite. The rewriter proceeded to remove our names and took full credit for writing the script, although all he did was mask all of our original ideas with his own dialog. This time action *was* taken. The Writers' Guild of America west employs an arbitration process to settle writer disputes, and we felt we had a doozy. The result: Our names went back on the script, where they belonged.

What continues to amaze me about all of this poaching and pilfering is that it is considered a standard way of doing business. You are forced to accept it and work within that system, but it's a sadly distorted state of affairs, and an especially tough part of the Hollywood survival game.

Accounts:

Suckers?

You pitch your idea, it's rejected, and you go home and mope. Then, months later, you're flipping the channels and see your proposal trotted out before you on the screen. "Robbed!" you cry. Or, how about this one: You get a story idea for a movie or a TV show—maybe you even submit a finished spec script—and then, all of a sudden, *similar* projects begin to sprout up all over the place like green fuzz on old meat. Is this simply a coincidence?

Greg Strangis: "Stolen from? In Hollywood? Hey, if you've never been stolen from, you must not have any good ideas. Since most thefts are difficult, if not impossible to prove in a court of law, and since violence is frowned upon, I usually shed a tear, down a Jack Daniels, and push on to something else."

Ralph Gaby Wilson: "Every writer in Hollywood has been stolen from. The best way to deal with it is not to own a gun."

Candace Howerton: "I thought a producer had stolen from me and I dealt with it. I confronted the producer, who was also a friend, which caused the friendship to end. He denied it, but I was never called in to pitch to him again."

Paul Mason: "I don't think I can actually say I have been stolen from, although I have seen some of my ideas done by others. . . . I've noticed at my learning annexes and book tours that the writers who come there are all terribly worried that people are going to steal from them. But I don't think they should let this stop them. What you've written isn't going to do you any good sitting in your drawer."

Jim Begg: "If you are creative, people will attempt to steal from you. You must stand up for your rights. If that means going to court, *do it!*"

Bob Schiller: "Stolen from? Think of all the *I Love Lucy* clones."

Franklin Thompson: "I had this feeling [that my work had been stolen], on one occasion, until I examined the material closely. I realized that another writer, reacting to similar creative demands, had simply contrived a workable solution similar to my own. Desperate men often take the same desperate measures."

Writer/producer *Dave Hackel*: "A dear friend of mine once told me that he thought we didn't generate ideas, but rather, ideas were 'out there,' and we found them . . . or they found us. If you subscribe to that notion, I suppose it's possible for more than one person to come to one idea. Hey, it's as good an explanation as any."

Arnold Margolin: "I have spent the last fourteen years working as an expert witness in numerous legal cases having to do with copyright infringement and it is clear to me from both my experience as a writer and producer and in these court cases that when similar projects appear, it is usually due to coincidence. That doesn't mean there haven't been cases of plagiarism and copying; I've seen those, too. But my formula for myself is, whenever I have an idea for a series or motion picture, I assume at least ten other writers are also having the same idea at the same time. These things are just in the air."

Jewel Jaffe Ross: "Yes, ideas are in the air, but so are thieves."

MIND PROTECTION

Theft happens, so cover your ass. *Register* your script or idea, so you have some proof that you had the idea in the first place in case you *do* decide to buck the system and make some noise about it.

You protect yourself by registering your script (or concept) with the Writers' Guild of America west. You do not have to be a Guild member to do this. I covered this in my book, *Writing Television Comedy*, but I'll repeat it here. You send a copy of your script or concept (unbound) to: Writers' Guild of America west, 7000 West Third Street, Los Angeles, California 90048 (Attn: Registration Department). Enclose a check for $20 made out to WGAw (Guild members send $10). You will receive a dated registration receipt from the Guild that will protect your material for five years. Registration is renewable. If you have any questions, call the WGAw Registration Department at (323) 782–4500.

THE GLASS LADDER DISCRIMINATES

In 1940s Hollywood, movie goddess Hedy Lamarr was quoted as saying, "Any girl can be glamorous, all you have to do is stand still and look stupid." This equation, stupidity equals enchantment, says a lot about Forties Hollywood, but I'm sure attitudes about women have changed since then. They have changed, haven't they?

Y'know, it's a funny thing. Even though there are many more women writers today, the principles of the Hedy Lamarr years still seem to be in effect. Female characters on TV are outnumbered by male characters, and it doesn't take a research study to see that there is an undue emphasis on actresses as sex objects who happen to be young, skinny, and usually white.

Today's TV sitcoms mix very little diversity with their canned laughter. The white-male character in his thirties is extremely popular, as is everyone in their twenties, and people over forty-five simply don't buy toilet paper. Carrying this even further, only about 15 percent of the sitcoms bother to show any kind of racial mix, but there are plenty of all-white and all-black shows. Why is that? I mean, every season, the networks pledge to improve the situation and they never do. It makes you wonder what kind of demographic vise is squeezing their creative little minds.

Granted, change has occurred in the way Hollywood discriminates, but it's cloaked in a climate that is more political than it used to be. Discrimination against sex, color, ethnicity, or religion exists and does not exist, depending on where you happen to be standing. Most Hollywood people are from somewhere else, and they bring their prejudices to town with them. A lot of lip service is paid to equality, but it's mostly just lip. There is no single, liberal mind in Hollywood, even though we are led to believe there is. It's all part of the democratic tinsel.

I think the greatest problem Hollywood faces is the growing pollution of *political correctness*, which uses discrimination as its tool and the common good as its rationale. Political correctness is nothing more than conformity through intimidation. This is unacceptable. It chokes off creativity and is in direct opposition to our freedom of expression. Positive change will only come about through free choice, not coercion.

ACCOUNTS:

Second-Rate Treatment for First-Rate Talent?

I asked the following female professionals if they believed that they had had the same career opportunities as men. Had they ever felt that they had been subjected to discrimination?

Judy Coppage: "You're not invited to the cigar and strip clubs. Also, you're not asked to play sports. There's the boys' club, the gay mafia, and women. Every year, in 'The Women In Business' issue of *The Hollywood Reporter*, most of the women work for powerful men. Very rarely does a women who runs her own business get in the top 50."

Sondra Bennett: "I was probably not treated equally but saw how people treated me more as a reflection of their character. To me, acting with self-importance reflects insecurity; disrespectful behavior toward others implies lack of self-respect. Seeing it that way helped me to not take it personally."

Brooke Bundy: "There is tremendous discrimination. If you look at *TV Guide*, men drive the shows. They're about *men's* problems, his job, his relationships and blah, blah, blah...."

Jewel Jaffe Ross: "Treated equally? Of course not. Not even close. People like to deal with people as much like themselves as possible. When I was looking for work as a solo woman writer, 98 percent of the people I was dealing with were guys. They looked on me as 'the other.'"

Laurie Scheer: "Yes, I feel that I have had the same career opportunities as men. Any woman that blames her lack of success on gender issues has a personal problem. I have never let that get in the way of my pursuit."

THE CASTING COUCH

"Come to my parlor, said the spider to the fly." You probably heard that little ditty when you were a child, but adults in Hollywood still hear its refrain now and then. The point I am making here is that actresses and actors are often manipulated in certain physical and emotional ways. To be blunt, they may be asked to sleep with somebody to get a job. Tales of the Hollywood "casting couch" echo through the industry as much today as they did back when 1940s movie legend Lana Turner was quoted as saying: "I like the boys, the boys like me." So much for playing hard to get.

Dorothy Parker once observed that "Hollywood is the land of yes men and aqui-yes girls," and quite a number of Hollywood professionals are very much in agreement that the tales of the casting couch do indeed have some validity. People love to think the worst of Hollywood when they see others achieve the success they think they deserve. There's a lot of jealousy, envy, backbiting. Someone rises to stardom, and word is instantly around that they slept their way into it. There's a tendency for us to believe a person is guilty before proven innocent, because that's the way Hollywood works. If a person really does sleep around, word gets out, credibility turns to quicksand, and a career gets sucked under. However, if there's some real spark there—a genuine love developing between, say, an actress and a director—the snide, sleep-around gossip will soon dissipate and people will start taking bets on how soon the break-up will occur.

ACCOUNTS:

Musical Chairs and Convertible Couches

There isn't a person in show business who doesn't have an opinion on the existence of the casting couch. Here's what some of those people have to say.

Sondra Bennett: "When I was very young, I had trouble with agents, managers, and producers trying to seduce me. Most of them repulsed me and I told them so."

Bob Schiller: "Yes, there is a casting couch, but writers never get to use it."

Franklin Thompson: "Trading sex for jobs is a part of everyday commerce; the culture of, 'use and be used,' is an accepted sexual-commercial transaction. No harm, no foul."

Ralph Gaby Wilson: "Well, there was this one woman producer with a pink on pink office. She cast. I didn't couch."

Candace Howerton: "I was friendly with a casting director. We had a fun relationship. I had heard 'things' about him chasing women around his office. One day, I jumped on his couch, lay down and kiddingly said, 'I've tried everything else.' We both had a good laugh out of that."

Ed Scharlach: "Casting couch? I'm still looking for it. [Laughs] I don't think anybody who's ever been successful in this business (except maybe Joan Crawford) ever got there through sexual favors. The casting couch may lead to one job, but it never leads to a career. People who think it might are totally deluded. Besides, it might not even be a couch; it could be the floor, the desk, a park bench, the back seat of a car...."

Jewel Jaffe Ross: "It was never a problem for me or any of my friends. Since we were all young and cute at the time, not being asked made us feel sort of sexless. I suspect that part of the casting couch syndrome comes from the other side. In other words, you probably have to make it obvious that you would accept a proposition if offered. Even casting directors don't like rejection."

Lawrence-Hilton Jacobs: "Oh, sure that exists. I know some people who have been in producing or casting situations and they would try to get some young girl or guy to do sexual favors for them in order to possibly get a part. And sometimes they even get the part, but to me you can only sell yourself out once and you can never get it back. If I start lying to myself, I am a lost soul."

SORTING THROUGH SORDIDITY

So, there you have them, Tinseltown's Top Five: *lying, cheating, stealing, lechery, abuse of power*. If Hollywood were a soap opera, it would sweep the daytime Emmys. It's no can of peaches living with these seamy realities on a daily basis, and it can be downright unnerving. Add to this a continual atmosphere of uncertainty and you have an opportune moment for masking those fears and frustrations by escaping into other realms of consciousness. Not always the best of realms. Not always conscious realms. In other words, rather than go nuts, you decide to do something crazy. Something self-destructive. Note the following popularly harmful behavior practices.

CHOOSING BOOZING

For quite a number of Hollywoodites, the anxiety suppresser of choice is alcohol. A couple of belts to steady the nerves and relieve the tension. Maybe a couple more because the first few are dulling the pain. Finally, one or two more until you forget why you're drinking, and could easily achieve the same result by whacking yourself over the head with a shovel.

A producer I once worked with dealt with the stress of running a TV show by drinking all day. He started early in the morning with the juice of a few martinis, all disguised in a nondescript plastic cup. He got funnier as the day progressed, until late afternoon, when he stepped over into the valley of complete idiocy. The show was a hit, the hours were long, and the entire staff had no choice but to deal with the man's bingeing.

Alcohol served as my very own Band-Aid during one depressive interlude in my own career. I was unemployed, unsuccessfully trying to sell writing projects to the uninterested, and the vagaries of the business were all beginning to eat away at me, so I choose to buddy-up to vodka with tonic. Fortunately, things got better and I no longer rely on booze to highlight my existence. The fact that I resorted to booze to get through was not a wise decision, but I did get a good joke out of it: "Did you hear about this new group? It's called 'Alcoholics Alias.' You continue to drink, only under a different name."

WIRED FOR LUNACY

Drugs are another elective numbing device in Hollywood. I know, it's not at all surprising that people take drugs; TV bombards us with ads for remedies that will relieve most anything that's ailing us. People are constantly urged, "Ask your doctor," or, "Tell your doctor," about whatever pill they happen to be pushing. If Moses came down from Mt. Sinai today, the tablets would be in a little plastic bottle.

My drug of choice, at another wayward period in my career, was cocaine. It wasn't all that popular with the general public at the time (the late Seventies), but in Hollywood (a mecca for trend-setting), it was all the rage with white on practically every other nose in town. It was a time of hanging out with different groups of strange, new friends, just dropping in for the free "blow" that was so generously provided. Not a period in my life that I point to with pride. (This cocaine interlude is more fully explored in my book, *Writing Television Comedy*, Allworth Press. A highly interesting read.)

In retrospect, I realize that (like alcohol) cocaine doesn't erase problems—it breeds them. You go through life misusing all of your virtues. You are subject to bouts of paranoia, and life provides enough things to work against you without you creating new ones. Cocaine is also extremely expensive and will devour your bank account quicker than an IRS auditor on speed.

Alcohol or drugs of any kind can always be relied on to ruin even the finest reputations. Word gets around that you drink or snort and suddenly your phone calls are not returned by nervous individuals who may also be drunks or druggies, and can't risk hanging out with someone like you, lest they be discovered.

ROOKIE UPDATE

Rachel Lawrence writes:

I finally found an acting teacher I like, and have been taking class, but the one bad thing was that the class was so huge that I didn't get to do scenes as often as I wanted to. Anyways, I told him how I felt, and he offered to give me some private coaching and the whole thing was a disaster! The man came on to me! He kept saying everyone does it. Well, I don't—and I ran out of the place and I will never go back. He can keep the money I gave him—the creep! ... This has not been a great few weeks. I sent out tons of pictures to agents and didn't get one single response. It's like the land of the dead out there. I finally had to get a job as guess what? I'm a waitress at a restaurant in Studio City. The pay's not great, but the tips should be good, and like Natalie Wood said to Rosalind Russell in *Gypsy*—"It's money, momma.". ... Not much progress on the movie I'm set to do, and I'm really not too sure about the whole thing. These guys who are "producing" this movie are always hanging out at my friend Melanie's place and they do a lot of cocaine. They tried to get me to do it, but I wouldn't. I'm just beginning to wonder about this whole thing. If they're trying to raise money for their movie, why are they spending so much on drugs? ... Oh, well, must keep a positive outlook. ... Onward! Rachel.

Kyle Kramer e-mails:

You know what I don't like about this business? The fact that it *is* a business. It really thwarts a lot of creativity—like executives putting the kibosh on something because they have not seen it before. You get a lot of repetition. I have been noticing that a lot on TV, where it's just spin-off after spin-off of the same thing. It's really a shock when there is something original on TV or an original movie that didn't have to be adapted from some novel. ... And another thing. I keep hearing that it's "Welcome to Hollywood and that's how it is." I hear things about the casting couch and how people get jobs, but there are more people who have made it in Hollywood by being loyal and friendly, and if I can't do it that way—where people really want to work with me—I don't want to do it. When I am compromised and forced to lie because I don't want things to blow up in my face, that's a position I don't like being in. I think that the real important things to me are honesty and just being myself and not getting nervous around certain people I meet, like huge casting directors. These are just people—they've got the same problems, the same insecurities as anyone has. I've heard about people who have gone into auditions and blown it because the producer's there, the director's there, and they're Godlike! Well, I am determined not to let that bother me. ... Defiantly yours, Kyle.

Chapter 11

POTHOLES ON
THE ROAD TO SUCCESS

*Challenges make you discover things about yourself that you never
really knew. They're what make the instrument stretch—what make
you go beyond the norm.*
—actress Cicely Tyson

By now you may have gotten a pretty good idea that the Hollywood experience is
no romp in the park. If you disagree and believe it *is* a romp in the park, I recommend you wear a sturdy helmet and sensible shoes, because challenges lurk
behind every tree in the Hollywood bewilderness. These challenges can be
likened to career *potholes* that litter the road to your creative goal, inhibiting your
ability to survive.

Now, career potholes are not to be confused with career blunders. Blunders
are self-inflicted goofs to which we subject ourselves along the way. Potholes, on
the other hand, are just there before us—clear *realities*, hard, cold facts that must
be recognized and dealt with. Your Hollywood survival will depend greatly upon
how you mentally manage these potholes. They will definitely affect your professional existence, so pay close attention as I review them in all their ego-
crunching detail.

POTHOLE #1: THE OVERWHELMING COMPETITION

The influence and projected glamor of Hollywood makes itself known on screens
all over our planet, and who knows where else?

A make-believe world to escape to seems like a swell idea, so individuals
from everywhere, all following a dream, flock to town every day. They seek their
Screen Actors' Guild card, their Writers' Guild card, and as the numbers increase,
it becomes more and more difficult to break into the business.

To all Hollywood aspirants, the Holy Grail is union membership—a must for any one wishing to succeed and survive. These memberships come with a hitch, of course, a sort of Catch-22 that comes with this territory: You can't join a union without having a job and you can't have a job without joining a union. So, it's really up to luck, contacts, and the possible kindness of a stranger. In addition, the union memberships are already large and, for the majority of these members, work is often pretty scarce. Here are some facts to ponder:

1. The current 2002 membership of the Screen Actors' Guild (SAG) numbers over ninety-eight thousand, with all of these members trying to land a couple of thousand jobs.
2. The American Federation of Radio and Television Artists (AFTRA) has around thirty thousand on its roster (including a couple of hundred who actually make a living out of it).
3. The Writers' Guild of America (WGA) counts over eleven thousand (the majority of whom have never written for money more than once).
4. The Directors' Guild of America (DGA) tallies more than ten thousand—a smaller membership, but then it's mighty slim pickings when it comes to directing jobs.
5. The major craft union—The International Alliance of Theatrical Stage Employees (IATSE)—is cram-packed with over ninety-eight thousand members, so you'd better know somebody before you come a' knockin'. (The easiest way to get into a craft union is to be born into a family of gaffers.)

Now, if I haven't completely ruined your day, here's something else to ponder. An enormous number of American productions (mostly TV movies and miniseries) are shot in Canada because of the cheaper Canadian dollar, so if you want to work up there, you'll have to pay some immigration lawyer in the hopes of getting a visa to work in Canada, where they will pay you in Canadian dollars—which takes all the profit out of it, so why bother?

ACCOUNTS:

Notes on the Struggle _____

Those who have worked in the corridors of Hollywood for years have witnessed a change in show business access due to the enormous growth in competition.

Sondra Bennett: "There is much more competition today. Anyone who sees themselves on a home video thinks they can be a professional actor."

Lou Wagner: "Every year it gets a little worse, a little tighter, a little harder to break in. Years and years ago, casting directors and producers would actually come and see a play, especially if it had good recognition and good reviews. Nowadays, they don't come, so, yes, it just gets harder and harder and the conglomerates eat up each other and there are less and less people to hire you. Pretty soon, there will be just one show on TV and you'll have to go through one casting director."

Peter Lefcourt: "I think it is more difficult today because of the sheer number of people who want to be screenwriters. The competition is brutal. Every college in the country has a screenwriting program. Nobody wants to write the Great American Novel anymore; they just want to write scripts and sell them for lots of money."

POTHOLE #2: THE DISAPPEARING TALENT AGENT

This particular dip in the road to conquer Hollywood concerns the steady disappearance of the smaller, boutique talent agent—a definite detriment to the opportunity for newcomers to secure representation.

The sought-after opening for that big break is getting smaller every day. Show business has not been spared during tough economic times, resulting in a trend where medium-sized agencies have merged in order to stay in business and compete with the huge agencies. In the meantime, smaller agencies are disappearing faster than free beer at a Super Bowl bash, and with all of this consolidation of power and talent, it's getting to a point where there are fewer and fewer agencies. The hard fact is, if you're not signed with a biggie, you're nowhere.

I am not claiming that the day of the small agency has passed—not entirely. There are still a few who continue to survive, but they are cutting down their client lists, and the entry into the business that they used to provide to their clients is being stifled as the Hollywood corporate culture grows.

As of this writing, Hollywood's monster agencies are making moves to expand their power. Specifically, they are out to grab things they've never been allowed to have before, like financial interests in TV and motion pictures, significant shares in distribution companies and advertising agencies, a piece of the project financing, sales, merchandising—they want to own it all. The big agencies no longer want to serve Hollywood: they want to *be* Hollywood with a stranglehold on production, which brings us right back to their efforts to squeeze smaller talent agencies out of business. Not a pretty picture, but a very real one.

ACCOUNTS:

Agent Eclipse _____

The current agency power-grab claims daily headlines in the trade papers, and you hear talk of it everywhere in Hollywood.

Greg Strangis: "The small, independent agent has gone the way of the buggy whip. The first to suffer will be nonstar talent. But nonstar talent is always the first to suffer."

Lou Wagner: "In TV and feature films, when a cast breakdown comes out with parts, they're going to go to the big three agencies—William Morris, CAA, and ICM. Casting directors need the big stars that these agencies have and, unless they placate the agencies with smaller parts for their young, up-and-coming people, they're not going to get a nibble on the Tom Cruises. So, politically, the rich get richer and the small agencies are having a horrible time. It will be deadly for older actors and young ones coming up if we dwindle down to just the big three, but we'll have to see what happens on that."

Peter Lefcourt: "Small agencies, like most small businesses, have difficulty surviving in a vertically integrated economic world. The loss of small agencies is a sad fact of life in today's business. It's not unlike the loss of the family GP in medicine. Nobody seems to have time or patience to nurture careers." [Vertical integration refers to a current business practice in show business, where the TV networks and other corporations are allowed to buy as many cable companies, stations, and satellites as they wish, consolidating power into the hands of a few.]

POTHOLE #3: THE SKINNY ON APPEARANCE

Looks are important to an actor's career, but there is also too much of an emphasis placed on conformity. By this I mean that there is less and less acceptance of what a person really is, and more of an insistence on current, faddish looks that have far too many people looking like far too many people, thus completely wiping out the whole concept of individuality.

"Things have gotten different in terms of what they want to buy," says actor **Lawrence-Hilton Jacobs**:

We are really into visuals, into flash cuts, we're into *types*. If you look at Tony Curtis in the movies of the Sixties, and he took his shirt off, he was reasonably built—he didn't have every chiseled muscle in place and that was okay. Today, you have to have every ab looking like an Adonis or something. We have gotten very, very into quick thrills.

There is also a current trend affecting women in the business. It's the promotion of anorexia as a necessary lifestyle, and it mainly involves the image of young actresses. This bony, emaciated, concentration-camp look affects far too many actresses, who feel that following this image is the only way to success.

Actress/teacher **Helaine Lembeck** sees this problem as a threat and she warns young women in the business to:

Watch out for the pressures to conform. Look at how many young girls have eating disorders because of the way that women look on TV and the covers of magazines. Several actresses have mentioned in articles that when they came to Hollywood, they were told to drop twenty pounds or so if they wanted to work.

We can only hope that this too is a cycle and, like the wearing of bloomers, it will pass.

POTHOLE #4: HOLLYWOOD SHELL GAME

Okay, it's time to talk about the practice of "scam 'n scram." The object of this game is to take your hard-earned money and flush it down the toilet. While I am sure that Hollywood offers many very legitimate outlets for career instruction, development, and advancement, it also provides a good share of shysteristic characters out to take advantage by picking your pocket. This shady practice has snuffed out many a Hollywood dream.

Actor **Max Manthey** left the Midwest for Hollywood, where he passed the audition and was accepted as a student at the highly reputable American Academy of Dramatic Arts in Pasadena, California. Despite having performed the lead role in an independent film, after only a brief stay in town, Max's Hollywood experience was cut short:

I enrolled at a place called Screen Actors Workshop. We did scene work in front of a camera and then the instructor would critique our work. This instructor had me believing that I was the next James Dean. In a town and industry where compliments were hard to come by, I was definitely enjoying the attention I was getting. Then one night, the instructor told the class about a deal some of us could get in on. He had connections and we could do prepared scene work on a local cable TV station. For about $1,000 each we would get to air thirteen weekly episodes of *The Show-Offs*. There was a small group of about eight of us. This seemed like our bridge to fame and fortune—the idea being that some agent or casting director would watch the program and, if they liked what they saw, they could contact us and we'd be on our way. There was a sincere feeling among us that this was our ticket into the industry. The day after the premiere show aired, none of us were exactly deluged with offers, but we felt that, as more shows aired, offers would generate. Just after that first show aired, our instructor told us he had to return home to New York for a funeral. He promised to return in time for the next show. He didn't. We never saw or heard from him again. . . . I was only in Hollywood for eighteen months. I guess my short stay was pretty insignificant.

Scam artists, flim-flammers, call 'em what you will, they cover Hollywood like slippery sharkskin seat covers. They are always there to prey on Hollywood wannabes, even though you may not know right away that you're being bamboozled. The only defense you really have is to approach these money-sucking situations in the most professional way possible. Ask for references from these people. Insist on a signed contract, and have it notarized. Let them know you're not an easy mark. I'm not saying that this is going to protect you, but when you appear sharp to a sharpie, there's a much better chance that you will save yourself some grief.

POTHOLE #5: HIGH ART? DREAM ON!

Many a young creative talent comes to Hollywood with the intention of realizing their "art." Only problem is, Hollywood has never been what one would call an artistic community. **Ed Scharlach** vividly illustrates this by revealing, "I wrote a film-noir take-off on a women's prison movie for *Duckman*, and I still remember the two most unusual notes I ever got on a first draft. The first was, 'We need more gratuitous sex,' and the other was, 'Another fart joke.'"

In addressing the concept of art, writer George Jean Nathan said, "Hollywood impresses me as being ten million dollars' worth of intricate and highly ingenious machinery functioning elaborately to put skin on a baloney." . . . And we know there's nothing artistic about baloney unless, of course, you ask a baloney maker who thinks he is an artist.

Hollywood is populated with various versions of baloney makers, all working in a business that strives to give a faceless public what it wants—something impossible to gauge. This "give 'em what they want" syndrome can have a very destructive effect, especially for actors and writers. Let's begin with the actor.

An actor will very often audition, not as him- or herself, but as someone he thinks those in power are looking for. This lack of faith and self-assurance can be tragic for an actor's career, as he quickly begins to lose control over his own, unique individuality.

Candace Howerton recalls facing this situation when she was a young actress: "I was always doing it somebody else's way, following what 'they' say, and not being myself (even though I could never figure out who 'they' were). I'm a little angry for not believing in myself—for not realizing that I could get the job just by showing up and reading the lines any way I wanted as long as I did it with confidence."

This tendency to lose creative identity appears in similar ways for writers too, as they are sucked into Hollywood's copycat mentality. A superb example of this is the sitcom *Friends*. When it became a huge hit, other series creators didn't have a chance of selling a new show to the networks unless it was a facsimile of *Friends*, so writers pitched copies of *Friends* (e.g., five or six young people instead of four). These copies sold, flopped, and the networks defended themselves by claiming that they were just trying to give the public what it wanted . . . even though the public didn't want it.

The same feeblemindedness goes for motion pictures—one high-grossing film is immediately followed by instant replicas. If they ever make a hit movie called *Clones*, you can be assured that the copies will look exactly like the original. This form of copycatechism has a very strong tradition in the Hollywood, and it is a surefire way of committing career suicide. Just like an actor, a writer can completely relinquish his or her unique voice by writing what she thinks will sell in order to please others. This is known as being "commercial." It is also known as being a dumbbell.

Franklin Thompson shares this little tidbit:

> Starting at the time of the big corporate takeovers of movies and TV, I've seen an effort to control creativity through insistence on formula. . . . Big business, through its executives and agents, is telling us that we're fungible, replaceable cogs in the entertainment industry machine. The kind of identity and individuality once known is gone or going. The successful rationalizing of the creative process produces identical formulaic material and, worse, an assembly-line mentality.

Well, I don't know what I can add to that. Maybe this. Today's writers, actors, whatevers, continue to be encouraged to alter their beliefs and to trade in originality for the company way. But conformity will never come up with anything new, and the real survivors are those who believe in themselves and promote the special individuality that separates them from the rest.

POTHOLE #6: THE AGEISM SCHISM

The Age Discrimination Act was passed by Congress in 1967 in order to protect workers forty years and older from age discrimination in the workplace. So, how is this working out in the corridors of Hollywood? Don't ask. The news has yet to reach Hollywood about this Age Discrimination Act—the specter of "ageism" is everywhere. Young is good. Young is cheap. Being over forty is fatal.

Former Hollywood screenwriter Dennis Palumbo (*My Favorite Year*) is a licensed psychotherapist specializing in creative issues. In his recent book, *Writing from the Inside Out*, he observed:

> The really insidious aspect of ageism is that it's based on certain 'givens' that rarely hold up under examination. Youth implies a more imaginative, more subversive, less rule-bound approach to creative work. Yet the facts say otherwise. Most young (or new) artists are often quite conservative, retro, and derivative. The way an artist learns craft is by apprenticeship, by using earlier artists as models. . . . A brief overview of history's most accomplished artists reveals that the majority of their best work was done during their middle-age years.

Age is, indeed, a defining factor in the industry—most certainly for comedy writers, actresses over forty, and everyone else over forty-five. At fifty, you're not only over the hill, you're buried under it. This type of roving dismissal is clearly the result of the tunnel vision of those in power, who insist on marketing to a specific demographic. The writing, the acting, and the setting of these screen fillers hardly reflect real life, with their focus on youth-oriented programming. What has been called the "art" of demographics is actually one of the world's most inexact sciences, which may explain its popularity.

Again, in *Writing From The Inside Out*, Dennis Palumbo points out that "Everybody knows, at a kind of gut level, that the marketplace's preoccupation with youth is ridiculous. Even a cursory look at who spends how much or what, and where, indicates that catering solely to the young as consumers is financially shortsighted, artistically bankrupt, and morally suspect."

The most frequently asked question in Hollywood (next to "Do you sleep around?") is, "How old are you?" And the majority of the replies tend to low-ball the truth. I always looked quite a bit younger than my actual years, so beyond thirty it was easier for me to survive by lying about my age. It became downright habitual. It got to the point where I actually forgot how old I really was and had to dig out my birth certificate.

ACCOUNTS:

You're How Old? _____

Many in Hollywood have pretty strong opinions about this blatant dismissal of age and experience. Here are some of them:

Candace Howerton: "It's awfully hard to get a job as a writer if you are over twenty-five. If you look over thirty or thirty-five, you automatically appear stupid; you can't have an original idea; you don't know the current jargon; and you are too old to write in this town!"

John Furia, Jr.: "The youth culture is emphasized by the companies' habit of hiring very young development executives who feel more comfortable with writers of their own age and attitudes. Designing movies and TV primarily to fourteen-year-old boys does suggest that you hire someone with a vivid recollection of what it means to be fourteen."

Coslough Johnson: "You have numerous gray writers with fantastic résumés who can't get arrested. My agent suggested that I throw away a page of my résumé because it would make me an older writer."

Arnold Margolin: "[Ageism] has become institutionalized. Networks and studios make it a policy not to hire older talent. . . . I don't know that you can legislate away ageism. Not until the advertisers decide they would rather target the over-fifty audience will it change."

Alan Sacks: "At fifty-nine, I am probably hipper and more contemporary than anyone I know. I am doing stuff now for teenagers that the network can't believe. I've got my ear to the ground, I've been pretty fortunate and blessed that way, so I don't have a problem with ageism at all."

Charlie Hauck: "I've noticed that it's the young writers who write the 'old' stuff. They saw it on TV when they were little kids, and now they're bringing it back again, thinking they're inventing it. Older writers tend to write new stuff, because they know what's old."

Look, I'm not going to harp on this putrid, unjustly wasteful practice of age discrimination. I have said enough—although I would like to add that all of this "graylisting" makes one wonder whatever happened to our system of free enterprise? When did the rules change? If this practice were based on race or gender, the outcry would shake the foundations of Madison Avenue.

THE HOLLYWOOD FAITHLIFT

According to a reliable fortune cookie I once opened in a Hollywood Chinese restaurant, "You cannot score if you stop at third base." A second fortune cookie read, "It's not the load that breaks you down, it's the way you carry it." And, yet, a third fortune cookie (it was a big meal) came up with: "Remember the mighty oak was once a nut like you." But, then, certain fortune cookies lose something in the translation. What's important is that the choice to survive is completely up to you. You have the option to give up or stick with it—to surrender your dream or engage in pothole confrontation and evasion. Keep listening to the words of the Hollywood professionals featured in this book. These people are mentors, sharing with you the best advice you'll ever get.

ROOKIE UPDATE

Rachel Lawrence writes:

> I wish I had better news, but I don't, and I guess I'm pretty depressed, so if I seem a little in the dumps, please understand. I got this call from this agent who got my picture in the mail, and I went to see him in his office on Hollywood Boulevard. This real, kind of smelly, old building—and the man was all by himself and very nice, and it looked like he was about a hundred years old. He had pictures of people on the walls who were all probably dead. At least that's the feeling I got. He told me he knew the business inside and out, and offered to sign me to a contract. He said I had "star quality." I told him I'd think about it and left, and, well, I thought about it and it just doesn't seem right. The guy seemed so out of touch. Just my luck that something good happens and it's not all that good. . . . My job is soooo boring! And the tips aren't as good as I thought they would be. The thing is, I really hate waitressing. I feel like a servant because that's the way a lot of people treat me. . . . You can forget about my motion picture debut, also my friendship with Melanie and her supposed "producer" friends. They're just a bunch of drug addicts. . . . One good thing. Daisy has been running like a charm. I think the smog agrees with her. . . . Oh, and one other thing, Brian called and I have to admit he cheered me up. He can be very funny. That's why he's the top car salesman where he works. . . . Oh, well, back to the Hollywood grind. . . . The best is yet to come, Rachel.

Kyle Kramer e-mails:

> Well, the career potential has fallen into place; now I just have to get the other pieces to fit. My initial goal was to get the acting thing going right away, but that hasn't happened. Plutonium is easier to come by than a SAG card, so I've been writing. I'm building my portfolio and getting scripts under my belt before I go for it. From things I've read, I have to have several scripts, so when they say, "Okay, what else have you got?"

I'll have something. . . . I haven't been going out on acting auditions, so writing keeps me sane and makes me feel productive. The problem is, when I get writer's block, then I feel like I'm not doing anything and it drives me nuts. . . . I think one of the reasons I don't have anything going up to this point is because of various things that have held me back—certain bad advice and promises that were not kept have slowed me down. I definitely had a naïve attitude coming out here, but I'm starting to branch out a little in forming my own opinions about things. I'm getting smarter every day. . . . Yours in Brilliance, Kyle.

Chapter 12

SURVIVING SUCCESS

*Real success is happiness. You enjoy what you have
and are satisfied, fulfilled, and peaceful.*
—Comedian Phyllis Diller

I've often heard it said that success is subjective, defined on an individual's own terms. In the above quote, funnywoman Phyllis Diller reveals her opinion, as did actor Michael York when he was reported as saying, "Success is the outward manifestation of inward fulfillment." To this, actor Levar Burton adds, "Success for me is all about being in alignment with what I know to be my true life's purpose. This is the only barometer I need in deciding whether or not I am succeeding as a husband, a father, or in my career."

Now, these are nice sentiments from people who have (coincidentally) achieved success, but let's get right down to the basic truth. Success in Hollywood is all about two words: "rich" and "famous"! Add to these other words, like "power" and "glory", and the phrase, "Nothing succeeds like excess," and you'll be getting real close to understanding the Hollywood meaning of "Bingo."

The most highly visible, grossly affluent, overly reported examples of success are your average everyday movie stars. These elite poobahs and poobahettes are literally crowned with fame and fortune—true manufactured U.S. royalty exuding an aura of the divine. England has their Sirs and Dames; we have Tom Hanks and Julia Roberts and others of that particular ilk. Heck, I'll bet the Queen of England curtsies when meeting the smirk of Brad Pitt. This is no surprise, of course. Stars' faces and other body parts on a giant screen can render these adored individuals bigger than life, and you have to admit that there's something pretty impressive about a person with a twelve-foot nose.

A mere step behind these movie stars in status are TV stars, only a smidge less regal than their movie counterparts because they appear on a much tinier screen and their noses are smaller. Whereas movie stars are pretty mum about the gazillions they pull down per film, TV stars seem to glow (or is it gloat?) over their spectacular incomes. The ungloating Ray Romano (*Everybody Loves Raymond*) has been reported to earn $800,000 for every episode, while the equally ungloating Drew Carey has to settle for a mere $750,000 for each show. But the all-time big-bucks champion is *Frasier* star Kelsey Grammer, who pulls down a nifty $1.6 million per show (as of this writing), including health benefits and a key to the executive washroom. *Frasier* has also made a star of Eddie the Dog, so his agent will likely request bones from Paris, an autographed dish that once belonged to Rin-Tin-Tin, and a larger dressing room with a four-mile dog run. (Talk is they may paint a circle around his eye and give him his own series.)

Sounds pretty impressive, doesn't it? Success in its giddiest extreme. You see, the images of these boob-tube sovereigns coming into your living room every week makes you feel somehow like you know them and secretly, in the back of your mind, you're sure you could've gone on to make that kind of big money, too, if you hadn't decided to major in business and finance.

WHAT PRICE FAME?

Okay, enough with the fantasy. Let's get real here. The truth is, these czars and czarinas of whichever screen do not, in reality, earn those excessive amounts of money. It's just not possible. After taxes, commissions to agents, managers, publicists, and hanger-on relatives, plus social expenses, high-end household disbursements, etcetera, etcetera, a star like Kelsey Grammer may net only $20 million a year, tops. So, as you can see, there is a definite downside to being as rich and famous as you thought you could be.

Now, as difficult as the pursuit of success may be, I have always thought that the *maintenance* of success demanded even greater effort than success itself. Success is basically a life change and things are seldom the way they used to be. How you handle that change will provide a real test to the strength of your character.

It's not easy being a Hollywood star. The more famous a person becomes, the harder it is to maintain a private life. When success appears for those focused, hard-working few, certain obligations surface and their lives are no longer their own. How these obligations and the lack of privacy are dealt with reveal true character—and quite possibly some occasional quirks in that character.

ACCOUNTS:

Fame and Fortune and Misfortune _____

Following are notes on the view from a few stars who have reached the summit.

Josh Hartnett: "I've always been the kind of person who liked to be alone, hang out, see things, travel around on foot. It's not the easiest thing to do when you're famous."

Jason Alexander: "The upside is that you certainly get a real sense of pride and accomplishment that you made that kind of impact on people with your work. The downside is the complete loss of anonymity. I can't just go to the gas station to get gas and a candy bar anymore. It always becomes a mini-autograph session. I do miss the peacefulness of anonymity, but fame is fabulous too. It has given me a great life."

Chris Rock: "The thing is, when you're famous, there is no such thing as a whisper. Everything you say is loud. Nobody views you as a subtle human being. If you think something is okay, it's like, 'He thinks it's horrible!' or 'He loves it'!"

Richard Dreyfuss: "The problem was that it [success] came too easily and quickly. I was very comfortable in pursuit of success. It turned out I wasn't happy in the attainment. I felt that success isolated me. I felt unsure of myself and out of place, which is why I got really badly into drugs. Drugs gave me the ability to enter a room without feeling so horrible. Of course, they also led me to behave terribly."

Actress Courtney Thorne-Smith: "I had to go into therapy to deal with it. All of my dreams came true, but I wasn't happy. I was scared and kind of sad."

Lawrence-Hilton Jacobs: "When *Welcome Back, Kotter* came on the air, almost overnight it was an event to walk down the street. People were pointing fingers, I was chased, it was strange, like a weird out-of-body experience, and I didn't know how to handle it. But, to this day—and I say this with pride—never have I *not* accommodated someone, never have I been nasty to a person."

Hank Jones: "When I was a regular on daytime TV, I'd stop at local furniture stores to make sure they had their television sets tuned to my show; then I'd casually remark that they were watching . . . me!"

STARS UNDER PRESSURE

The words "Hollywood" and "tragedy" are all too often intertwined. Fame invites pressures and expectations, and the average Joe or Josie Dingfelder from Milwaukee who suddenly rockets to fame in a film or TV series may have difficulty dealing with this newly minted reality. It's no picnic handling sudden responsibility with huge degrees of attention. Situations like this often result in tragic Hollywood stories, the kind of Tinseltown occurrences that the press gobbles up like sharks on a ham hock. The media is always overjoyed when they can sadly report the incidence of some Hollywood notable crashing nose-first from atop the Hollywood heap.

Speaking of noses, substance abuse is always big and treated with overabundant relish—as in the cases of John Belushi and River Phoenix. It was splashed all over that Ben Affleck went into rehab to kick alcohol. The media overwatched as Mariah Carey spent weeks in a hospital for treatment of a physical and emotional breakdown—and again when, soon after her release, she had to return. Innuendo about Mariah flew in the press and across the airwaves like pies at a Three Stooges convention. Of course, guys like Charlie Sheen and Christian Slater have always been around to display socially unacceptable behavior with their younger counterparts waiting in the wings. And then there's always Robert Downey, Jr.—well, you know the story. The tabloids love the antics of characters like these; it saves them the trouble of having to make up anything. A majority of stars handle themselves decently and responsibly, but we never hear about it. Attributes like "nice" and "normal" kill ratings and are a death to circulation.

MANAGING THE FISCAL WINDFALL

Hollywood success can come swooshing into your life at a rapid, often unexpected, pace. But there it is: Dreams do come true. Yesterday you were chuck; today, you're sirloin. These are very often lucrative, providential interludes that may present a huge test in fiscal responsibility. The hoo-ha joy that money engenders is often in great conflict with whatever else money engenders, so just watch out for the financial traps that could lie ahead.

High on the list of these traps is to *spend* lavishly, with hurried frequency like there's no tomorrow, because you're young and working and making big bucks and what's wrong with a big house, expensive car, and a charge account at Greenblatt's Deli? Have to keep up with the richies (who now live next door and are trying to keep up with you). I fell into this trap, and why not? I could now do all my dreaming when I was awake. I bought the house, the car, hired a maid, a gardener, a rowing machine that sleeps eight, and if I seem to be exaggerating it's not *that* far from the truth.

Earlier, I talked about budgeting your money during tough times. One of the not-so-secret ways to grapple with insti-wealth is to continue to watch where your money goes. And I don't just mean *watch* it go; I mean don't go there. When the numbers on income checks pass three digits, don't start spending money to make up for all those times when you didn't have it.

I'm not suggesting you become Ebenezer Scrooge, just don't be a spendthrift. Show some financial responsibility. There's nothing wrong with treating yourself now and then, but palaces are expensive to keep up, and do you really need to spend thousands on a used piece of gum chewed by a major leaguer? I don't think so.

ACCOUNTS:

Fast Cash _____

Attitudes vary on how higher earnings should be dealt with, so learn from the following.

Judy Coppage: "I handled finances pretty well. It's easy to overspend. I've invested pretty well, but I'm probably more conservative than most."

Coslough Johnson: "No writing job is permanent, so I knew that I'd better save money to cover for the dry times. I handled it quite well, and that is why I never have to write for money again!!!!!"

Charlie Hauck: "I don't have many extravagant tendencies. I've been accused of still having my First Communion money. Every year, after our annual state-of-my-finances meeting, my business manager used to say, 'Well, you'll be fine as long as you don't buy a boat.' Now he says, 'You'll be fine as long as you don't buy an island.' So I guess my financial state is improving."

Arnold Margolin: "My wife and I would deliberately try not to let this [the Hollywood trap] happen, but it sneaks up on you, and then one day you realize you have the cars, the house, the pool, and the bills. So we would sell the house and cut back to smaller and, five years later, find out that we had done it all over again. It was a constant struggle. I think I have, in the end, won over it, but it is insidious."

Lloyd Garver: "There are certainly times that I wonder if we should have bought a cheaper house. But these thoughts only cross my mind while I'm awake or sleeping."

Paul Mason: "When I made money, I didn't handle it as well as I should, considering I am a man who very carefully and very successfully manages three-hundred-million dollars a year for the companies I serve. But for myself . . . I came from a family that had very little and I see my own money very differently. I have enough and have been very fortunate in that I have been able to take care of my family, and still have enough to make me reasonably comfortable. . . . But, no, I have not been a great saver or shrewd financial investor."

THE INSTANT BUDDY SYSTEM

When you achieve success in show business, there will definitely be people around who always knew you would. Interesting people, these. Achieve a Hollywood ranking, and a whole cast of characters come out of the woodwork and into your life—a whole flock of old friends and new buddies you never knew you wanted. When dealing with these people, exercise caution and don't be afraid to doubt their motives. You're making it, and they want a piece of it, but don't act defensive or aloof, just be careful and be yourself. *Always* be yourself: It's the best way to survive success.

The Instant Buddy System works in another way. "I had a sleazeball accountant, and it all ended very badly," recalls **Robert Hegyes**. "But when you're in your twenties and successful, you think it's never gonna end. You don't notice what's going on—You're gonna be rich!"

When you're making huge amounts of money, you'll be approached by individuals who will want to "help" you manage your finances. I'm talking about *business managers*, individuals who, for a standard commission of 5 percent, will take care of all your monetary needs, often investing your money, and lifting that nagging burden of monthly bill paying.

Now, there are responsible, honest business managers, but unfortunately, there are also business managers of other shades and stripes. How do you know who's who? Beats me. I could never figure it out. Even the most honest-looking twerp can turn out to be a crook, as **Lou Wagner** reveals in his own story:

It's the classic story of finances for the actor. I am usually very, very good with money—I make my own decisions and I save, but with the series at the time (*CHiPs*) and the McDonald's commercials, for a while it was all coming together, so I decided to get a good business manager—ha, ha—well, you know the story. I mean, I was in everything—all the shelters possible. This guy assured me it was all on the up and up. I was in cattle, I was in oil and, fortunately, a couple of real estate things. At the end of the year, they would prepare my taxes and I would get these outrageous refunds from the IRS. Then, one day, the IRS sent me a letter stating that they had second thoughts and all these shelters were no good and I owed "x" amount of money, plus penalties and interest, and they treated me like I was a crook. I just barely got out of it by the skin of my teeth. Practically everybody who starts making big money fast, they get a money manager and, boy, the percentage of good ones are few compared to the ones that steal you blind or don't know what they're doing.

If I myself had it to do all over again, I probably would have paid much more attention to my personal finances instead of delegating it to others. Or maybe I would've made the same gaffes all over again. (Yeah, I probably would have.) But enough about me—enough with the confessing, I'm getting my shirt all wet.

My simple bit of financial advice is: When you make the big dough, be on your guard. Be wary; learn from my mistakes and those of so many others—mistakes that can be avoided by reading an excellent book like this one. Keep in mind that an agent's commission is 10 percent (no more, no less); a business manager will ask 5 percent (I remember one who asked for 6 percent, the slimy creep); a personal manager will charge 15 percent (some charge more), but for those just entering the business, a manager may be the best, and only, way to get started. It's up to you to decide how much it's worth to promote your survival. It's your choice. While you're choosing, pick an income tax firm familiar with show business deductions that charges a flat fee for its services.

TAKING IT TO EXTREMES

We've all at one time or another read about the stereotypical situation where success turns a person into someone she's not, into some kind of arrogant monster whose ego has burst at the seams, rendering her so self-absorbed that she squishes when she walks. This kind of Jekyll-and-Hyde transformation happens a lot in Hollywood—more often than one may think.

In his autobiography, *Aaron Spelling: A Prime-Time Life* (with Jefferson Graham), producer/writer/former actor Aaron Spelling states:

> Hollywood's a very strange town, and it can do weird things to people. It's not easy getting used to fame. One week you're reading for a part and six weeks later you can't walk down the street in peace. You're making more money than you've ever made, you're suddenly being asked for interviews, and that's hard to cope with, especially for young actors.

Success makes a failure of many people. In a business filled with me-first types, it's a very short trip to becoming the kind of person whose ego spins out of control. These big-headed galoots and galootesses can be immediately spotted by the manner in which they treat others. You've surely run into the types (in any business) who go around with the mistaken idea that they can make themselves great by showing how small someone else is.

Success is rarely permanent in Hollywood, and like I've said, no one ever has it made, so it's best not to let it go to your head. People with oversized heads topple very easily. The world didn't used to revolve around them—why should it now?

I am reminded of another fortune cookie (I eat a lot of Chinese). This cookie's message was "He who gets on high horse is ready for a fall." Translated, this is a warning that if you get too big for your britches you're in great danger of blowing a promising career, so it's best to stay grounded, unaffected, and loyal to the real you that got you the success in the first place. Take *Frasier* star Kelsey Grammer's lead. According to Jane Leeves (who plays Daphne on the series):

He's a huge talent with a huge TV presence, but he never makes us feel like we're underlings, you know? Like we're second best. He's not on a star trip. Kelsey's always trying to push us into the spotlight by getting the writers to give us all more lines. . . . He's a smart, sensitive guy who is very caring, very generous, and very funny. I adore him.

Kelsey Grammer's professional behavior is as much of an asset as his talent. In a high-pressure business, he's found a way to lead, to ease the pressure and create a positive environment. It's no wonder that *Frasier* has continued to entertain us for as long as it has. Positive leadership begets good fortune.

In my experiences in the sitcom world, I've witnessed several personality changes linked to stardom. One actor (whose name I dare not mention lest I be poisoned) dealt with success by turning moody, churlish, and receptive to a host of other unsavory traits. Reverting to his demanding, childish self, he caused those around him to focus heavily on thoughts of corporal punishment. This man became manipulative with the show's staff, often resulting in petty and more than petty hostilities. He made enemies, he burned bridges, and now he occupies a place as one of those "Whatever happened to . . . " people. But nobody knows what happened to him because nobody really cares.

What this actor and (former) star failed to realize is that successful people never get that way without the help of others. Hollywood show business is a collaborative medium involving the best efforts of an enormous number of people, so anyone who goes around acting like a prima donna is laying the groundwork for that fortune-cookie fall. The responsibility for handling success is up to the individual. Once again, it's an inside job.

ACCOUNTS:

Wearing the Crown

I like it when famous people handle their good fortune without increasing their hat size. These people show a lot of class.

Actor Robert Montgomery (former star of films and TV and father to Elizabeth of *Bewitched*): "If you achieve success, you will get applause, and if you get applause, you will hear it. My advice to you concerning applause is this: Enjoy it, but never quite believe it."

Laura San Giacomo, star of TV's *Just Shoot Me*: "I can't accept the fact that (being on) a TV show makes me a star. That's something that is earned through a body of work over a long period of time."

Actress Charlize Theron: "You have to surround yourself with people you trust. People who really know who you are . . . people who really do love you and are willing to show you your flaws."

FAMILY AND FRIENDS

Success can have a significant effect on family life. The effect can often be detrimental, as indicated in this quote from actor/writer Sylvester Stallone: "When you're living in the fast lane, you tend to overlook the basic components that give your life meaning—relationships, getting to know someone really well, putting someone else first. People who are highly ambitious often don't focus on the needs of their immediate family, especially their children."

During my thirty-year tour of duty in Hollywood, I have repeatedly noticed a rather idiosyncratic pattern of behavior involving the effects of success on family and friends. Even if you're not stuck on yourself, a friend or family member may display awkward reactions to your sudden providence. The dynamic may change as you are subject to envy, jealousy, and possible problems in the relationship. The only way for any successful person to handle this kind of situation is to stay in touch with reality and remain true to who he really is. The others will likely come around. Meanwhile, take a tip from **Arnold Margolin:**

Success can be terribly isolating and insulating, which is especially bad for a writer. I first saw this among successful playwrights in New York City who had lost their touch because they had lost touch with the real world. Once I was successful and could see the same thing happening to me in Hollywood, I made a conscious effort to avert it. My own, peculiar way of doing that was to become a reserve deputy with the L.A. County Sheriff's Department. Being out on patrol once a week or more and having to deal with criminals, suspects, victims, witnesses, and tragedies of all kinds, certainly kept me in touch with a certain kind of reality. On the street, no one knew or gave a damn that I produced a hit series or made lots of money. It was—and still is—a great way to keep a perspective on just who you are.

PRESERVING THE LUSTER

True and lasting success is built on *reputation*—and the foundation of a good reputation is our trusty colleague, *strength of character*. I refer here to remaining sincere, free from affectation, unimpaired by hypocrisy or falseness. You take care of your character and your reputation will take care of you. Success is not an end-all; it is a continuation of growth, a creation of a person you can trust, who enjoys life and whom you don't mind living with. Success is not found in power or prestige; rather, it manifests itself in openness, goodness, and positive personality. Always remember that it takes no time at all to lose a reputation, and a very long time to regain it.

SLIPPERY SUCCESS—AND HOW YOU MEASURE IT

It often takes a person years to become an overnight success in Hollywood—for everyone from Lucille Ball to Michelle Pfeiffer to Kevin Spacey. But, once attained . . . well, you know, nobody has it made.

You've heard the phrase "Fame is fleeting." Well, it certainly can fleet. Here today, fled tomorrow. One flop, you're in trouble; two flops, it's worse; three flops, and you're out. Check out the crop of celebrities from a year ago. How many are still around? Count the amazing number who made a big splash, then headed right down the Hollywood flusher. Agent **Gary Cosay** reflects on this in his own experience. "Sometimes people are on hot shows, get big deals, and they think it's going to go on forever—then, suddenly, they hit the wall. They struggle—can't get an agent. They disappear. I don't know what happens to them."

As I said earlier, a star doesn't achieve success without lots of help. Among those helpers are faces without names (supporting actors and bit players), and names without faces (writers, directors, producers, agents, managers, craftspeople). These are the people who make it all work—who make stars stars. For this nonstar majority, success is not necessarily fame, although there may certainly be degrees of fortune.

To those who populate the former onion fields of Hollywood, success is looked at not so much in terms of fame or fortune but in professional accomplishment blended with personal happiness. True success isn't so much material wealth as it is a wealth of the spirit: the satisfaction of having accomplished that which makes for a happy, emotionally fulfilling life.

ACCOUNTS:

The Abstract Reality of Success _____

I've heard it said that success is a journey and not a destination, and that's a good way to look at it, as long as you enjoy the trip.

Tom Cherones: "I considered myself successful even when I wasn't making much money because I always loved my work."

Robert Hegyes: "I still feel that I'm very, very successful. It's a rarity when anyone has one television series, let alone two hit shows (*Welcome Back, Kotter* and *Cagney and Lacey*). That's the frame of mind you've got to keep . . . and, God willing, I'll get a third series."

Coslough Johnson: "I never had problems with success, probably because I always equated success with getting a paycheck after the job was done. To me, a little adulation on a job well done was nice, but mostly the payment at the end of the job was my measure of success."

Jed Allan: "I loved every second of my success and I didn't have enough of it to get in my way. It wasn't big enough to bother me, just wonderful enough to make me happy. I needed better work, but I didn't need any more success mentally. . . . I was never impressed by myself. Very honestly, I really wasn't. I enjoyed it, I got a kick out of it, but it never made me change."

Bob Schiller: "Success is so fleeting for TV writers that you can think of yourself as a success only a bit at a time. Once you're retired, then you can evaluate your entire career and conclude, yes, it was a successful career or, no, I didn't achieve what I set out to do. If your goal was to make a living and you did, you can consider yourself a success. However, if you set out to become a household word, that's another matter."

John Furia, Jr.: "Success is always relative. No matter how successful you are, someone else is doing better. And a healthy attitude is to recognize that you are always one script away from an Oscar or an Emmy, and one script away from never working again."

BABES IN HOLLYWOOD

It's time to take a brief look at the survival of children in show business. But first a word about me. I recall when I was a mere babe in Racine, Wisconsin. Seems like only yesterday that my mother would enter my finely powdered body into these baby contests, usually run by a photography studio or the local movie palace. The newspaper ad would say something like: "Make Your Child a Movie Star!" or some such come-on. I did win once, scooped up the prize for best smile . . . and the memory haunts me until this day. (Jeepers, I could have been a child star!)

The survival factor is at its highest point of risk when it comes to child actors. Throughout the nearly century-old existence of Hollywood, thousands of horror stories have been repeatedly splattered all over the media about child stars gone wrong, broke, or crazy. We see and hear all about their tragedies in the tabloids and on shows like *Entertainment Tonight*. It's always a case of too much success too soon:

tragic stories of lost childhoods and adult lives enveloped by immaturity, confusion, and bitterness. Burned-out young minds that have slipped through the faults of the Hollywood landscape. (Whew! Lucky for me, I never became a child star.)

Former actor **Paul Petersen** started in the business at the age of six, and he has the rare distinction of having been fired as an original Disney Mouseketeer for conduct unbecoming a mouse. "It's a fiction to think that a child can be a star on a TV series and not be affected," says Paul. "It's unnatural for a child to be working in a high-pressure, high-visibility environment. It upsets the balance of childhood, which depends on the rough-and-tumble of socialization. . . ."

Money is always a major issue when parenting a young breadwinner, and unfortunately, there is a grim history of financial shenanigans, dating back to early Hollywood. In her book *Hollywood's Children*, Diana Serra Cary (who was Baby Peggy in silent films) offers this candid assessment on parents:

> Nearly every one of us was an innocent where money was concerned, having handed over every cent we earned to our parents since we were infants. And in many cases our parents worked to keep us ignorant of financial matters, not even showing us how to make out a check or deposit slip on our own.

Hey, put yourself in these kids' little shoes. They spend their early professional years being expected to act like mini-adults, and then when they become real adults, their successes (with few exceptions) dry up and blow away. **Paul Petersen** puts it this way: "Leaving the business isn't something you really ever do, the business leaves you. When Spanky McFarland (*Our Gang*, *The Little Rascals*) came back from the Second World War and tried to pick up his theatrical career, he said, 'Hollywood's not buying what Spanky McFarland has to sell.'"

When a child actor is able to survive the transition into a healthy adult life, it is usually due to positive parental support, understanding, and responsible financial planning. The best example I know of is Ron Howard and his brother, Clint. Despite fame and money, Mr. and Mrs. Howard saw to it that their boys didn't "go Hollywood." They stayed in the same house, in the same neighborhood, with the same friends, leading as normal a life as possible. Ron and Clint's folks were the best friends a child could ever have.

ACCOUNTS:

Parental Influence

Parents have always played an essential role in a child actor's survival. Some good, some not so good. So, if you are a parent, plan to be a parent, or even had a parent, pay close attention to the following voices of former child stars. Would they subject their children to Hollywood?

Paul Petersen: "People ask me how I got started in show business, and I tell them my mother was bigger than me. It's a joke, but yet it's the truth. . . . She says that she enjoyed my successes far more than I did, but in later years she suffered the defeats much worse than me. . . . I've always told my three children, 'When you show me that college sheepskin, I will support you because you will not have to be a bartender, chauffeur, or a waiter.' . . . But, of all the kid stars who have ever been, only six have put their kids into the industry, and half of those wish they hadn't."

Debbie Watson Taylor: "My parents never pushed me, it's what I wanted to do. They were very supportive, very proud. . . . I have two sons and I wouldn't discourage them from going into show business. My boys have very strong personalities and, if it was something they really wanted to do, I would support it."

Bernadette Withers Lynch: "My mother pushed me. She was just damn crazy, and I was having such a horrible childhood life. . . . I just wish my home life had been happier. . . . Well, now that I have grown children, I can say that I did not want them to act professionally. I didn't want them to miss being an all-around kid, getting poison oak, all the things I missed."

Fame is a hard drug for children to swallow, but kids who are troubled are now getting help. **Paul Petersen** is founder and president of a nonprofit organization called A Minor Consideration. "There's trauma that comes with realizing that their time in the spotlight is over," Paul explains. "Their money is gone, their education has been sacrificed, and this is where A Minor Consideration comes in. We're a group of over six hundred former kid stars who have decided to take care of our own. Former and current child actors receive professional counseling, financial career management, educational advice, and the shared experience of participants who have either survived or succumbed to the lures of stardom, fame, and sudden wealth. Our gatherings really serve like group therapy—suddenly we're all in a room, realizing the common themes we're dealing with. . . . It's a winning hand."

For those of you who wish to learn more about A Minor Consideration, the Web site is *www.minorcon.org*.

Chapter 13

FAMILY BUSINESS

*Some people in Hollywood pronounce "nepotism" like a dirty word,
but I tried to make it an acceptable art form. I worked with my
family for two reasons: They were talented, and they made me feel
more comfortable. There aren't many people in Hollywood whom
you can trust completely and if a family member can do the job,
then it can only help you, too. I believe this is true of any business.*
—Garry Marshall

Hollywood has a grand old tradition of hiring its own—the "own" being family members—the tribal rite known as "nepotism." According to **Ralph Gaby Wilson**, "Nepotism is a synonym for Hollywood."

Ever since the venerable film pioneers trekked westward to Hollywood, nepotism has been in full flower. Studio heads always kept a lot of relatives on the payroll. A few of these relatives had talent; the rest were just relatives. Those showing absolutely no talent for anything seldom lasted past lunch and went into politics.

You're probably wondering how this applies to you, since you're not related to anyone in Hollywood show business. Well, that could be a problem, especially early on. You may sometimes see yourself overlooked in favor of those with family connections.

ACCOUNTS:

Primogeniture _____

Everyone with experience in Hollywood has an opinion on the existence of nepotism—opinions like these:

Judy Coppage: "Nepotism is alive and well. Show business kids have the advantage of long-standing relationships and parents who help. Someone new has to prove themselves, while someone less talented, but with a well-known last name, has a definite advantage. I first learned this as an actress at UCLA. The show biz kids got cast first."

Franklin Thompson: "From my perspective, nepotism, while still around to some extent, is in steep decline. The stakes are too high, the punishment for failure too severe to permit incompetents to hang around on salary. You do see some nepotism in the writing game, father-son teams in which youth fronts for age and experience."

John Furia, Jr.: "Nepotism is fine as long as you keep it in the family (as the saying goes). Many businesses are father/son or daughter oriented. This is no different. We hear about the occasional absurdities, but then the kings of Europe often appointed their children as heads of state to protect their power."

Hollywood often exemplifies the ideal that the best way to make it in show business is to be born into it. Michael Douglas, Jamie Lee Curtis, Jane and Peter Fonda, Beau and Jeff Bridges were children of movie stars, so they are singled out as having made it through family connections. Well, stop me if I'm wrong, but I believe these individuals made it because they had talent and determination. Family ties, though they may offer access, provide no guarantees of success. There are many sons and daughters of stars who tried and failed, but we never hear about them because it would de-tinselize the concept of royal succession.

Laurie Scheer notes that although nepotism can be a factor in show business, "It still doesn't guarantee that you will make it. I know the daughter of a well-known Academy Award–winning actor who can't get her scripts sold. . . . She gets meetings because of her name, but it still hasn't been a sure thing for her."

The real issue here is not so much connections as it is influence. Would these stars have chosen to pursue their acting careers if they hadn't been brought up in the business? Maybe, maybe not, but daily exposure to the TV and movie industries can make a huge difference to an individual's direction in life. "My older son has been with *Saturday Night Live* for about fifteen years," says **Bob Schiller**. "He's writing, acting, directing, and is now in big demand directing comedy commercials. My younger daughter formed her own production company to produce a movie script she and a partner wrote."

Family support can be very important to survival in show business. Let me illustrate by introducing you to a Hollywood family representing three generations in show business. They're not household names. They all work behind the scenes, and they are all definite *survivors*. Welcome to . . .

BREAKFAST WITH THE STRANGIS FAMILY

I had a chance to sit down over eggs, waffles, and such to talk to these four friends of mine who all have the last name of Strangis.

Sam Strangis has been in the business all his life, and is currently the co-executive producer of the CBS series *CSI: Miami*.

Greg Strangis, whom you have already met in previous pages, is Sam's eldest son. Greg has enjoyed a thirty-year career as a writer, producer, and now a personal manager.

Gary M. Strangis, Sam's youngest son, formerly served as producer of the ABC series *The Practice* and is currently involved in ABC's *Dragnet*. He shares two "Outstanding Drama" Emmys, a Peabody Award, a Golden Globe, and a Producers Guild of America Award, and he managed to get us the best table in the restaurant.

Walker Strangis, Greg's son, is new to the business. He's an aspiring writer who has an entry-level job at David E. Kelley Productions.

Listen in to what they said.

Jerry: You're pretty new to the business, Walker, so let's start with you. Tell us about your job.

Walker: Well, I work as a writer's assistant on *The Practice*, which means I do a great deal of legal research and fact-finding. I help set up the writer's meetings, keep the writers and their scripts organized and their refrigerators stocked. I answer phones, do some proofreading, and generally try to keep them happy, but a great deal of my energy is going into writing on my own.

Jerry: How did you get the job?

Walker: I got this job because I worked as a production assistant a few years ago on another David E. Kelley show. I stayed in touch with people in the corporate offices, and when the position came around, I never let up. I made it clear that I wanted to come in and interview for it until they relented. . . . I should add that I found out about the production assistant job through my Uncle Gary. His involvement, however, was restricted to telling me that a position had opened up and that he thought I should send in a résumé. Beyond that, he refused to intervene.

Greg: Walker has to develop a career like we all did. He has the beauty of having access, but he's got to parlay that access into his own networking, create his own generation of contacts and friends and associates; he has to prove himself to others and himself that he's got what it takes to develop a craft. He has to demonstrate that he has the skills. You don't just walk into a room and say 'I'm a writer'; you walk into a room and drop a bunch of (spec) scripts down and say, "Read these, and tell me, am I a writer?"

Jerry: Spoken like a true father.

Greg: Thank you.

Jerry: Sam, tell me a little about your career.

Sam: I'm seventy-two years old and started in the business when I was four, working as an actor, then as a dancer and doing stunts. I became an assistant director, then worked my way up to where I produced a lot of shows—two of my favorites were *Batman* and *The Six Million Dollar Man*. When I was running production at Paramount, I stopped them from merging with Universal by showing them we could shoot shows cheaper than they could. Universal was the biggest then, now it's Paramount. I've had many high points—about every ten or twelve years, I get a new one, which is kind of nice.

Jerry: Gary, did your father encourage you to get into the business?

Gary: No, my father preferred that we *not* get into the business. We were all discouraged and, like my father, I would prefer my kids would not get into the business.... I mean, many of the people in the industry—well, they're not a group of characters that I would really embrace a lot. That's not to say there are not good quality people out there....

Greg: ... But there is a lot of backstabbing, avarice and greed, dishonesty, duplicity, inflated egos. These things run rampant through the business. People kill each other stepping down to pick up the dollar.

Walker: Now you can see why my father asked me not to get into the business. He felt strongly that I should get an education with a different career in mind. The struggles and disappointments that he lived through—and had continued to live through—were not things he wanted me to have to experience.... Without sounding like too much of a cynic, the people I see around me doing the best are concerned with little other than themselves. Talent and teamwork seem to have very little to do with it.

Jerry: Okay, Sam, the truth now—did you really encourage your sons to go into the business?

Sam: No, I don't think I did. If I did, I did it unknowingly, 'cause I always wanted my children to make their own decisions. I don't think I ever pushed anything on Greg or Gary.

Greg: Actually, you wanted us all to have legitimate careers.

Sam: I think Greg fell in love with it when I took him on location in Boston. That's when I think he decided that's what he wanted to do.

Greg: Yeah, you got to eat oysters and ride in limousines. I thought that was what I was looking for... and to fly first class.

Sam: Gary surprised the hell out of me when he went to college and decided he wanted to take a motion picture course. I thought he was going to be a lawyer.

Gary: Dad, I've been meaning to talk to you about that.

(*Laughs*)

Jerry: Are a lot of your relatives in the industry?

Sam: Our family *is* the industry. Uncles, nephews ... you pick them, we've got them.

Gary: Oh, yeah, we have everything from production, writing, camera, post-production, acting, we've covered the gamut.

Greg: Directing, assistant directing ...

Gary: Music ...

Greg: Yeah, music. We have people in all fields .... In many ways it all dates back to my grandfather who was in the produce business in Tacoma, Washington. He got the idea to go down to Hollywood and get into show business. So, basically, the entire family, like a group of gypsies, got on trains, got in cars, and came down to L.A. to break into the industry.

Jerry: So, this really *is* a family business?

Gary: To a certain extent I would say it's a family business because you can't go to any family gathering without somehow backing into a conversation about this show, this schedule, this budget, or something related directly or indirectly to what someone in the family is doing. So, yeah, it is a family business, and I think it's going to keep going.

Greg: Well, Walker certainly hopes so.

Walker: I don't know if I would have gone into the business without the family influence, but I do know that I could never see myself doing anything else.

Greg: It's understandable. My mother wanted me to become a doctor or lawyer or something legitimate. But the lure of show business was too strong. With family members in features, TV, with cousins and uncles working in the business, how could I *not* be influenced? Besides, doctors and lawyers spend like a million or more years in school, and I hated school.

Jerry: Do the four of you see a lot of each other? Is there a strong family bond?

Sam: We don't see each other as much as we'd like because we're all working in different places. I talk to the boys .... I talk to Greg everyday, Gary and I talk about every other day. He, like me, is either on location or having his problems, so we don't get a chance to talk as much as we'd like.

Greg: As far as the rest of the family ... Well, you have to understand, the family is huge.

Walker: There is a definite bond between the four of us; I would say that being in the business has strengthened and encouraged stronger relations.

Jerry: Are your spouses all supportive of your work?

Sam: Absolutely. Bonnie was also in the business at one time.

Greg: I *finally* found a spouse who was supportive.

Gary: Mine was probably more supportive early on than she is now. The hours in production are brutal, and I feel that I always have to be there at first call until the end of the day because, as a producer, I am responsible for the show and the well-being of the crew. I can't expect my crew to work these hours if I'm not there with them. I spend more hours with my work family than I do with my real family. And when I do have free time, I spend as much time as possible with my wife and kids. If I don't I'd have to pay a price, and I would rather not pay that price.

Jerry: What would you recommend to someone who wants to break into the business?

Greg: Keep driving to San Diego. (*Laughs*) Gary, you want to tackle that one?

Gary: I don't know that there is an easy way—so much rides on luck and timing. Writing has always been a ticket, and if you happen to sell that screenplay to people that can make it happen, that's a fast track up the ladder. Post-production is an incredibly fast track now. If you have any sort of knowledge and know-how in the new technologies, particularly in post-production, editing, and visual effects.... Well, a lot of people are moving up that were bagging groceries two years ago.

Greg: And they live with their Mac G-4s.

Jerry: Any other comments anyone would like to make?

Greg: Let me say just one thing. My dad, he'll speak for himself, but he has been through all the ups and downs and peaks and valleys of a career. He's had a fifty-year career, which is very unusual by today's realities. And my brother, still at a very young age—he's only forty—has had a twenty-year career. I've had a thirty-year career. We're really lucky.

Jerry: Sam, how would you describe your feelings at seeing your kids succeed in show business?

Sam: It's probably the most satisfying thing in the world. Nothing is better than people coming up and telling you how good your children are. I mean, I constantly get it on both of my sons. 'I just worked with Gary, I just talked to Greg'—it's wonderful to see them successful.... And, by the way, I've got to tell you something—nobody got a job by me making a phone call to my friends. I know a lot of people in this town, but everybody in my family got it on their own.... And we know how to survive because we work hard and we know what we're doing. When I started, people said I wouldn't work past forty. Today, I'm seventy-two, I'm on the top shelf and making more money than I have ever made in my life.

Greg: If I asked you to name three other seventy-two year olds in the same situation, you probably couldn't name one.

Sam: It's a good business. You get out of it what you put into it. And if you give a lot to it, you'll come out rich. It's a well-deserving business, and talent will always win out over the bullshit.

Jerry: Thanks for the breakfast, guys.

Sam, Greg, Gary, and Walker (in unison): We thought *you* were paying.

Chapter 14

THE PSYCHOLOGY
OF HOLLYWOOD

*I have an everyday religion that works for me. Love yourself first
and everything else falls into line. You really have to love yourself
to get anything done in this world.*
—Lucille Ball

Wise words from the funniest of women. Lucy was obviously referring to the
importance of self-esteem in a person's emotional makeup. As necessary to life
as the food we eat—and as difficult as hell to hold onto amidst the mentally
distorted atmosphere of Hollywood. Being repeatedly clubbed over the head with
an emotional tire iron can knock a person down a few pegs. The fact is, you'll get
depressed, and it's perfectly normal to feel down—just don't go overboard. If you
feel depressed, feel depressed...for a while...just don't wallow in it. Wallowing
gets real boring real quick, so put aside those self-defeating thoughts. Watch the
Marx Brothers in *Duck Soup*, then get on with your life.

Unfortunately, there are some people who don't bounce back well from times
of adversity. They decide to punish themselves for not accomplishing their goals, so
they become intensely focused on beating themselves up. They're mad, dammit, and
this is the way you're supposed to act when you're mad. They dedicate their life to
expecting the worst because, by golly, they're gonna be ready when it happens!

Boy, some joyous individuals they are—paying interest on calamity before
there is any. I used to know people like that. I say "used to know" because I don't
see them anymore, which only goes to prove that that sort of behavior is not only
an effective exercise in self-sabotage, but can cost you friends as well. It's like that
line from the *Pogo* comic strip: "We have met the enemy and he is us!"

Now, since a head-first plunge into show business can be detrimental to
a person's mental health, I thought it would be a good idea to talk a little
about this. In fact, you should get used to talking about this, because sooner
or later you may be talking these things over with a therapist in order to keep

your brain in first gear. There is no shortage of shrinks in Hollywood—it's the town's largest growth industry.

OUT OF MIND

All of us in the arts seek approval—and we are more than often shot down in mid-seek. There's a lot of cruelty out there being bandied about by basically very insensitive individuals. Oh, yes, these shallow nutcases, who seldom choose therapy for their own vicious demeanors, are free to roam around Hollywood destroying the minds, the spirit, and self-respect of those who don't take actions to fortify themselves. Those who remain unfortified will feel physically spent, suffer headaches, loss of energy, and difficulty in concentration, even memory. And, of course, worming around in their brains will be old standbys like fear, anger, and guilt (the usual Hollywood crowd).

These binding emotional traits must be recognized and dealt with or Hollywood will turn you into someone you're not, and it's real creepy to have to reintroduce yourself to yourself every other day or so. That's why I decided to take responsibility for my own life and seek professional help.

Yes, it's true, I've been in therapy. Several times for a variety of problems engendered by a Hollywood career. The first time, I entered group therapy because I was having trouble dealing with success. I'll never forget the looks on the faces of the others in the group. Here were a bunch of people who were having trouble getting out of bed in the morning and I was going on about how tough it was adjusting to success. As you may have guessed, this quickly led me into private therapy, where I was able to deal with my problem without having someone throw a chair at me.

I also sought refuge in sessions with psychics and then went out and tried to make the good things they said come true. On a physical level, I put my body through a rigorous "rolfing" procedure that, despite certain amounts of discomfort, freed my body so that I could become the dancing fool I am today.

Therapy is a very useful instrument for survival no matter which Hollywood endeavor you pursue. And it certainly shouldn't be difficult for anyone creative to go into therapy because it's all about *you*. Wow, what a great subject!

Creativity can only emerge when you have some understanding of yourself. Knowing what makes you tick—how you relate to the world around you—is a fantastic aid when it comes to creation of a character (as an actor or writer) because you'll find that a whole lot of yourself goes into that creation.

Finding a good therapist is like finding a good agent or photographer, and you should approach it in the same way: by asking around. I found my therapist by reading a book he wrote. When I found out he practiced in the Hollywood area, I made an appointment. When we first met, I felt I already knew a lot about him. Hollywood has more than its share of therapists who are constantly on call as tour guides to help show business folk steer their way through the insecurities and anxieties that endanger Hollywood survival.

There is a slight hitch, however: shrinking costs money. These people are in business like anyone else. You could liken them to a plumber, since they help to clear obstructions and tighten the nuts in your mind. Other therapies, or sources of therapy, are there to help—options like AA, ALANON, even free clinics—so, help is there should you really need it. If it gets to psycho-ward time, you might seriously consider a less stressful line of work, like sky-diving.

ACCOUNTS:

Celebrity Psyche

A great number of show business professionals seek help from a variety of therapeutic methods in order to piece together their cognitive debris. Let's hear what they have to say.

Lloyd Garver: "I have had a small amount of psychiatric therapy—it will be twenty-five years next February."

Brooke Bundy: "I was in psychoanalysis for a long time, and it was wonderful. I was so fortunate to have such an incredibly fine doctor who I just cherished. I think often about the wisdom she imparted over the years, and the just and courageous statements she made to me. She helped me immeasurably with the quality of my life."

Judy Coppage: "Therapy greatly helped my confidence. However, my husband (who's a therapist) was my biggest supporter and still is."

Candace Howerton: "I believe in therapy. It has kept me alive. . . . Later, I discovered Adult Children of Alcoholics, where I met a lot of people in the business. That was support, let me tell you!"

Laurie Scheer: "When things got tough, my methods of survival turned to the metaphysical realm. It's very easy to begin to look for a higher power out here in Hollywood through the use of tarot cards, crystals, or astrology. . . . I have found comfort in these methods. . . . So have many in the industry."

EMOTIONAL DOWNERS

As you may have wisely surmised by now, Hollywood is not easily conquerable—more often, it's the other way around. (If this is beginning to sound familiar and you'd like me to shut up already, I promise I will as soon as I'm through.) Until then, I have a few more things to say, so hush up and check out the following list of emotional downers.

EMOTIONAL DOWNER #1: DISAPPOINTMENT. Disappointment is a huge given in any Hollywood career, but there is a positive way of dealing with it. In *The Practical Dreamer's Handbook*, Paul and Sarah Edwards advise, "When times are tough, remember your time will come. It's not unusual to experience a round of disappointments when you start to follow a dream. In fact, at one time or another, it may even seem like everything is going down the tubes. The best antidote we know for such times is to decide that they're a sign that something better is coming your way."

EMOTIONAL DOWNER #2: STRESS. Always a biggie. Known to flatten everyone in its path, but hopefully not you. Stress begets uncertainty, insecurity, and ulcers(also sadness, headaches, constipation, stuttering, depression, and the heartbreak of psoriasis. It's a long list. In *Learning to Control Stress*, author M. W. Buckalew, Jr. states:

> Try talking to yourself in ways that are "descriptive" rather than "judgmental." Judgmental self-talk usually involves labeling yourself or your actions with words like *bad, clumsy, awkward, dumb, foolish*. Descriptive self-talk, on the other hand, involves the use of words that simply portray the event as a movie camera might, without putting a value judgment on it.

I, myself, follow Mr. Buckalew's recommendations with great zeal, describing my actions with descriptive words like *sensational, astounding, stupendous, enchanting, charming*, and *sexy*. It works.

EMOTIONAL DOWNER #3: ANGER. The sinister brother of stress. Begins with madness and ends with regret. Anger is like steam that's ready to explode, and it's a lot better to *manage* your anger before your anger manages you. In *Your Erroneous Zones*, Dr. Wayne Dyer notes, "anger is a choice as well as a habit. It's a learned reaction . . . a form of insanity."

In *If Success Is a Game, These Are the Rules*, Dr. Cherie Carter-Scott suggests that you "give yourself the chance to feel all of your feelings. Brush none aside, and consider none too frivolous or indulgent to experience. Cry if you need to, laugh, stomp around, *get angry*, even allow yourself a little self-pity. It is important that you let your emotions come up and through you and release them. All feelings have a natural course that they need to run. *Blocking them* will only block you from moving on."

EMOTIONAL DOWNER #4: FEAR. Probably should precede stress and anger, but there's no predictability in this kind of behavior, so why should there be in this list? I've experienced fear a lot during my career. And, although I have never sought it out, learning to work under extreme pressure has done wonders for my survival.

On the subject of fear, psychologist Abraham Maslow is quoted as saying, "You can turn back, but if you want to grow you must be willing to go forward and face your fears again and again and again. Fight against letting fear take over so it controls you. Fear has no power of it's own—the power to overcome is in your hands."

EMOTIONAL UPPERS

Now, I know that these various negative elements are not pleasant to think about, and the last thing I want to do is discourage anyone from taking a shot at enjoying their very own Hollywood Babylon. So, allow me to point out a few emotional uppers that beat the downers by a long shot and will actually keep you young, or (for older folks) as young as you feel yourself keeping. So, let's take a gander at those frames of mind that put you in the winning column.

EMOTIONAL UPPER #1: MENTAL RESOURCEFULNESS. You can shatter negative emotional habits by replacing them with active optimism. I've always been good at that and could always think up ways to get through, if not get ahead. Hawking hot dogs at Dodger night games allowed me to write every day and produce a "spec" script, which began my writing career.

In his book *Live Your Dreams,* motivational speaker Les Brown says, "You may not always be able to control what life puts in your path, but I believe you can always control who you are."

EMOTIONAL UPPER #2: LUCK. Luck is what happens when preparation meets opportunity. Max Gunther has written a book titled *How to Get Lucky.* In it, he affirms that, "You have to have good luck. Without it, nothing will work right for you. Good luck is the essential basic component of success, no matter what your personal definition of success may be."

Now, luck is a difficult thing to pin down, but you can't survive without it. Some believe luck comes when it comes, and that's that, but I don't agree. Sure, it's nice to be in the right place at the right time, but you have to *put* yourself in the right place. There must be effort in one's approach, an attempt to *generate* luck and to have something to do with its creation. Sure, you may have to wait, but the luck is there if you reach for it. (Do not use this theory in Las Vegas.)

EMOTIONAL UPPER #3: HUMOR. A "sense" of humor to be precise. If you think you don't have one, think again. I believe we are all born with a sense of humor. It just has to be whipped out and developed. That sixth sense you hear about is not seeing dead people: It's our innate ability to appreciate, and occasionally initiate, humor. You simply have to admit to what you're really thinking without being afraid to sound stupid. Humor is fearlessness at its best. For, as Dr. Wayne Dyer writes in *Your Erroneous Zones*: "It is my belief that you cannot deal with the most serious things in the world unless you understand the most amusing."

In his autobiography, *Wake Me When It's Funny* (with Lori Marshall), Garry Marshall recalls that he and (then partner) Fred Freeman decided that it was too easy to get depressed and feel sorry for themselves, so they approached it with humor:

> We made a pact: We would devote one half hour of each day to self-pity. We pledged to sit in our cold fifth-floor apartment for thirty minutes each day and say things like: "No one will hire me. I will never work. I will fail. I am sad." However, at all other times, we had to maintain an air of supreme self-confidence.

When Robin Williams graduated from California's Redwood High School, he was voted the funniest in the class and the least likely to succeed. Oh, how much we have yet to learn about the value of humor. Humor generates laughter, and laughter is a healing wonder drug that cuts the stress and has an uncanny power over pain. If you can laugh at it, you can live with it. If you can laugh at yourself, you can live with yourself. Humor is your ally: It protects the heart.

EMOTIONAL UPPER #3: SELF-ESTEEM. If you don't think you need self-esteem, don't ever attempt a career in Hollywood. It's the most important mental tool you'll ever need to work with. It opens all kinds of doors and keeps those doors from shutting behind you. And I'm not talking about self-esteem as being stuck on yourself or having an overly insolent ego. People who act like that are just trying to overcompensate for their immense doubts about who they think they might be.

"No one else can give you self-esteem." I first heard these words at a seminar I attended some years ago conducted by Nathaniel Branden who, with a Ph.D. in psychology and a background in philosophy, is a practicing therapist in Los Angeles. Nathaniel is a personal friend and a mentor who has been a great help to me with emotional guidance. In *The Six Pillars of Self-Esteem*, Branden defines self-esteem as: "1. Confidence in our ability to cope with the basic challenges of life; and 2. Confidence in our right to be successful and happy, the feeling of being worthy, deserving, entitled to assert our needs and wants, achieve our values, and enjoy the fruits of our efforts." Branden then goes on to point out that, "When we eliminate negatives, we clear the way for the emergence of positives, and when we cultivate positives, negatives often weaken or disappear."

Among Branden's published works is *How to Raise Your Self-Esteem*. In this book he writes, "Just as the acclaim of others does not create our self-esteem, neither do knowledge, skill, material possessions, marriage, parenthood, charitable endeavors, sexual conquests, or facelifts. These things *can* sometimes make us feel better about ourselves temporarily, or more comfortable in particular situations; but comfort is not self-esteem." Continuing on, Branden adds, "The higher our self-esteem, the better we are to cope with life's adversities; the more resilient we are, the more we resist pressure to succumb to despair or defeat."

To me, the Branden phrase (from *The Six Pillars of Self-Esteem*) that best defines the subject is this: "The need for self-esteem is a summons to the hero within us."

COGNITIVE CONCLUSIONS

The majority of the American public thinks that Hollywood people are crazy; I mean, anyone who would attempt to make it in show business should definitely have their head examined!

The funny thing about this public perception is that there is a lot of truth in it. The stresses of show business will often demand that we talk through our feelings with someone—not someone close to us like a spouse or a parent, but an objective professional with a background in understanding these matters. Your ultimate survival may depend on it.

ROOKIE UPDATE

Rachel Lawrence writes:

All my life I have believed that we are on this earth to make our dreams come true. I still believe that—it's just that I wonder if some dreams are really worth going after. I've been in Hollywood almost a year, and I have so little to show for it. And for a while now I've been wondering whether or not I'm doing what's really right for me. I'm only nineteen, and I think I might be wasting my life. I know this sounds like I'm taking back all that talk about goals and commitment and stuff, but I'm miserable! Life is really crummy at the moment. I'm not happy....I miss home. I need time to clear my mind and feel comfortable and figure out what I'm going to do with the rest of my life. I am trying very hard and it's not happening, and I know it could take years, but I don't know if I am willing to take those years. The thing is, I've made up my mind. I'm going home. Sorry I didn't have happier news. Sorry I didn't become a star. But it's my life and I so much want it to be happy....Sincerely, Rachel.

Kyle Kramer e-mails:

I am addicted to writing, and write in some form or another every day. When I finished my last script, I felt empty and bored, going through writing withdrawal. I knew I had to start again right away, so over the last few days, I wrote out the beginning of three different script ideas, finally settling on one. I got the first five pages in my computer yesterday and I'm hoping to get the first draft finished in a month. (Yes, I have a great deal of time on my hands.) . . . All I really want to do is sustain a lifestyle doing something I love. Whether it's writing or acting or eventually getting into directing or something like that. I want to do something creative and do it well, and be able to support myself and my eventual family. Success for me is also keeping my life simple and free of the needless drama that tends to creep in every once in a while. I am not one of those people that need dramatic things going on in their life all the time. I just want everything to be simple, happy, and nice, and maybe it's naïve of me to think I can do that, but my parents are my models—they rally well—and that's what I want for myself. . . . Later, Kyle.

Chapter 15

TO QUIT OR NOT TO QUIT

*I'd made a choice. I'd gone to L.A. because I had to find a
challenge. I believe that, as long as I didn't quit on myself,
I couldn't fail. Nothing could stop me but me.*
—Freddie Prinze, Jr.

Actor Freddie Prinze, Jr. demonstrates the eager commitment of a young person new to Hollywood—a commitment that will face constant trial and require enormous strength of character. It's never easy to make a living in a business overloaded with risk.

The hardest, grittiest fact to be faced is that show business is seldom a lifetime career. In fact, the average tenure for those seeking their dream is generally five years at most. I would estimate that even a smaller percentage of those with Hollywood career dreams actually wind up having much of a career at all. A great number of aspiring actors, writers, directors, producers, agents, and executives are around for a brief sojourn and then disappear, never to be heard from again.

INSECURE SECURITY

Everyone strives to attain some semblance of security in his or her life, but in Hollywood, security is only the name of a bank (or used to be before it vanished from the scene). This lack of security seems to be a daily reality in more and more businesses these days, but it is most visible in Hollywood because practically everyone is a freelancer hoping to land a temporary gig. Not a whole lot of permanence in that. In a *TV Guide* article, actor Michael Ian Black, who plays the manager of the Stuckeybowl on TV's *Ed*, admitted to his own feelings of impermanence when he said, "In three years, when I'm working at Starbucks, I'll be able to look back on this with a certain amount of fondness."

A sense of justice is nowhere to be found in Hollywood. The town chews up talent, then spits it out like sand on a pizza. I've worked with several writers, actors, producers, directors—one-time, top-of-the-heap folks who are completely absent from the scene today. It's no patch of petunias living a daily existence where you're grappling with fate, as this gnawing sensation of peril, and even jeopardy, lingers in the bowels of your mind. (Wow, what a great sentence!)

"Most actors will tell you, after every job they do, that they will never work again," says **Lou Wagner**. "You go through months and months and months without any work and you always feel like you're starting over again."

Several times in this book I have avowed that no one in Hollywood show business ever has it made. You'll be tested, accepted, rejected, insulted, loved, hated, and betrayed in an industry where you have to prove yourself over and over again. There were many, many times as an actor and a writer when my spirit was weak and I was so broke my pockets couldn't afford pants. At times like these, I seriously began to think about abandoning my quest and giving it all up. This question will appear with great frequency, and how you address it will definitely determine your aptitude for survival.

ACCOUNTS:

Thoughts on Desertion _____

Hey, look, it's a fact. The human mind is capable of occasional deflation, especially after being assaulted with all-too-frequent rounds of crushing negativity. Creeping thoughts of abandonment and resignation will scramble around in your brain like an egg at Denny's. How you process these thoughts—how you defend yourself against this mental deflation—is of vital importance to your career survival.

Robert Hegyes: "I think about giving up the business constantly. There's a frustration level—I want it, I don't want it, I'm letting go, I'm not letting go. . . . The thing is that I feel as though I'm better now than ever. I'm not losing my skills; I'm getting better at being able to translate that into a performance. I know the right opportunity will come along and, as long as I can stay at the table, I have a chance to get a hand."

Jed Allan: "You don't give up the business, it gives you up. That's what happens—they stop calling. I was working for thirty years, then nothing. . . . It's virtually impossible to believe it could happen. It really is. Now, I'm asked to audition more than once for a three or four line part—I can't believe these people would even ask. It's like starting all over again. I'm still working, just not as much. I don't need as much—don't care as much."

Lawrence-Hilton Jacobs: "There is no giving up. I don't have that defeatist attitude where you need something to fall back on. If I need something to fall back on I'm deciding up front that I will fall, and I don't believe that. I am a musician, an actor, a writer, a director, and I'm nuts, and I get excited about the possibility of pulling off something that is interesting, far-reaching or hard to do. There is no such thing as chucking it."

I used to resign from show business on an average of once a week, but something pulled me back, and it wasn't long before I was in the business again. My sense of eternal optimism always provided an impetus for me to continue on with my quest, but all too often I felt like I was tilting at windmills. After all, I would remind myself, I had a mission to accomplish, a personal vow to persevere and succeed. If I ran from my goal now, some clown would take my place and seize upon my soon-to-be well-deserved success. I figured that even Mickey Mouse had long periods where he wasn't working, and if he could come squeaking back, so could I.

CAREER ADJUSTMENT

When the action stops, the strong generate new action. Painful periods of "fading" Hollywood success lead many professionals to survive by turning to other areas of show business. Many writers (like me) began as actors. Directors were writers. Producers don't generally begin as producers, but as assistants and gofers. A person may initiate a career in TV and end up in motion pictures, or vice versa. It's whatever keeps you in and gets you there.

ACCOUNTS:

Switching Gears _____

Take a gander at these examples of career adjustments.

Jim Begg: "Once, a director asked me if I had ever considered going into production. I told him 'yes,' and about one month later, he called me and offered me a job as his assistant in filming an industrial film for Chrysler in Palm Springs. I did everything, including payroll and casting. What a way to learn. The next year, the company that we both had worked for offered me a job producing an industrial film for Volkswagen, and that is where my producing began."

Sondra Bennett: "I never sold my body—only body parts. I became a hand model."

Coslough Johnson: "While the freelance sitcom market was slowly shrinking and my hair was getting grayer, I found myself writing cartoons. It was quite a thrill to write the words, 'Hi Ho, Silver!' in a *Lone Ranger* cartoon."

Dave Hackel: "Years ago, I was working as a writer on a show and got a call from the producer inviting me to come to the post-production sound mix. This was not my area, and not in my job description, so I asked why I was being asked to attend. He told me he knew one day I'd be producing shows of my own and that this would be a valuable aspect of the business for me to learn. I went. I learned. A knowledge of post-production techniques has proven to be invaluable."

Those who find other niches within the business are definite survivor material. For others, the Hollywood dropout rate is in constant motion. Players come and go, and those who struggle on are in dire need of some kind—any kind—of self-help.

REASSESSING YOUR LIFE

I don't think there's anyone in the business who does not undergo constant *self-analysis*. It's unavoidable, while living in the unpredictable world of Hollywood nuttiness. There are various ways of engaging in this analysis, my favorite being that trusty old bathroom mirror, where I can converse with myself on a one-on-one level.

The last time I talked to myself about the career scenario I had created, it went something like this:

Mirror Me: Why the long face?
Real Me: Don't ask.
Mirror Me: You might as well tell me, I'm not gonna go away.
Real Me: Look, I don't even know who I am anymore, so how do you know you're even talking to me?
Mirror Me: Because I know you. You're smart, creative, strong. The very image of me.
Real Me: Yeah, well, I've changed. I'm jaded and angry—and I complain a lot more than I used to.
Mirror Me: Well, you'll have to learn to release that tension.
Real Me: I did! This morning I slammed the door in this little Girl Scout's face!
Mirror Me: That was a dumb thing to do.

Real Me: You're telling me. I had to buy six boxes of Thin Mints just to get her to stop crying.

Mirror Me: Y'know, it seems to me that, deep down inside, you're starting to lose faith.

Real Me: Well, I can't keep living this way. I'm beginning to talk to myself.

Mirror Me: Hey, no big deal. Just keep in mind the words of Albert Einstein: "In the middle of difficulty lies opportunity."

Real Me: Yeah, sure, but Einstein never had to pitch a story to an insane twenty-year-old producer.

In the midst of this conversation with myself, I was reminded of the *Practical Dreamer's Handbook,* in which authors Paul and Sarah Edwards pose three self-analytical questions. The first is, "How much do you want this?" The second is, "Okay, so you still want it, but how much?" And the third, "Do you want it enough to put up with whatever it takes?"

Now, how I answered these questions revealed to me a lot more about what I was really thinking than I thought I was really thinking. Once I had a clearer idea of where I stood, I realized that life does not stand still, it is constantly being revised and rewritten. As situations change, we must face them and deal with them directly. These revisions are what sustain a person. They strengthen our ability to adapt, and as I've pointed out earlier, an aptitude for adaptability is directly related to our talent for survival.

A PENCHANT FOR REINVENTION

You cannot survive in Hollywood if you are not open to change—to *reinvent* yourself at various levels. Another fortune-cookie message comes to mind here: "When fate hands you a lemon, make lemonade." (Those Chinese cookie writers should put out a book.)

Face it, Hollywood is filled with lemons. They're a cash crop and things are not always going to turn out as sweet as you would like them to—the glitter seldom blows that way. Feelings of failure are natural responses to disappointment and rejection. The danger lies in thinking that you really *are* a failure.

Always keep in mind that failure is not so much a fact as it is someone else's opinion of you, and that can be pretty unreliable, so the only thing you can really rely on is *you.* Trust yourself. You'll know what to do—you're talented, you're resourceful, you'll think your way through this. Your life was meant to be lived consciously and happily.

Many Hollywood professionals have reinvented (or readjusted) their lives so that they could stay in the show business game. As I've indicated before, several have employed a shortcut method to reinvention, where they marry spouses who support them, usually in jobs well outside of show business. As long as this does not engender resentment or guilt, it's an effective way to remain afloat, but the least sign of friction can result in day-to-day misery, so I don't really recommend this approach unless your spouse is a saint.

Then, there are those individuals who have that thing your parents always urged you to have: "something to fall back on." A number of these people use their education to perform as writing instructors, acting coaches—jobs closely allied to the business that enable them to supplement their professions. Actor/writer **Robert Hegyes** teaches English composition at Brooks College in Long Beach. Writer/producer **John Furia, Jr.** is the founding chair of the division of writing at the University of Southern California School of Cinema-Television. Producer/writer **Alan Sacks** is chairman of the Media Arts program at Los Angeles Valley College. Actor **Eddie Applegate** teaches acting workshops at various locations in the L.A. area. And actress **Helaine Lembeck** is one of the premier teachers of comedy in Hollywood. I know a writer who is a lawyer, an actor who is an accountant, a director who is a skilled mason, and they all employ these services whenever survival demands it.

Among those individuals who successfully reinvent themselves within the business, writer/producer **Ed Scharlach** has proven himself to be the ultimate Hollywood survivor. "Garry Marshall, one of my mentors, has given me lots of advice through the years," he says, "and one piece of advice was to 'keep popping out of different holes,' which I have managed to do." (Marshall attributes this quote to Noel Coward.) By following this advice, Ed has managed to avoid being pigeon-holed in one particular area or venue. During his career, he has written successfully for sitcoms as well as making the near-impossible crossover into musical/variety, mystery-drama, animation, and, today, is a writer for European television. Ed explains:

> Columbia Tri-Star has an international arm, and there is a very popular German series called *Nikola*, where they use American comedy writers because—astounding as it may seem—there are not many German comedy writers. The show is wonderful; good comedy actors, and they just flourish with our writing. I've been able to work on that show now for four years and counting. Columbia Tri-Star is owned by Sony, so I am working for the Japanese writing for the Germans, and I eat a lot of Italian food, so I've covered all the Axis countries.

By the way, other American funnymen contributing to German shows are **Arnold Margolin** and **Lloyd Garver**.

So, you get the idea here—*flexibility* is a big key to endurance. *Reassessment, reexamination, adaptability,* and *reinvention* all play a part. They can renew your determination, sustain you, or have you deciding to enter other areas of occupation.

Accounts:

Reinventing a Life _____

Reinvention is an important key to happiness. And happiness is not always achieved through the achievement of a Hollywood dream. Often, other roads appear and are taken. Life changes, people move on—these people, for instance:

Sondra Bennett: "Ultimately, I lost interest in the Hollywood scene. I saw that everybody 'acting,' particularly off stage. I used my performance skills and spiritual overview to develop a 'Life Performance Training,' which I teach in corporations today. I now use the art of acting as a tool to help people better understand how the way they act affects the outcome of situations in business and life."

Hank Jones: "I just channeled my energies into what was first my hobby, genealogy. Also, my inner voice was telling me that it was time for a change. I began having trouble remembering my lines (something that I never used to do) and became nervous on camera. It was time to leave the biz and the universe was telling me exactly that. Now, when I do my genealogy seminars in front of hundreds of people, I'm cool as a proverbial cucumber, and I'm never nervous, just full of confidence and joy. It's what I'm supposed to do at this stage of my life—no doubt about it!"

Candace Howerton: "I gave up the business when I had a stroke in 1992. I felt like I was starting over as a baby, learning to walk, talk, and read. I went back to school two years after my stroke to obtain a Bachelor's degree in psychology, and then to USC to earn a Masters of social work in 2001. I found something that I really feel passionate about, working with people who have had their lives ripped out from under them."

Lloyd Garver: "Success only started to 'fade' for me this year. I worked on the Norm show and it was canceled. So, after we wrapped in March, I had no job lined up. For the first time in about thirty-two years, I'm not on the staff of a show. I have dealt with it by being afraid most of the time, by not buying any new shirts or jeans, and by exercising a great deal to reduce stress. My agent was extremely unsupportive and disgustingly treacherous. . . . After a couple of months being unemployed, he completely bailed out on me. Even though I had known him for twenty-five years, and he'd been my agent for about nine years, he refused to speak to me on the phone for six weeks.

His behavior didn't surprise anybody. As my ex-partner Ken Hecht put it, 'It's not surprising that he bailed on you, but it's amazing how quickly he did it.' . . .

I started writing short stories during this period, and even though nobody has bought any of them yet, I certainly don't feel I've wasted any time. Also, in September, I became a weekly humor columnist for a small daily newspaper called *The Kansas City Kansan*. I love writing the columns, and possibly it will develop into a career. I'm also writing for a German sitcom, so you have to live in either Kansas or Germany to see my work." (Note: Lloyd's column is now seen weekly on the opinion page of *www.cbsnews.com*.)

WHATEVER HAPPENED TO ME?

I don't work in Hollywood anymore. Some may say that I quit, but I see it as a form of reinvention for the sake of joy. As I reviewed my Hollywood career, I recalled those glorious hills and stinking valleys, and all the times I had been counted out only to come roaring back more determined than ever. Agent **Gary Cosay** told me I was the most tenacious client he'd ever represented, and that was a helluva compliment from a pretty tenacious guy. But, it also brought certain issues much more into focus, and I realized it was time for another round of mirror-talk.

Mirror Me: So, how are we feeling today?
Real Me: Show business sucks.
Mirror Me: You don't have to keep pursuing this dream, you know.
Real Me: Hey, whose side are you on anyway! I'm a writer, and writers write.
Mirror Me: Then you'll hang right in there.
Real Me: No, I can't keep going on like this. I'm not happy. I want to be happy.
Mirror Me: You're free to quit at any time.
Real Me: Maybe I already have and nobody told me.

So, as you can plainly see, at this point I was seized by the possibility that I had worn out my Hollywood welcome. Changes were occurring in a business that runs in fluctuating cycles and the current fluctuation didn't seem to include me. The horrible specter of ageism had hit the business hard, and I was a comedy writer past forty who had apparently dislocated his sense of humor. The youth cycle had firmly planted itself and was weeding out those considered incapable of coping with the current scene. The writing was on the wall, without a joke to be found, and I had to face up to the fact that I was a weed.

Mirror Me: You're actually thinking of quitting?
Real Me: I'm just being realistic—reversing my course.
Mirror Me: Give me one good reason for quitting.
Real Me: I'll give you a whole list. I haven't worked in eight months; my agent retired and I can't get another agent; I've had it with all the phoney baloney

Tinseltown schmooze; I'm sick of the struggle, the problems, and I can't keep closing my eyes hoping they'll all go away!

Mirror Me: Boy, *somebody* got up on the wrong side of the bed this morning.

Real Me: And you wanna know the worst thing? It's *no fun* anymore!

Mirror Me: I can't believe you're going to quit writing.

Real Me: Who said anything about quitting? I could never quit writing. I have to pop out from one of those Noel Coward writing holes and figure how to quit without giving up.

Thomas Wolfe once wrote, "You can't go home again," but I could and I did. I moved back to my hometown of Racine, Wisconsin, where I hoped to live a happy life—a real life—just like in the movies. In the meantime, I began the process of reinventing myself as a writer.

Dennis Palumbo, in his book *Writing from the Inside Out*, states, "How does a writer (or actor) go about reinventing himself or herself? Here's a clue: In describing Zen training, Shunryu Suzuki said it was like emptying all the furniture and knicknacks out of a room. Then, if you wished, you could put them all back in. But with renewed awareness. . . . This mental 'spring cleaning' is a prerequisite for reinventing yourself."

Meanwhile, back in my hometown, I opened my own writing company (a company of one) called The Write Connection. Cute, huh? It was tough at first, but the survival tactics I had learned in Hollywood—*drive, resilience*, and *tenacity*—came to my rescue. I did a lot of footwork, selling myself and my background, and slowly smart minds began to respond. Luckily, geography was on my side; living between Milwaukee and Chicago allowed me access to many prospective clients. My first gig was writing a speech for an executive at S. C. Johnson and Son (purveyors of wax, scrubbing bubbles, and associated products). The speech was funny, made a big splash, and I was brought back for an encore. Thus began a business that provides speechwriting, video scripting, live shows, newsletters, TV and radio commercials, and print advertising—all with a humorous slant. Among my clients are Kimberly-Clark and Allstate Insurance Company, to whom I have introduced a drastic new concept: Humor in Business (not an oxymoron). I recently received an *Addy Award* for excellence in advertising, and whatever else I accomplished was due to the skills and the savvy that I had acquired and honed in Hollywood.

Wait, there's more! The Write Connection was merely a means to an end—allowing me to explore new forms of writing. This is my second nonfiction book; the first, *Writing Television Comedy* (Allworth Press, 2000) was well received. I finally wrote that play I had been meaning to write for all those years, and I have completed my first novel—a comedy tome that has gotten me a literary agent in New York City. Yes, I'm still in the process of dream completion, and I'm writing better than ever—but I never could have succeeded without paying my dues in Hollywood.

Oh, and let me add this. I went to college to be a teacher, and here I am teaching at my Alma Mater, the University of Wisconsin–Milwaukee. The course is titled "Writing Television Comedy," using my own book as the text. Now, *there's* a sweet feeling. I also present speeches and writing seminars around the country and have recently focused on school-faculty groups, where I approach another drastic new concept: Humor in Education (not an oxymoron).

Acting is a hobby now; it keeps me sharp and I do enjoy it so. I'm also directing plays—at times, even for money (another drastic new concept). Directing keeps me fresh, alert, and a better writer. Fact is, I've never been happier in my life. Everything creative that I have ever had to offer is being put to use. But, as I said, I never could have done it without my Hollywood experience. Did I survive? Was I a success? There's no doubt about it.

ROOKIE UPDATE

Rachel Lawrence quit Hollywood and returned home to her family. In a recent letter she writes:

> It's so nice to be back where I feel loved and wanted and happy. Looking back I know I've done the right thing, and I haven't really given up, I've just decided to have something to say about my future. . . . I'll be entering the university in the fall. I'm going to major in business, and who knows? I might end up back in Hollywood someday as a big producer! . . . My parents are really happy to have me back, and believe it or not, Daisy is still running like a charm. I wouldn't trade her in for the world. . . . I am currently a star! Playing the lead in a community theater production of *Born Yesterday* and I'm really good in the part. The newspaper reviewer said I "stole the show"! What I find really interesting is that people around here treat me like a star—I'm the one who went to Hollywood! . . . Now, I've been saving the best news for last. Brian and I are engaged! We haven't set the date yet, but I'm so happy. Thanks for letting me be a part of your project, Jerry . . . My best to you always, Rachel.

Kyle Kramer e-mails:

> I now know that it's not going to be easy, but I'm here to stay. I want to be famous, or at least well respected in the industry, doing what I love and still retaining my values and my morals. I want to show people that success doesn't change you and that you don't have to be a cutthroat to get to the top. I want to find success without stepping on people. I want to set a good example and help people wanting to get into the business, just like people in the business will help me. I want to create. I want to

make a Hollywood marriage last. More immediately, I want to sell my first script. I want to direct my second script. I want to star in my third script. I want to make enough money to afford my apartment on my own, eat well, own a BMW 540, and buy as many records—not CDs, but records—as I want. And I want to do this for the rest of my life, maybe even starting my own production company along the way. I don't think that's too much to ask, do you? . . . Sincerely, Kyle

Chapter 16

SUMMING UP

Throughout my life I've faced adversity, but it has taught me a valuable lesson. If you get knocked down, you have two choices: Lie there and be defeated or get up stronger for the experience. I have always chosen to get up.
—Actor/Dancer/Singer Rita Moreno

My purpose in writing this book has been to give you a clear and realistic picture of a fantasy business. I hope you have enjoyed the ride and will tell your friends to run out and buy this book (because my current goal is to have written a bestseller).

I was the eldest of six children, and had lost two fathers by the age of sixteen. My mother depended on me a lot, and while acting as surrogate father to my siblings I quickly learned that life put up a lot of obstacles to be faced and nobody was ever going to hand me a free lunch. I became used to hustling for what I got, so I guess I was already in basic training for my trip to Hollywood. I never lived with expectations that things would come to me; I had to come to them. It was up to me to make my dreams come true. By nineteen, my dream was a career in show business. There was no question about it—I could not *not* do it. I wasn't going to live a life of regrets because I didn't at least give it a shot, and now I look back at my Hollywood career with everlasting pride.

Sure, there were things left undone. I never had a motion picture screenplay produced (came close a lot); I never had one of my seven TV comedy pilots picked up by a network (came close a lot); nobody ever threw me a testimonial dinner (no, I never got a dinner). What I *did* have was a lengthy, productive, highly interesting career filled with exceptional victories. I wrote over two hundred produced teleplays, and not a lot of TV writers can match that. I did a guest-star role on *The Beverly Hillbillies* and got to jump in the cement pond, and very few actors can say that. What I am most proud of is that, personally, I never changed; I remained true to myself and my values. I never "went Hollywood"—I held on to my Midwestern values. My character was never diminished, and it added years to my survival.

FINAL PAYOFF

Before I go, I'd like to say something nice about a union. Actually, I belong to five of them (six if you count the Waiter's Union I had to join when I sold hot dogs at Dodger Stadium). The five unions I speak of are Actors Equity Association, the Screen Actors Guild (SAG), the American Federation of Television and Radio Artists (AFTRA), the Writers Guild of America west (WGAw), and the Association of Canadian Television and Radio Artists (ACTRA). Today, I'm on honorary withdrawal from all but the Writers Guild because I have been awarded a life membership and am officially vested in the WGA's pension fund, which issues me a generous check every month, making all those hours walking the picket lines completely worthwhile. It's a thrill to realize that the WGA was looking out for my welfare, and I'm very grateful to find a kind of actual "security" that will pay off for the rest of my life. (A good thing, too, since all my other residuals have pretty much run their course, except for the two fifteen-dollar checks I have received every year for the past thirty-five years for a Twentieth Century Fox movie I did called *Tora, Tora, Tora*. Hey, thirty bucks a year for thirty-five years amounts to one thousand fifty smackers, and there's no quibbling over a figure like that.)

HOLLYWOOD TO COME

There are a great many theories about the Hollywood of the future. A number of theorists are concerned that reality TV shows are the wave of the future and a threat to writers and actors, but I think they're more of a threat to the TV audience, which will soon tire of them and want to go back to being entertained on a legitimate basis. It's just a matter of another cycle passing in and out of favor.

The future expansion of entertainment markets, like cable and the Internet, have been predicted, and are now a reality with thousands of channels to choose from—many of which will be devoted to *I Love Lucy* reruns. (Some cycles last a lot longer than other cycles.)

Synthetic actors, virtual performers, digital stars, "creative"-writing software: There's a kind of fear of the continued growth of technology leading to manufactured people, stories, and environments, rendering human actors and writers extinct, although I doubt this will be the case (which is sure to come as a great disappointment to producers and directors).

It's difficult to accurately foresee what Hollywood's future holds—the place is just too damned unpredictable. Heck, radio comedy and TV variety shows could become hot all over again, which would neatly complete that cycle. Look, whatever is in store, I think it will still require real people with real talent. You can be sure of that.

ACCOUNTS:
Final Shots from the Pros _____

I posed this final question to many of my Hollywood friends and colleagues: "If you were writing a 'How-to-Make-It-in-Hollywood' book, what would you advise? What to do? What not to do?" Here's what they had to say.

Writer/Producer *Arnold Margolin*: "Never appear desperate. There is nothing that puts off potential employers like the stink of desperation. Keep doing whatever it is you do—acting, writing, directing. Don't turn your nose up at the work you have to do for nothing to await the big payday."

Writer/producer *Dave Hackel*: "Don't just know what or who you want to be, know what and who you are. You'll set more realistic and attainable goals. And be honest enough to judge your own talent at different stages to determine how you're doing and analyze your chances for success—i.e., maybe you want to be a writer, but your talent lies in producing. Go with your strengths."

Agent *Gary Cosay*: "I don't think there are any rules of the game. I think you have to have a passion for what you do that gives you a vision to fulfill it, even make mistakes, but, ultimately, get something out of it. If it's about money, go into the stock market."

Director/producer *Tom Cherones*: "Never lose your confidence. Keep busy while you wait. I wrote a cookbook and learned to fly airplanes. Always do the best you can whatever the job may be. When you apply yourself, it leads to bigger things."

Writer/Producer *Ed Scharlach*: "Know that you want to do it more than anything else in the world. If there is one thing you would rather do, if you are not willing to kill yourself to do this, then you shouldn't be doing this. You have to be willing to give up everything else. You have to feel that there is nothing else you can do."

Personal manager/actress *Brooke Bundy*: "Watch television and go to the movies. This is your craft; know what is going on. Know who your competition is, what they are doing. Know the rhythms of the shows—their rhythms are different (for example, *Friends* versus *Frasier* or *NYPD Blue* versus *Law & Order*). Know the characters—know the dress—that's your homework. When you go to an audition, know who the casting director is. Know what the casting director has done. Do your research. Don't get pushed—be proactive."

Producer/writer *Alan Sacks*: "What I teach my students is that they need a full knowledge of the industry. They need to know digital editing; they need to know cinematography, writing, producing, and directing. The more knowledge you have in any given area, the more successful you are going to be. . . . And one more thing. Never put five minutes of music on your answering machine. No exec wants to listen to Eminem before leaving a message."

Writer *Franklin Thompson*: "Everyone who wants to should try show business in Hollywood for a while. When discomfort, in the form of anxiety, loss of identity, violation of moral values or erosion of personality strikes, it's time for self-analysis and career review. If the rigors of the trade make you unhappy, get out. If you don't feel any uneasiness, you're in the right business. You're also a moral imbecile."

Actor/writer *Robert Hegyes*: "First of all, I would say to any kid who wants to go to Hollywood: Get your college degree. Follow your dream, but use common sense and make sure you have a degree before you even begin this thing. . . . Have something to fall back on. Lives fall apart when there's nothing to fall back on. There comes a time when you're not working and you've got to do something to bring in money—so, thank God, I have a teaching degree."

Actress/teacher *Helaine Lembeck*: "Be true to yourself—don't get cocky—leave your ego at the door. There are too many people for every role, so be grateful and thankful. When you're on a set, conduct yourself in a professional way—and don't complain if your line is cut, the important thing is the final product. Put a premium on education whether it's dramatic classes, comedic classes, dancing, singing—whatever it is, be good at it."

Writer/TV executive *Laurie Scheer*: "Wimps need not apply. If you are not willing to give up your entire life for your career, then stay at home and work at the local radio or television station. You'll be eaten alive in Hollywood if you maintain your local work ethic of leaving your nine-to-five job at 5:00 P.M. This is a town where you have to love your work because your work becomes your life, your identity, your existence. . . . Hollywood is for the dreamers, those that love the wonderment. The pay-off is divine. Don't ever give out—don't ever give up."

Writer/producer *John Furia, Jr.*: "Love the unpredictability. You have to have some gambler's blood to enjoy this."

Actor/writer/director/*Lawrence-Hilton Jacobs*: "Always brush your teeth. When you smile, try to feel it a little bit because we do a lot of it. If you have only one good suit, don't wear it out. Presentation is everything and you are going to need it. If you're going to sweat, put cotton balls under your arms, because you never let them see you sweat. . . . I'm an accomplished musician, been on Broadway as an actor and singer, done successful movies and television shows, and I still get an electric excitement about it. Wow, let's take this on and make it work! I know the game I'm in and there's no end to it."

ADIOS

I hope the information gathered in this book has been of some help to you. If not, I did all this work for nothing—but I'm sure that's not the case, so why bring it up? I expect many of you to take a crack at Hollywood, and live out the career plan you have created. As a talent, you have a responsibility to entertain, educate, and, at the very least, rise above the mundane and stop the dumbing-down of our society—what humorist Steve Allen tagged as "dumbth." Lots of dumbth out there. As poet Alan Ginsberg once suggested, "Follow your own moonlight." I followed mine, and I hope you do the same, making a life of sunlight in the doing.

Appendix A

NOTES ON THE CONTRIBUTORS

Jed Allan has appeared in over 150 television shows and movies of the week. He began his acting career in the original Broadway productions of *Oliver* and *Barefoot in the Park* and starred in the L.A. revival of *Guys and Dolls*. Jed is best known for his long-running TV roles on *Days of Our Lives, Santa Barbara,* and *Beverly Hills 90210*.

Eddie Applegate's acting credits span the Broadway stage, motion pictures, commercials, and innumerable TV roles. Eddie is well recognized as Patty Duke's boyfriend, Richard, on *The Patty Duke Show*. Today, Eddie continues to entertain, appearing in media everywhere, and he currently teaches acting in the Los Angeles area.

Jim Begg has acted in countless commercials, motion pictures, and TV shows. He has directed over one hundred TV commercials, produced numerous pilots and Movies of the Week, and served as senior vice president of TV production for New World Pictures. Today, Jim serves as a media production consultant.

Actress **Sondra Bennett** initiated her career with theatrical roles in her native Dallas, Texas. Moving to New York City, she worked on and off Broadway, then to L.A., where she appeared in guest spots on TV shows and in commercials. She now lives in Ojai, California, where she conducts corporate retreats in Performance Training for several of America's largest corporations. Her company, *Trans*Acting Organization, produced performance seminars all over the world.

Brooke Bundy began as a New York model at the age of thirteen. She appeared on Broadway in the Tony Award–winning play *JB* directed by Elia Kazan. Upon her arrival in L.A., she was signed to a contract by Columbia/Screen Gems, and she appeared in hundreds of TV and movie roles, and as a regular on *Days of Our Lives* and *General Hospital*. After ten years as an agent, Brooke has turned to developing the careers of others, working for Bob Noll at Monster Talent Management.

Tom Cherones was director/producer of the NBC series, *Seinfeld*, for which he received an Emmy, the Directors' Guild Award, and the Golden Globe. He has also served as the director of numerous pilots and episodes of such shows as *NewsRadio* and *Caroline in the City*. Tom got his break as production manager/associate producer on *Welcome Back, Kotter*.

Judy Coppage is the president of The Coppage Company, a literary and talent agency. Prior to starting her own agency, Judy was director of development at Paramount Television, and vice president and executive in charge of production at Hanna-Barbera. Judy sold the *Die Hard* novel to Twentieth Century Fox, and the rest is cinematic history.

Gary Cosay initiated his agenting career in the mailroom of the William Morris Agency, then moved on to develop writers at Creative Management Associates, International Famous Artists, Leading Artists, and, today, as a founding partner of United Talent—the fourth-largest agency in the world.

Rich Eustis was co-creator and executive producer of ABC's *Head Of The Class*, as well as four other TV series. In feature films, he co-wrote *Serial* and *Young Doctors In Love* with Michael Elias and did extensive rewriting on *North Dallas Forty* and Rodney Dangerfield's *Back To School*. Rich has five Emmy nominations and one Emmy.

Writer/producer *John Furia, Jr.*, is past president of the Writers' Guild of America west. He has written and/or produced a number of Movies of the Week and miniseries, and served as show-runner for the series *Kung Fu*. A recipient of multiple Emmy nominations, John is the founding chair of the division of writing at the University of Southern California School of Cinema-Television.

Lloyd Garver served as writer/producer/executive producer on such classic TV comedy series as *Frasier, Home Improvement*, and *Family Ties*. He has received several Emmy nominations, the Humanitas Prize, and the Planned Parenthood Award. He now has an agent who returns his calls and he is co-executive producer of ABC's *8 Simple Rules*, starring John Ritter.

Writer/producer *Dave Hackel* started his career in radio broadcasting, then moved to television, where he arranged for prizes on *Let's Make a Deal*. Today, David has risen to executive producer/creator of the hit NBC series *Becker* with Ted Danson. Prior to that, David served as writer/producer/creative consultant on *Frasier, Wings*, and *Dear John*.

Charlie Hauck began in the entertainment industry as writer, then producer of *Maude*. He went on to create or co-create seven network comedies, and has most recently served as executive producer on *Home Improvement* and consulting producer on *Frasier*. He has just completed a script for Showtime based on his novel, *Artistic Differences*.

Actor/writer *Robert Hegyes* is best known for his starring roles as Juan Epstein in *Welcome Back, Kotter* and as Detective Manny Esposito on *Cagney and Lacey*. He has also served as a sitcom director and is the author of several TV pilots and motion picture screenplays. Robert is adjunct professor of English literature at Brooks College in Long Beach, California.

Actress/writer **Candace Howerton** has acted in more than sixty TV shows, movies, commercials, and industrial films. Her writing career includes the sitcom *Blossom* and thirteen animated films, among them *Ghostbusters* and *Yogi Bear*. She has worked as a production coordinator/associate producer for ABC, and has recently received her master's degree in social work from the University of Southern California.

Lawrence-Hilton Jacobs is best remembered as Freddie "Boom-Boom" Washington on ABC's *Welcome Back, Kotter*. He starred on Broadway in the musical *I Love My Wife*, and has appeared in such motion pictures as *Claudine*, *Cooley High*, and as the father, Joe Jackson, in ABC's mega-hit miniseries, *The Jacksons: An American Dream*. Larry is an accomplished musician, writer, and director.

Coslough Johnson has written for several comedy classics like *Rowan and Martin's Laugh-In*, *The Sonny and Cher Show,* and *The Monkees*, resulting in nominations for two Writers' Guild Awards, seven Emmy nominations, and one Emmy. Coslough is the author of two published children's books, along with scripts for a great number of sitcoms, variety shows and motion pictures.

Actor/writer/musician **Hank Jones** is a recording artist, ASCAP songwriter, and comedian. As an actor, he has been featured in numerous sitcoms, several motion pictures (including eight for Disney Studios), and over five hundred national radio and TV commercials. Today, as an author and speaker, Hank is one of the foremost genealogists in his field.

Kyle Kramer is an aspiring actor/writer.

Rachel Lawrence is an aspiring actress/star.

Peter Lefcourt is the author of five published novels, and has written and produced such miniseries and Movies of the Week as *Beggars and Choosers* and *The Woman of Windsor*. Among his TV series are *Eight Is Enough*, *Scarecrow and Mrs. King*, *Due South*, and *Cagney and Lacey*, for which he was the recipient of an Emmy Award. Peter is a member of the WGAw board of directors. His new novel, *Eleven Karens*, will be published by Simon and Schuster in January 2003.

Actress/teacher **Helaine Lembeck** (with brother, Michael Lembeck) runs The Harvey Lembeck Comedy Workshop in Beverly Hills. Her first acting role was as "Judy Borden" on *Welcome Back, Kotter*, and then as a regular on the children's live-action sitcom *The Krofft Super Show*. Helaine has appeared in several television pilots, guest-starred on many TV shows, and performed in feature films, as well. She's acted with such stars as John Travolta, John Ritter, and Robin Williams.

Bernadette Withers Lynch began acting in motion pictures at the age of three. She worked steadily through her teens as a TV regular on *Bachelor Father*, and in the films *The Trouble with Angels*, *All Fall Down*, and *I'll Cry Tomorrow*. Bernadette is now a strategic partner manager for Oracle, a computer software company.

Actor **Max Manthey** studied at the highly regarded American Academy of Dramatic Arts in Pasadena, California. He admits to having been a naïve kid with Midwestern sensibilities, and due to an unfortunate experience, his promising Hollywood career was cut short after only eighteen months.

Arnold Margolin began as a Broadway actor in *The Diary of Anne Frank*. His TV writing credits include over sixty episodes for comedies like *The Mary Tyler Moore Show*, *Growing Pains*, and *Love, American Style* (co-creator). He has penned numerous pilots, feature screenplays, and was awarded an Emmy for his lyrics to the theme for *Love, American Style*.

Paul Mason is senior vice president of production for Viacom, and co-writer of the cult movie *King Kong vs. Godzilla*. He has served as producer/writer on such TV classics as *Ironside*, *It Takes a Thief*, *MacMillan and Wife*, and as production executive on *Roots*, *Chico and the Man*, and *Welcome Back, Kotter*. Paul is the co-author (with Don Gold) of *Producing for Hollywood* (Allworth Press, 2000).

Commercial agent **Kim Muir** began her career as a receptionist at the renowned Wilhelmina Agency. Five months later, she was franchised as an agent. After a five-year stint with Wilhelmina, she formed a fourteen-year partnership with Joan Messinger at the Herb Tannen Agency. Kim and Joan recently formed their own agency, Pinnacle Commercial Talent, a division of AEF.

Paul Petersen is well remembered for his role (from ages twelve to twenty) as Jeff Stone on *The Donna Reed Show*. Paul has since gone on to publish a total of sixteen books, and is now an advocate for change in the treatment of young professionals as founder and president of the nonprofit organization A Minor Consideration.

Del Reisman is past president of the Writers' Guild of America west. He began his career as story editor on *Playhouse 90*, followed by stints as writer/producer on *The Twilight Zone*, then *Rawhide*, *The Untouchables*, *Peyton Place*, and *The Streets Of San Francisco*. Del represents the Writers' Guild on the National Film Preservation Board and is a senior lecturer at the American Film Institute.

Writer/actress **Jewel Jaffe Ross**'s TV acting roles include *Gunsmoke*, *Gidget*, and *My Three Sons*. In feature films, she appeared in *The Trouble with Angels*, *West Side Story*, and as the young Bette Davis in *Hush, Hush, Sweet Charlotte*. Jewel served as executive script consultant on *Welcome Back, Kotter*, and as a contributor to *House Calls*, *Love, American Style*, and *Days of Our Lives*.

For writer/producer/creator **Alan Sacks**, two accomplishments stand out: co-creating *Welcome Back, Kotter* and serving the role of executive producer of *The Color of Friendship*, which won the Emmy Award as "Outstanding Children's Program." Alan began at the ABC network, where he rose to the position of executive in charge of current programming. He has conceived more than twenty produced TV movies, is currently producing movies for the Disney

Channel, and is the chair of the Media Arts program at Los Angeles Valley College.

Writer/producer **Ed Scharlach**'s résumé lists more than two hundred hours of comedy and drama series, variety shows, and specials. He wrote and produced *Mork and Mindy, Happy Days, Chico and the Man,* and *Mike Hammer,* and he was on the writing staff of *The Odd Couple, Love, American Style,* and *The Dean Martin Show.* Ed has written for several animation series and is currently producing the all-new *Scooby-Doo.*

Writer/TV executive **Laurie Scheer** was instrumental in developing the initial formats of MTV, Showtime, Nickelodeon, and AMC's Romance Classics. She has taught film and TV at Northwestern University, DePaul University, the University of Chicago, and American University. Laurie is the author of *Creative Careers in Hollywood* (Allworth Press, 2002).

Comedy writer **Bob Schiller** (with partner Bob Weiskopf) have written and produced a number of classic TV shows, including *I Love Lucy, The Carol Burnett Show, All in the Family,* and *Maude.* All of this writing garnered them two Emmy Awards, two Writers' Guild Awards, the Humanitas Prize, and a Peabody Award. Bob claims that he pursued a career in Hollywood because he couldn't afford bus fare to New York.

Gary M. Strangis formerly served as producer of *The Practice,* and is now currently involved in ABC's *Dragnet.* He has also served as producer of the CBS pilot *RHD/LA,* and has been fortunate enough to work with Dick Wolf, Michael Mann, David E. Kelley, and Steven Bochco. Prior to producing, Gary worked as both unit production manager and assistant director on a variety of television and feature projects.

Writer/producer/personal manager **Greg Strangis** has written and produced such TV series as *Eight Is Enough, Star Trek, Falcon Crest, Soldier Of Fortune,* and *JAG.* A longtime member of the board of directors of the Writers Guild of America west, Greg has now drawn upon his collective experience and become a personal manager with Marvin Dauer and Associates.

Sam Strangis has enjoyed a fifty-year career in Hollywood, starting as an actor, dancer, and stuntman. Having formerly served as co-executive producer of the top-rated *CSI: Crime Scene Investigation,* he is now co-executive producer of *CSI: Miami.* Among the other successful series Sam has produced are *Batman* and *The Six Million Dollar Man.* Sam served for many years as vice president of production for Paramount Studios.

Walker Strangis is new to the business—an aspiring writer with an entry-level job as a writers' assistant on ABC's *The Practice.*

Debbie Watson Taylor was discovered in her teens in a production of *Bye, Bye, Birdie,* and was signed to a seven-year contract by Universal Studios, where she starred in two TV series, *Karen* and *Tammy.* Motion pictures followed with leading roles in *Tammy and the Millionaire,* as Marilyn Munster in *Munster, Go Home,* and in the Warner Bros. musical hit *The Cool Ones.*

TV and film story editor–writer **Franklin Thompson** served as vice president of literary affairs for Quinn Martin Productions (*The Fugitive, Streets of San Francisco*) and as executive script consultant for such series as *Matlock* and the *Perry Mason* two-hour specials.

Actor **Lou Wagner**'s list of credits spans from *Happy Days* to *Columbo* to a regular role on *CHiPs,* to recent appearances on *Yes, Dear*, and *Providence*. Lou played a major simian role in the original *Planet of the Apes*, and this past season was featured in *James Dean: An Invented Life*. Lou is known by many for his fifteen-year run as "The Little Professor" in the original McDonaldland commercials.

Writer/producer **Ralph Gaby Wilson** recently wrote the critically acclaimed *The Trial of Old Drum* for The Animal Planet. He is the author of several screenplays, including *Outside Chance*, which was selected for showing at the Edinburgh, Deauville, and Montreal Film Festivals. He currently has several feature film scripts in development.

Appendix B

RESOURCES

Actors Equity Association
5757 Wilshire Boulevard, Suite One
Los Angeles, California 90036
(323) 634–1750
www.actorsequity.org

American Federation of Television and Radio Artists
5757 Wilshire Boulevard
Los Angeles, California 90036
(323) 634–8100
www.aftra.org

A Minor Consideration
14530 Denker Avenue
Gardena, California 90247
(310) 532–1345
www.minorcon.org

Association of Canadian Television and Radio Artists
625 Church Street, Third Floor
Toronto, Ontario, Canada M4Y 2G1
(800) 387–3516
www.actra.ca

Backstage West
5055 Wilshire Boulevard
Los Angeles, California 90036
(323) 525–2356
www.backstage.com

Cenex Casting Network
(Extra work for non-union members)
220 South Flower Street
Burbank, California 91502
(818) 562–2700

Central Casting
(Extra work for SAG/AFTRA members)
220 South Flower Street
Burbank, California 91502
(818) 562–2700

Daily Variety
5700 Wilshire Boulevard, Suite 120
Los Angeles, California 90036
(800) 323–4345
www.dailyvariety.com

Directors Guild of America
7920 West Sunset Boulevard
Los Angeles, California 90046
(310) 289–2000
www.dga.org

East Los Angeles College Theatre
Director of Theatre, c/o Theatre Arts
1301 Avenida de Cesar Chavez
Monterey Park, California 91754
www.perspicacity.com/elactheatre

The Harvey Lembeck Comedy Workshop
P.O. Box 57946
Sherman Oaks, California 91413
(310) 271–2831

Hollywood Creative Directory
IFILM Publishing
1024 North Orange Drive
Hollywood, California 90038
(800) 815–0503
www.hcdonline.com

The Hollywood Reporter
5055 Wilshire Boulevard, Fifth Floor
Los Angeles, California 90036
(323) 525–2150
www.hollywoodreporter.com

The Hollywood Reporter Blu-Book Directory
(The Yellow Pages for the entertainment industry)
c/o The Hollywood Reporter
5055 Wilshire Boulevard, Fifth Floor
Los Angeles, California 90036
(323) 525–2150
www.hollywoodreporter.com/hollywoodreporter/thrblu/letter.jsp

International Alliance of Theatrical Stage Employees
1720 West Magnolia Boulevard
Burbank, California 91506–1871
(818) 841–9233
http://ia33.org

Larry Edmunds Bookshop, Inc.
6644 Hollywood Boulevard
Hollywood, California 90028
(323) 463–3273

Producers Guild of America
8530 Wilshire Boulevard, Suite 450
Hollywood, California 90028
(310) 358–9020
www.producersguild.org

Samuel French Bookstore
7623 Sunset Boulevard, Department W
Hollywood, California 90046
(323) 876–0570
www.samuelfrench.com

Screen Actors Guild
5757 Wilshire Boulevard
Los Angeles, California 90036
(323) 954–1600
www.sag.org

Theatre LA Theatre League Alliance
644 South Figueroa
Los Angeles, California 90017
(213) 614–0556
www.theatrela.org

Writers Guild of America west
7000 West Third Street
Los Angeles, California 90048
(323) 951–4000
www.wga.org

Appendix C

REFERENCES CITED
AND OTHER BOOKS

Branden, Nathaniel, Ph.D. *How to Raise Your Self-Esteem* (New York: Bantam, 1987).

Branden, Nathaniel, Ph.D. *The Six Pillars of Self-Esteem* (New York: Bantam Books, 1995).

Brown, Les. *Live Your Dreams* (New York: Avon Books, 1996).

Buckalew, M.W., Jr. *Learning to Control Stress* (New York: Richard Rosen Press, Inc., 1979).

Carter-Scott, Cherie, Ph.D. *If Success Is a Game, These Are the Rules: Ten Rules for a Fulfilling Career and Life* (New York: Broadway Books, 2000).

Cary, Diana Serra. *Hollywood's Children: An Inside Account of the Child Star Era* (Dallas: Southern Methodist University Press, 1997).

Dyer, Wayne, M.D. *Your Erroneous Zones* (New York: Harper Mass Market Paperbacks, 1997).

Edwards, Paul and Sarah. *The Practical Dreamer's Handbook* (New York: Jeremy P. Tarcher, 2000).

Green, Joey. *The Road to Success Is Paved with Failure: How Hundreds of People Triumphed over Inauspicious Beginnings, Crushing Rejection, Humiliating Defeats, and Other Speed Bumps along Life's Highway* (New York: Little Brown and Company, 2001).

Gunther, Max. *How to Get Lucky* (New York: Stein & Day, 1986).

Jones, Henry Z. *More Psychic Roots: Further Adventures in Serendipity and Intuition in Genealogy* (Baltimore: Genealogical Publishing Co., 1999).

Katselas, Milton. *Dreams into Action* (Beverly Hills, Calif.: Dove Books, 1996).

Marshall, Garry (with Lori Marshall). *Wake Me When It's Funny: How to Break into Show Business and Stay There* (New York: Newmarket Press, 1997).

Palumbo, Dennis. *Writing from the Inside Out* (New York: John Wiley & Sons, Inc., 2000).

Prochnow, Herbert V. and Herbert B., Jr. *The Toastmaster's Treasure Chest* (New York: Harper & Row, 1979).

Spelling, Aaron (with Jefferson Graham). *Aaron Spelling: A Prime-Time Life* (New York: St. Martin's Press, 1996).

Viscott, M.D., David. *Risking* (New York: Simon and Schuster, 1988).

Index

ABOUT THE AUTHOR

Jerry Rannow began his show business career as a professional actor with guest appearances on such popular TV shows as *The Beverly Hillbillies*; *My Three Sons*; *Love, American Style*; *The Red Skelton Show*; *The Jonathan Winters Show*; and *The Carol Burnett Show*. Jerry went on to make the successful transition to writer/producer on many network television series, including *Welcome Back, Kotter*; *Happy Days*; *Room 222*; *Love Boat*; *All in the Family*; and *Head of the Class*. He won exclusive contracts to develop television series with the ABC network, Columbia Pictures, Twentieth Century Fox, and the CTV network in Canada, where he was the recipient of a Canadian Emmy nomination. Jerry has taught humor and television screenwriting at the University of Wisconsin (Madison and Milwaukee), DePaul University, Carthage College, and the USC Film School. His first book, *Writing Television Comedy* (Allworth Press, 2000) is now at bookstores everywhere, and he just completed his first comedy novel, *This One'll Killya*.

BOOKS FROM ALLWORTH PRESS

Creative Careers in Hollywood
by Laurie Scheer (paperback, 6 × 9, 240 pages, $19.95)

Acting for Film
by Cathy Haase (paperback, 6 × 9, 240 pages, $19.95)

Writing Television Comedy
by Jerry Rannow (paperback, 6 × 9, 224 pages, $14.95)

The Screenwriter's Legal Guide, second edition
by Stephen F. Breimer (paperback, 6 × 9, 320 pages, $19.95)

Career Solutions for Creative People
by Dr. Rhonda Ormont (paperback, 6 × 9, 320 pages, $19.95)

Hollywood Dealmaking: Negotiating Talent Agreements
by Dina Appleton and Daniel Yankelevitz (paperback, 6 × 9, 256 pages, $19.95)

The Filmmaker's Guide to Production Design
by Vincent LoBrutto (paperback, 6 × 9, 216 pages, $19.95)

Technical Film and TV for Nontechnical People
by Drew Campbell (paperback, 6 × 9, 256 pages, $19.95)

The Health & Safety Guide for Film, TV & Theater
by Monona Rossol (paperback, 6 × 9, 256 pages, $19.95)

An Actor's Guide—Your First Year in Hollywood, Revised Edition
by Michael Saint Nicholas (paperback, 6 × 9, 272 pages, $18.95)

Shoot Me: Independent Filmmaking from Creative Concept to Rousing Release
by Roy Frumkes and Rocco Simonelli (paperback, 6 × 9, 240 pages, $19.95)

Directing for Film and Television, Revised Edition
by Christopher Lukas (paperback, 6 × 9, 256 pages, $19.95)

Producing for Hollywood: A Guide for Independent Producers
by Paul Mason and Don Gold (paperback, 6 × 9, 272 pages, $19.95)

The Directors: Take One
by Robert J. Emery (paperback, 6 × 9, 416 pages, $19.95)

The Directors: Take Two
by Robert J. Emery (paperback, 6 × 9, 384 pages, $19.95)

The Directors: Take Three
by Robert J. Emery (paperback, 6 × 9, 400 pages, $19.95)

Please write to request our free catalog. To order by credit card, call 1-800-491-2808 or send a check or money order to Allworth Press, 10 East 23rd Street, Suite 210, New York, NY 10010. Include $5 for shipping and handling for the first book ordered and $1 for each additional book. Ten dollars plus $1 for each additional book if ordering from Canada. New York State residents must add sales tax.

To see our complete catalog on the World Wide Web, or to order online, you can find us at www.allworth.com.